SSSP

Springer Series in Social Psychology

Advisory Editor:
Robert F. Kidd

Springer Series in Social Psychology

Advisory Editor: Robert F. Kidd

Attention and Self-Regulation:
A Control-Theory Approach to Human Behavior
  Charles S. Carver/Michael F. Scheier

Gender and Nonverbal Behavior
  Clara Mayo/Nancy M. Henley (Editors)

Personality, Roles, and Social Behavior
  William Ickes/Eric S. Knowles (Editors)

Toward Transformation in Social Knowledge
  Kenneth J. Gergen

The Ethics of Social Research:
Surveys and Experiments
  Joan E. Sieber (Editor)

The Ethics of Social Research:
Fieldwork, Regulation, and Publication
  Joan E. Sieber (Editor)

Anger and Aggression:
An Essay on Emotion
  James R. Averill

SSSP

The Ethics of Social Research
Fieldwork, Regulation, and Publication

Edited by
Joan E. Sieber

Springer-Verlag New York Heidelberg Berlin

Joan E. Sieber
Department of Psychology
California State University—Hayward
Hayward, California 94542
U.S.A.

Robert F. Kidd, *Advisory Editor*
Department of Psychology
Boston University
Boston, Massachusetts 02215
U.S.A.

Library of Congress Cataloging in Publication Data
Main entry under title:
The Ethics of social research.
  (Springer series in social psychology)
  Bibliography: v. 1, p.   ; v. 2, p.
  Includes indexes.
  Contents: [1] Surveys and experiments—[2] Fieldwork, regulation, and publication.
  1. Social psychology—Research—Moral and ethical aspects—Collected works. 2. Social
sciences—Research—Moral and ethical aspects—Collected works. I. Sieber, Joan E. II.
Series.
HM251.E76   174′.9301   82-5486
                    AACR2

Printed in the United States of America

9 8 7 6 5 4 3 2 1

ISBN 0-387-90691-6   Springer-Verlag   New York   Heidelberg   Berlin
ISBN 3-540-90691-6   Springer-Verlag   Berlin   Heidelberg   New York

Preface

Social scientists are unprepared for many of the ethical problems that arise in their research, and for criticisms of their ethics that seem to ignore such cherished scientific values as objectivity and freedom of inquiry. Yet, they possess methodological talent and insight into human nature that can be used to understand and resolve these problems. The contributors to this book demonstrate that criticism of the ethics of social research can stimulate constructive development of methodology.

Both volumes of *The Ethics of Social Research* were written for and by social scientists to show how ethical dilemmas arise in the day-to-day conduct of social research and how they can be resolved. The topics discussed in the companion volume include ethical problems that arise in experiments and sample surveys; this book deals with the ethical issues involved in fieldwork and in the regulation and publication of research. With candor and humor, many of the contributors describe lessons they have learned about themselves, their methods, and their research participants. Collectively, they illustrate that both humanists and determinists are likely to encounter ethical dilemmas in their research, albeit different ones, and that a blending of deterministic and humanistic approaches may be needed to solve these dilemmas.

The aim of this book is to assist investigators in preparing to meet some of the ethical problems that await the unwary. It offers perspectives, values, and guidelines for anticipating problems and devising solutions. Many of its chapters even offer specific methodological and procedural solutions to clearly defined problems. However, no ethical dilemma in social research is solved once and for all, and no procedure or value orientation, however broad and sophisticated, is acceptable to all or universally effective in confronting potential problems. Consequently, an equally important aim of this book is to provide role-models and a learning set that will enable investigators to effectively focus their moral sensitivity and scientific creativity on the unique problems that arise in their own research.

Appreciation is due various people who made this book possible. First, I acknowledge some intellectual debts: to Herbert Kelman, whose book, *A Time to*

Speak, compelled me to recognize that there is an important place in social science for conscience, humanism and social activism, along with intellect, determinism and objectivity; to Ian Mitroff and Ralph Kilmann, whose book, *The Methodologies of Social Science,* helped me to understand why social scientists find it hard to discuss the ethics of their research without getting upset (at one another and at society), and hard to agree on what their ethical problems are or how they should be handled; and to Donald Campbell and Robert Boruch who have been demonstrating for a long time that social scientists can use the tools of their trade to cope effectively with ethical problems in their research.

Second, I acknowledge my thanks to those who have worked with me: to the contributors for being so patient with my efforts; to my students and numerous colleagues who read chapters and commented on the organization of the book, especially my colleague, Conrad Taeuber, who kept me supplied with good ideas during the critical period of development of these volumes; to Diana Smith and LaVonne Dillian for their assistance with the preparation of this manuscript; and to the people at Springer-Verlag, who worked with speed, competence, and graciousness to transform a big box of paper into two attractive volumes.

Finally, I thank my long-term co-worker, my husband, Ben Zeitman, for his encouragement, and for the love and energy he has contributed to our creation of a two-career household in which activities such as book editing and wine making can exist side-by-side with a minimum of chaos.

Shenandoah Valley, California   Joan E. Sieber

Contents

Preface v

Part I. Ethnographic Fieldwork and Beneficial Reciprocity 1

1. Harms, Benefits, Wrongs, and Rights in Fieldwork 7
   Joan Cassell

   Comparing Experimental Research with Fieldwork 8
   Relations between Investigators and Investigated 10
   Relations between Fieldworkers and Informants 14
   Applying Kantian Ethics to Fieldwork 17
   Analyzing Wrongs 20
   Conclusions 27

2. Research Reciprocity Rather than Informed Consent in Fieldwork   33
   Murray L. Wax

   The Context of the Moral Challenge 34
   Openness, Deception, and Consent in Fieldwork 36
   The "Consent Process" in the Community Study 41
   The Relativity of "Informed" 43
   Reseach Reciprocities 44

3. The Threat of the Stranger: Vulnerability, Reciprocity, and
   Fieldwork 49
   Myron Glazer

   The Pain of Words and the Right of Refusal 50
   The Fear of Retaliation and the Problem of Fidelity 55
   The Plight of Survivors and the Promise of Advocacy 58
   The Face of Death and the Call of Compassion 62
   A Word of Summary and Acknowledgment 67

4. **Risks in the Publication of Fieldwork** 71
   Carole Gaar Johnson

   Lessons in the Ethics of Publishing Fieldwork Exemplified by the
   Studies of Springdale and Plainville 72
   Scientific Responsibility 84
   Consent to Risk Violation of Confidentiality 85
   Publication of Secrets 86
   Guidelines for "Ethical Proofreading" of Fieldwork Manuscripts ... 87
   Directions for Future Research on the Ethics of Publishing Fieldwork 88

**Part II. The Roles of Social Scientists in Research Regulation and in
         Giving Social Science to Society via the Mass Media** 93

5. **A Proposed System of Regulation for the Protection of Participants
   in Low-Risk Areas of Applied Social Research** 97
   Donald T. Campbell and Joe Shelby Cecil

   Proposed Regulations 101

   Critique of Campbell and Cecil's Proposal: Subjects Need More
   Protection 122
   Ernest R. House

   Critique of Campbell and Cecil's Proposal: Don't Throw Out the Baby
   with the Bathwater 125
   Norman M. Bradburn

6. **Regulation and Education: The Role of the Institutional Review
   Board in Social Science Research** 131
   Elizabeth Decker Tanke and Tony J. Tanke

   The IRB and the Review Process: Examining the Research Proposal   132
   Communication between the Board and the Investigator 141
   Conclusion 147

7. **Social Science in the Mass Media: Images and Evidence** 151
   S. Holly Stocking and Sharon L. Dunwoody

   Research on the Process 154
   Research Needs 158
   Some Implications and Practical Suggestions 162

Author Index 171

Subject Index 179

Contributors

Norman M. Bradburn, Department of Behavioral Sciences, University of Chicago, 5848 South University Avenue, Chicago, Illinois 60637, U.S.A.

Donald T. Campbell, Maxwell School, Syracuse University, Syracuse, New York 13310, U.S.A.

Joan Cassell, 19 Monroe Place, Brooklyn, New York 11201, U.S.A.

Joe Shelby Cecil, Federal Judicial Center, 11520 H Street, Washington, D.C. 20005, U.S.A.

Sharon L. Dunwoody, Department of Journalism, University of Wisconsin— Madison, Madison, Wisconsin 53706, U.S.A.

Myron Glazer, Department of Sociology and Anthropology, Smith College, Northampton, Massachusetts 01060, U.S.A.

Ernest R. House, University of Illinois, College of Education, Center for Instructional Research and Curriculum Evaluation, 1310 South Sixth Street, Champaign, Illinois 61820, U.S.A.

Carole Gaar Johnson, Department of Sociology, Washington University, St. Louis, Missouri 63130, U.S.A.

S. Holly Stocking, 712 E. Cottage Grove, Bloomington, Indiana 47401, U.S.A.

Elizabeth Decker Tanke, Department of Psychology, University of Santa Clara, Santa Clara, California 95053, U.S.A.

Tony J. Tanke, Knudson, Tanke and Scholz, 45 Franklin Street, San Francisco, California 94102, U.S.A.

Murray L. Wax, Department of Sociology, Washington University, St. Louis, Missouri 63130, U.S.A.

Part I

Ethnographic Fieldwork and Beneficial Reciprocity

Ethnography is the study of people and their culture. The fieldworker stays in the habitat of the host culture for an extended period of time and becomes closely acquainted with one or more members of that culture. The fieldworker participates in the host culture, and strives to understand it, to learn as far as is possible to speak, think, feel, perceive, and act as a member of that culture, and yet to examine and describe it critically from the trained perspective of his or her own discipline and culture.

Fieldwork is the main method of cultural anthropologists and is increasingly a research method chosen by social psychologists, sociologists, political scientists, educators, nurses, criminologists, management scientists, and others who seek insight into a particular subculture, e.g., that of the school child, the alcoholic, the sick and dying, the draft dodger, the white collar criminal, or members of the feminist movement. When the fieldworker sets out to understand an exotic or deviant culture, it is necessary to participate in that culture over an extended period of time in order to interpret the meaning of the events that occur there. However, when field workers seek to understand some aspect of their own culture, much information often can be gained through extended conversations or unstructured interviews. In fieldwork, there is no experimental design, no observation or interview schedule, no treatment, and no measuring instruments. The fieldworker *is* the measuring instrument, and the method of gathering information is to create a natural human relationship with one or more members of the group to be studied and to learn their culture by interacting with them, talking with them, and observing them.

In contrast with sciences that deal with radiation, gene splicing, or social experimentation, fieldwork, with its use of Conceptual Humanist and Particular Humanist approaches to learn about the lives of others, would appear to be quite safe and free of serious ethical dilemmas. However, while the method of fieldwork resembles that of creating an ordinary human relationship, fieldwork is not an ordinary human relationship: Fieldworkers are strangers who enter another culture to learn its ways, and then leave and write a report describing certain aspects of that culture from the perspective of their discipline and their own culture. They typically have support from a funding agency, and that agency may have more than an academic interest in the nature and potential uses of the findings. Usually, fieldworkers achieve entrance into the host culture by creating a relationship with someone who has considerable power within or over that culture. Once they have gained entrance into the host culture, fieldworkers are faced with the task of creating relationships with members of the host culture that are fair and respectful, of establishing a viable way to survive and gain knowledge of the host culture, and of allaying fears and preventing stresses that might otherwise arise among people who are visited by a powerful stranger. Although it may be difficult to communicate in a precise way about the scientific nature and purpose of fieldwork to those being studied, fieldworkers must take care not to wrong members of the host culture by lying or betraying their trust. Fieldworkers must quickly learn the ways in which information might be used harmfully in the host culture, so that confidentiality can be protected in relevant ways. After developing what may be a deep moving relationship with members of the host culture, fieldworkers must be both sensitive and detached enough to complete the fieldwork by writing a report that is incisive enough to be of scholarly value, yet compassionate enough to warrant the confidence of the informants. Finally, fieldworkers should disseminate the findings in a responsible and nonharmful way, preserving privacy and confidentiality as appropriate.

In short, fieldwork is still social science research, replete with problems of creating respectful relationships with research participants, obtaining valid data from them, assuring privacy and confidentiality, interpreting data correctly, and disseminating data responsibly. However, these generic similarities to the ethical problems of other kinds of social science research are misleading, for the specific contextual characteristics that induce risk or harm in fieldwork are quite different from those in other social sciences. Not surprisingly, many of these problems are akin to ones that arise in ordinary social and business relationships where there are conflicts of interest, failures to understand or empathize with the needs of the other party, or a desire on one or both sides to exploit the other. Problems of this kind (wrongs, as opposed to harms) call for a reversal of the ethical problem solving approaches that are used in other areas of social or human research: The fieldworker who seeks to engage in ethical problem solving typically *begins* with the intense Particular Humanist experience of surviving among members of a strange culture, creating somewhat intimate relationships there, and seeking to understand his or her experience and that of the host. Stepping back from the relationship, the fieldworker takes a Conceptual Humanist role from which to examine the personal experience of fieldworker in its many facets. Finally, the fieldworker uses the tools of the Conceptual Theorist to differentiate, taxonomize, analyze, and create new understanding of their research relationships, of ethical dilemmas inherent within those relationships, and of ways to resolve ethical dilemmas of fieldwork.

In Chapter 1, Joan Cassell takes the role of Conceptual Theorist and taxonomizes and analyzes the concept of social science and then the concept of fieldwork. Next, she takes the role of Conceptual Humanist and considers what it means, ethically, to do fieldwork in each of these roles. Thereby, she is able to show what special ethical problems inhere in fieldwork of various kinds, problems not taken much into account in most ethical and regulatory considerations of human research.

Specifically, Cassell clarifies ways in which fieldwork differs from research that is patterned on the Analytic Scientist or deterministic model. She stresses the symmetry or parity that exists in the relationship between fieldworker and informant, the lack of conceptual or experimental control exercised in fieldwork, and the relative lack of harmful manipulation of respondents. In a comparison of fieldwork with biomedical experimentation, psychological experimentation, and survey research (from whence most ideas about the ethics of human research are drawn), Cassell shows that most ethical problems connected with fieldwork are somewhat different from those arising in other areas of human research.

She then distinguishes among five varieties of fieldwork, that is, the verandah model, noblesse oblige, going native, undercover agent, and advocate, and identifies the major ethical problems that may arise within each: tangible or measurable harm to those studied is rarely at issue; at issue are *wrongs* to persons, that is, uses of persons as means to the fieldworker's ends, e.g., deceiving, lying, and revealing kinds of information in publications that those studied would wish kept secret. Because the verandah and undercover agent models and some versions of the advocate model necessarily involve wrongs, Cassell rejects them in principle unless it can be shown that these are the only feasible ways of doing research that is worth doing. Cassell concludes that in fieldwork the principle of beneficence cannot be construed to mean maximizing benefit over harm, but rather the active search for *reciprocal benefits*. Although Cassell does not tell us precisely what reciprocity means, she provides some of the taxonomic and analytic tools needed to discover when and how beneficial reciprocity might be possible in various kinds of fieldwork.

In Chapter 2, Murray L. Wax shows how and why reciprocity forms the ethical basis of fieldwork, and challenges us to conceptualize the various forms and functions that reciprocity might take depending on the setting and goals of the fieldwork. We see that the initial contact between fieldworker and hosts is very different from that between most social scientists and their research subjects. It is marked by the fieldworker's efforts to cope and survive in a foreign culture and by the hosts' efforts to understand whether the alien being in their midst will be acceptable and useful to them. In the beginning, fieldworkers and informants view each other as objects, research objects and purveyors of technological benefits, respectively. Most informants are not concerned with the scientific purpose of the fieldwork, but with such matters as the sponsorship of the fieldworker and the advantages he or she may bring. Then, depending on the character and needs of the parties involved, certain reciprocities are established, a peer relationship develops, and suitable moral norms are enforced on one another. It is this emergent reciprocal relationship, not an informed consent procedure, Wax argues, that is the moral basis of fieldwork. Inherent in this relationship is the establishment of participants and fieldworkers as peers and fellow human beings.

Wax shows that covert fieldwork precludes processes of reciprocity. He defends some instances of covert fieldwork, when it is the only way to obtain socially valuable information, but explains its inherent methodological drawbacks: maintaining a cover interferes seriously with the process of fieldwork in various ways, for example, it deprives the fieldworker of the insights that are possible through the development of reciprocity.

Wax examines some of the motives and perceptions that arise as fieldworker and informant begin to create a relationship, and some ways in which the particular character of the relationship may limit the information that can be gained. Argyris (Chapter 1, p. 30, companion volume) has done a similar analysis of social psychological research. Both Wax and Argyris remind us that a Conceptual Humanist orientation provides special kinds of useful knowledge, e.g., kinds of self-knowledge and knowledge of other persons that can only grow out of mutual self-disclosure in a trusting relationship. We are challenged to understand more about the potentials for data gathering, dissemination, and application that are overlooked by a social science geared primarily to an Analytic Scientist or Particular Humanist model.

In Chapter 3, Myron Glazer enlarges our sense of these possibilities. Moreover, if Wax leaves the reader believing that reciprocity occurs only in exchanges of cultural information in return for technological assistance, Glazer makes it abundantly clear that there is much with which to reciprocate in fieldwork in modern society. Focusing largely on fieldwork in Western cultures, Glazer begins by considering the vulnerabilities and fears of the researched and shows how various forms of reciprocity serve to reduce fears of harm on the part of both the fieldworker and the respondent. Through excerpts and analyses of interviews with noted fieldworkers, insights are given into the way in which establishment of trust then makes possible a second type of reciprocity: the giving of information in return for friendship, understanding, support, and emotional release. As the relationship ensues, reciprocal encouragement and support help both the fieldworker and the respondent to overcome the feelings of despair or uncertainty that are likely to arise at times in the relationship. Given the depth of the relationship that may ensue, the burden on the researcher to make the final report worthwhile, scholarly, and also compassionate and respectful of those studied, becomes enormous. This is so particularly when the fieldwork delves into extraordinary settings where, for example, war, death, or financial disaster form the context. Questions such as the following may arise:

1. How does one repay the trust of dying children or troubled, despairing adults?
2. When are words painful to the teller?
3. How can fieldworkers be sensitive to informants' need not to disclose information?
4. How can a fieldworker compensate an informant for the emotional pain of disclosure?
5. In what ways can a fieldworker give compassion?
6. Is it ethical to write and publish information that others have shared in their most anguished moments; is it ethical not to publish such information when it was given with the expectation that it would be used to enlighten others?
7. When might it be dangerous to be an informant? How can that danger be minimized?
8. What do informants want in the way of having their story told to the world and can the fieldworker really provide what is wanted or promised?
9. What obligation might a fieldworker have to serve as an advocate for her or his informants?

We see that the fieldworker must move sensitively through the roles of Particular Humanist, Conceptual Humanist, Conceptual Theorist, and Analytic Scientist as required to serve the interests of ethical fieldwork, humanitarian concern and good, critical scholarship. The complex richness of the reciprocities that Glazer describes are not what one learns about in most social science research methodology texts. Yet, one can hardly avoid the conclusion that Glazer has told us something of paramount ethical and methodological importance. If the fieldworker's own sensitivities are the instrument through which fieldwork data are gathered, and if reciprocity is the means of creating and developing ethical and effective fieldwork relationships, then Glazer has scratched the surface of a vast realm of ethics and methodology in fieldwork.

How can we further our understanding of processes of reciprocity as they may occur in the wide range of settings where fieldwork is now done, e.g., with members of organizations, criminals, police, socially and sexually deviant persons, the aged, and cultural minorities? By what means can fieldworkers discover, share, and sharpen ideas and sensitivities about reciprocity? Reciprocity, in the actual process of relationship, is clearly a Conceptual Humanist and Particular Humanist activity, and it seems inconceivable that it could be studied and shared except by case study and experiential means. The knowledge gained about reciprocity, thus, will be experiential and affective as well as intellectual. As such, it promises to provide useful understanding of ourselves and humanity, over and above its usefulness in fieldwork.

Cassell, Wax, and Glazer emphasize that the two ethical issues of paramount importance in fieldwork are establishment of beneficial reciprocity and the avoidance of harm in the publication of findings, but they devote little attention to the latter problem. In Chapter 4, Carole Gaar Johnson addresses one subset of these risks: those connected with the publication of fieldwork done in communities. When publishing the findings of community studies, there are risks of breach of confidentiality that include upsetting informants by the way they are portrayed, enabling others to locate and pry into the lives of those described in the study, and damaging the reputation of fieldworkers. Yet, the point of community studies is to describe significant aspects of the culture of a community with accuracy. The truth about persons is not always attractive, and the identity of accurately described communities may be difficult to hide as may the identity of persons saliently described in the study, pseudonyms notwithstanding.

Drawing on examples of harmful and destructive reporting of community studies, Johnson discusses some of the harms that have resulted. Then drawing on examples of ethical reporting, she shows that it is possible to create reports that are objective and accurate, yet respectful and beneficial to those studied. We see that promises of confidentiality, given in good faith, have turned out to be impossible for the unwary fieldworker to keep: the real locations of studies and the real identities of the persons described have become known. Information that was never meant to be seen by those who were studied has become available to them. Worse, some members of the communities studied have taken an interest in intensifying the upset caused by the invasion of the privacy of other community members. Thus, paternalistic attempts to cloak identity have backfired mightily.

Johnson goes beyond the usual reactions of a fieldworker to his or her community hosts to consider the kinds of reciprocity that might be appropriate, given the very real risks of publication. She also considers the objectives of doing this kind of science in the first place, presumably to provide general and objective knowledge and understanding based on a specific example. (Thus, she moves from a Particular Humanist perspective across the spectrum of Conceptual and Analytic orientations.) What emerges is a set of recommendations based not on the assumption that secrecy can be maintained, but on such foundations as respectful communication and collaboration between fieldworker and informants, the use of descriptive rather than evaluative language, and the analysis of the fieldworker's own biases. We see that a sensitive blend of scientific and humanistic concerns can produce community study reports that are instructive and valuable to all, including those described therein, which is the realization of a Conceptual Humanist goal.

Johnson concludes, not surprisingly, with a challenge to the Conceptual Humanist in each social scientist. She proposes that the last stage of social science research involve assessment of the harm and benefit done by the publication of the findings. She further proposes that more work be devoted to analysis of the consequences of publication by type or class of social science research. Finally, she recommends that a more concerted effort be made to discover ways to use this new knowledge constructively, both in the conduct of future research and in the education of undergraduate and graduate students of social science.

Chapter 1

Harms, Benefits, Wrongs, and Rights in Fieldwork

Joan Cassell

The term "research with human subjects" is frequently used to describe a wide variety of biomedical, behavioral, and social investigations. Unfortunately, the phrase obscures significant differences between methods. Investigators who carry out fieldwork, or participant observation, traditionally call the people they study "informants," as opposed to the "respondents" of survey research, or the "subjects" of psychological (and biomedical) experimentation. These terms describe radically different relationships between those who study, and those who are studied (Spradley, 1979, chap. 3). The various modes of research also differ in the narrowness or breadth of research focus, in the incidence and seriousness of harms and benefits and, consequently, in the ethical problems associated with each method. As a result, procedures designed to improve the ethical adequacy of one kind of research (such as signed consent forms, or randomized response methods) may have little effect on the practices of another.[1]

This chapter discusses some differences between research methods, and explores their ethical implications. My primary focus is on fieldwork, on the distinctive ethical problems associated with this method, and on possible solutions. After a

---

[1] When the Federal government began to regulate the conduct of research involving "human subjects," it recognized no significant differences among the several varieties of research (biomedical, behavioral, social), but sought instead for concepts and principles that were universal in application. In partial consequence of the critical analyses represented by the present essay, as well as by the essays in this and kindred volumes (e.g., Wax & Cassell, 1979a; Cassell & Wax, 1980), the revised regulations, issued January 27, 1981, by the Department of Health and Human Services, make appropriate discriminations among the varieties of research involving human beings. Because of this happy outcome, some of the critical passages of the present essay have lost their relevance to contemporary issues in the politics of science and have become of historical interest. The very nature of such essays makes it impossible to suspend them in time for the purposes of book publication; nevertheless, I believe the arguments and analyses developed herein have a conceptual and logical validity that goes beyond the initial occasion for their writing.

brief review of the issues, I present two schemes to clarify the differences between (1) four kinds of research on human beings (biomedical experimentation, psychological experimentation, survey research, and fieldwork), and (2) five varieties of fieldwork (which I have called the "verandah model," "noblesse oblige," "going native," "undercover agent," and "advocacy research"). I then offer a Kantian analysis of the five modes of fieldwork and, finally, introduce the concept of wrong, as opposed to harm. This concept, based on Kant's categorical imperative, can lead to a broader view of ethics and fieldwork, which has implications for analysis of the ethical problems associated with every variety of research.

Comparing Experimental Research with Fieldwork

The various modes of research can be arranged on a spectrum (Cassell, 1980), based on the asymmetry or parity of the relationship between investigator and investigated, the narrowness or breadth of research focus, and the magnitude of potential harms and benefits. At one pole is biomedical experimentation, which serves as the model for the Federal regulations to protect the human subjects of research. Next is psychological experimentation, then survey research and, at the opposite pole, fieldwork or ethnographic research. Comparing experimental research with fieldwork emphasizes the differences in research modes. I shall now compare the asymmetry or parity of the research relationship, the researcher's "conceptual control," and harms and benefits.

Asymmetry of Relationship

The asymmetry or parity of the research relationship is based on (1) the perceived power of the investigator, and (2) control of the research setting. In experimental research, investigators are, or are perceived to be, relatively powerful. Patients depend on physicians for medical care, students on psychology professors for good grades, and physicians, professors, and psychologists all have relatively high status in our society. Experimenters generally control the hospital, laboratory, or classroom setting where research takes place (with the exception of social psychology field experiments, where deception frequently gives experimenters a different kind of control).

In fieldwork, the research relationship is more symmetrical. Fieldworkers have little power over those studied; when conducting research they lack even the symbolic props of power, e.g., the white coats, professional jargon, impressive technology, and obedient assistants, that exemplify the superior status and authority of the scientist. In fact, fieldworkers frequently downplay whatever status and authority they possess in their own milieus, assuming the role of novice or learner, and asking those studied to teach them how their hosts perceive, classify, describe, and react to their world. The host people control the setting of research, and fieldworkers may be dependent on them for food, shelter, and protection.

Asymmetry in the relationship between investigator and investigated facilitates coercion. The more powerful and controlling researchers are, or are assumed to be, the more difficult it is for the researched to refuse to take part in a study, submit to painful procedures, or continue as research subjects if they find participation unpleasant. The asymmetrical research relationship between experimenters and subjects, then, allows a kind of control and subtle coercion that is inhibited by the more balanced relationship between fieldworkers and hosts. Fieldworkers are not necessarily more scrupulous or less controlling than experimenters; it is the structure of the research situation, rather than the personality of researchers, that allows investigators to coerce the investigated to a greater or lesser degree.

Conceptual Control

Experimental research and fieldwork also differ in the extent of what might be called "conceptual control,"[2] exercised by investigators. Narrowly focused research controls both (1) the background or contextual features of a study, and also (2) interpersonal elements; broadly focused research controls neither. In experimentation, the more narrowly a research design focuses on a few relevant variables, the more effective the experiment. Background features, such as ethnicity, social class, structural elements, or characteristics of the research setting, must be held constant, excluded, or controlled for if they are not to interfere with the research process. Similarly, uncontrolled interpersonal elements may invalidate experimental findings. Experimental interaction is carefully designed to exclude irrelevant ideas, feelings, and interactions: the independent variable is the experimenters' manipulation of subjects; the dependent variable is subjects' reactions to this manipulation. Whatever else goes on between experimenters and subjects, whatever interpersonal elements impinge on the research situation, is irrelevant, at best, and interference, at worst. Thus, if subjects react to something besides the experimental manipulations, such as the wishes or unconscious cues of experimenters, this reaction may confound the findings.

Unlike experimenters, fieldworkers exercise little or no conceptual control; their research is so broadly focused that many critics refuse to classify it as science. It is difficult to ignore or control for contextual features in the field, and few ethnographers would wish to do so. Rather than interfering with what is studied, the physical, structural, social, and cultural contexts of research are significant data in their own right. Interaction is not controlled in fieldwork: it ebbs and flows freely, and a wide range of interpersonal features serve as a source of data. Experimentation consists of the physical, social or psychic manipulations by the investigator. Social and psychic manipulation occurs in fieldwork, as well. The difference is that those who are studied are in a position to manipulate fully as much as those who study, and are frequently more skilled at it. Fieldworkers manipulate their hosts to obtain data; their hosts manipulate fieldworkers to obtain whatever it is

---

[2] In social research, it is the structure of concepts of the investigator that shapes the pattern in which the data are analyzed and the findings are presented. Instead of "conceptual control," one might speak more narrowly, and precisely, of control over the design and execution of the research investigation. Whatever the phraseology, the notion is basic to the ethical analysis of the research process.

they want at that particular moment (and they usually want something, if only social interaction). In fieldwork, the significant manipulation is that of the field-worker by those studied; this provides data on customs, ideas, and expectations. The subject of study in fieldwork, then, includes those contextual and interpersonal features that must be excluded or controlled for in experimentation.

The narrower the focus of research, the easier it is for an investigator to predict what will occur during, and as a result of, the limited and circumscribed interaction between researcher and researched. Because experimenters exercise high conceptual control over their research, they have greater ability to predict risks, benefits, and findings than fieldworkers, whose conceptual control ranges from low to nonexistent. Consequently, requiring a fieldworker to predict what is going to occur before research is carried out, as do the Federal regulations to protect human subjects, leads to an exercise in futility, creativity, or mendacity.

Harms and Benefits

Similar variation emerges when the potential harms and benefits of experimentation and fieldwork are compared. In experimental research, especially biomedical experimentation, the magnitude of possible harms is generally higher; benefits, too, tend to be greater. Contrasted with the threats to life and bodily integrity, and the promises of restoration of health proffered by biomedical experimentation, the harms and benefits of fieldwork are minimal and difficult to measure (Cassell, 1978b). In experimentation, harms and benefits are likely to occur during, or as a direct result of, the manipulation of subjects by experimenters. In fieldwork, on the other hand, the most serious harms result from the manipulation of data, not people, and occur at a later date when research findings are disseminated (or data are subpoenaed). Many of the most serious risks to those studied by fieldwork are posed not by researchers, but by what sponsors, legal sources, and governmental agencies may do with the findings.

Let us turn now to a more systematic and differentiated comparison of differences between various research methods, and then, of differences between varieties of fieldwork. This analysis will indicate what kinds of ethical decision making are most suited for the problems that arise during, and as a result of, fieldwork.

Relations between Investigators and Investigated

Differences in relations between those who study and those who are studied by various types of research become apparent when research modes are compared along four dimensions: (1) the relative power of investigators, as perceived by subjects; (2) control of the setting where research takes place; (3) control over the context of research, and (4) control over research interaction. These dimensions are continua, and the relationships in different types of research vary systematically along them. I shall now review four ideal typical forms of research on human beings, measuring each along the four dimensions: biomedical experimentation, psychological experimentation, survey research, and fieldwork. Table 1-1 summarizes the argument.

   Biomedical Experimentation is located at the far end of the four dimensions. Biomedical experimenters are likely to be perceived by subjects as having great power, since subjects may depend on these physicians for their medical care. Under such conditions, patients may be afraid to refuse to take part in an experiment. For example, in a large American teaching hospital, physicians recruited their own female patients as subjects. Despite the fact that the women had signed forms consenting to the experimental procedures, 39% of those interviewed said that they did not know they were participants in a research project, and an additional 8% felt coerced and would have preferred not to participate (Gray, 1975, p. 128). Biomedical investigators control the hospital or laboratory setting in which research is carried out. In addition, they have high conceptual control: the research design controls for as much contextual interference and interpersonal variation as possible. As a result, the research interaction is primarily in one direction: experimenters act on subjects and their diseases. This is not to say that there is no personal flow of two-way interaction between experimenters and subjects; there may be a great deal. But this personal interaction is excluded from the research design and must

Table 1-1. Relationships between Investigators and Investigated

	Biomedical experimentation	Psychological experimentation		Survey research face-to-face (structured close-ended)	Fieldwork (participant observation)
		Lab	Field		
Asymmetry of relationship					
Investigators' power as perceived by those studied	H	H-M	H-M	L	=
Investigators' control over research setting	H	H	0	0	Negative (control by those studied)
Conceptual control					
Investigators' control over context of research	H	H	M	H-M	0
Investigators' control over research inter- action (direction of interaction)	H I→S one-way	H I→S one-way	H-M I→S one-way	H-M I→S one-way	= I⇌S two-way

Note. I, investigator; S, those studied; H, high; M, medium; L, low; =, equal; 0, none.

be controlled for if there is a possibility that it might influence the experimental outcome.

Psychological experimenters generally have less power over their subjects than biomedical researchers. Rarely are the subjects of psychological experiments hospitalized or ill. Admittedly, experimenters may invoke the prestige of a university or other large institution, as well as the more generalized prestige of "science," all of which subjects may perceive as authoritative. For example, Milgram's controversial experiments on the human disposition to be cruel in an authoritarian setting took place at Yale and were later carried out in a New Haven research laboratory (1963, 1965). It is possible that the subjects' obedience to the commands of the authoritarian experimenter reflected a trust that Yale University and "science" would allow nothing dangerous to happen. In laboratory experimentation, the researcher controls the research setting and exerts high conceptual control, with a narrow focus on a limited number of relevant variables. In field experimentation, the perceived power of the experimenter is medium-to-low and the researcher has no control over the setting of research. The experimenter has less conceptual control than in the laboratory: it is difficult to exclude or control completely for contextual features in the field. Control of interaction is comparatively high, however, with the experimenter focusing narrowly on a limited number of relevant variables. In laboratory and field experimentation, research interaction is primarily one-way: when an experimental subject reacts inappropriately, for example, by trying to "read" or "please" experimenters (Orne, 1972; Orne & Scheibe, 1964), investigators perceive this behavior as "noise." In psychological experimentation, then, researchers have high-to-medium perceived power, high-to-low control of the setting, and high-to-medium control over contextual and interpersonal features.

The situation differs in *survey research.* (I shall concentrate on face-to-face surveys using structured close-ended questionnaires; the interested reader can easily calculate relationships for mail and telephone interviews, and for surveys using less structured or open-ended questions.) Although researchers may be perceived as prestigious, especially when a powerful institution or "science" is invoked to increase response rate, interviewers lack power and have little perceived ability to exact compliance or to punish for noncompliance. Investigators do not control the setting of research. Conceptual control, however, is relatively high, since structured questionnaires preselect those contextual and interactive features considered important and minimize or suppress those considered irrelevant. Consequently, research interaction is, in effect, one-way, with investigators applying verbal stimuli, and those who are studied (respondents) producing responses. (Interaction becomes increasingly two-way in an unstructured interview; although investigators try to assume primary control over the form, and time involved, of the research interaction, they are not always successful.) In structured close-ended survey research, then, investigators have little perceived power, no control over the research setting, and high-to-medium control over contextual and interpersonal elements.

While conducting *fieldwork,* investigators have comparatively little power over those who are studied: informants are usually free to leave the situation or to decline to enter interaction. In point of fact, those who are studied frequently have some power over the investigators, who may depend on the hosts for food, lodgings, protection, and social sponsorship (Wax, 1977, p. 323). Those who are studied control the research setting. Conceptual control is low: neither contextual nor interpersonal features are excluded or controlled for; instead they provide significant data.

Unlike other modes of investigation, fieldwork does not place human interaction outside the research paradigm: instead, the paradigm is based on human interaction, in all its richness, variety, and contradiction. (See, for example, the descriptions in this volume of the fieldwork conducted by Erikson and Bluebond-Langner, in Glazer, Chapter 3.) In addition fieldworkers are their own measuring instruments. It is the fieldworker rather than the informant who changes as a result of participation, and these changes serve as a source of data. (See Fox's account of how she learned the function of gallows humor, Glazer, Chapter 3.) Fieldwork interaction is controlled by both the researcher and the researched, and flows freely in two directions. Contradictory definitions of the research enterprise and its relationships, by those who study and those who are studied, may lead to conflict or misinterpretations, but these contradictions can also lead to the investigators' deeper understanding of how informants organize and define reality. On some occasions it is the observers, and on others the observed, who initiate interaction, with the extent of participation determined by individual situations and personal predilections. (This analysis does not characterize deceptive fieldwork, which is discussed below.) In overt, as opposed to covert, participant observation, fieldworkers have their research agenda and have acquired skill in directing interaction and eliciting information, but those who are studied also have their own agenda and frequently exhibit remarkable skills in elicitation (R. Wax, 1971, pp. 181-229). In fieldwork, then, power is shared between investigators and investigated, with those studied having somewhat more power to frustrate research than researchers have to compel them to participate. The hosts control the setting of research, and investigators have little or no conceptual control over contextual or interpersonal features.

Similar variation between research modes is found when potential harms are weighed against benefits. Subjects of biomedical experimentation, for example, may suffer serious harm, or even loss of life, from certain procedures; on the other hand, they may benefit greatly from the same procedures: their lives may be prolonged, their health improved, their symptoms alleviated. Subjects of psychological experimentation are not exposed to the same degree of easily calculable harm as biomedical subjects, but then, rarely do they benefit to the same degree, although a larger class of individuals may benefit, and the findings may contribute to human knowledge, which is, of course, a benefit (see Kelman, 1968, 1972). Survey research would seem to have less potential for serious harm than experimental research, with the greatest injury being violation of privacy or confidentiality. The benefits to individual respondents are probably less substantial, as well, with the greatest benefit being to science or human knowledge. There is a comparatively minimal level of harm associated with fieldwork, this being primarily the violation of privacy or confidentiality (see Johnson's discussion of these issues in Chapter 4). The most serious harms in fieldwork occur not during the process of fieldwork but as a result of its products (this distinction follows Kelman, 1978): the research data or findings. The tangible benefits of fieldwork may also be somewhat amorphous, being primarily the correction of misperceptions about various groups and the advancement of knowledge.

Moving along the spectrum of research, from biomedical research at one pole to fieldwork at the other, the asymmetry of the research relationship and the investigators' conceptual control diminish. It follows logically that investigators will have increasing difficulty predicting what will occur during interaction, or defining in advance what will be considered "legitimate" or studiable behavior as opposed to "noise." Because investigators are unable to predict exactly what is going to happen during the course of research interaction, it becomes self-contradictory, as Wax points out in Chapter 2, to secure "informed" consent before the research is initiated. In addition, in the move from one end of the research spectrum to the other, calculable harms become less serious and benefits less immediate. As a result, weighing potential harms against benefits before research is carried out becomes an exercise in creativity, with little relevance to the ethical dilemmas and problems that may emerge during the research. In such research, utilitarian calculations of risks versus benefits become ever less appropriate in judging the value or ethical adequacy of a research project.

A more appropriate ethical framework for judging fieldwork might be constructed on respect for the autonomy of individuals and groups based on the fundamental principle that persons always be treated as ends in themselves, never merely as means—the Kantian categorical imperative (Kant, 1959; see also Englehardt, 1978, p. 19).

Before applying the categorical imperative to the conduct of fieldwork, I would like to examine participant observation more closely. The preceding discussion of relationships between investigators and investigated dealt with fieldwork as though it consisted of a comparatively homogeneous set of relationships.

The position of fieldworkers can be understood as a role that is negotiated over time, a social construction, composed in part by the ways in which those who are studied will tolerate a stranger, in part by the temperament and interests of the investigator. (The chapters by Wax and Glazer underline this point.) Thus, there are a variety of relations which merit separate analysis. Table 1-2 summarizes the argument.

Relations between Fieldworkers and Informants

Fieldwork is at the far pole of the research spectrum when compared with methods where there is an asymmetrical relationship between investigators and investigated and where investigators excercise high conceptual control. Nevertheless, variations do exist within fieldwork, and these can be measured along the same dimensions used for the other modes of research.

At one extreme, by now historically obsolete in many parts of the world, is the *verandah model* of ethnography. (This argument follows the lead of Wax and Cassell, 1979b). Think of the fieldworker, sitting on the verandah of the government station, sending for a "native" who will be subjected to several hours of systematic ques-

Table 1-2. Relationship between Fieldworkers and Informants

	Verandah model	Noblesse oblige	Going native	Undercover agent	Advocate
Asymmetry of relationship					
Fieldworkers' power as perceived by informants	H	H-M	L-0	0	H-M
Fieldworkers' control over research setting	H	M	L-0	L-0	L
Conceptual control					
Fieldworkers' control over context of research	H-M	L	L-0	L	M
Fieldworkers' control over research interaction (direction of interaction)	M-L F⇌I limited two-way	= F⇌I two-way	= F⇌I two-way	M F∿I distorted	L negative variable

Note. The varieties of fieldwork are rated relative to each other, and the categorizations are not comparable to those of Table 1-1. F, fieldworker; I, informant; H, high; M, medium; L, low; =, equal; 0, none.

tioning about indigenous language and customs. (I understand that this model was utilized by Radcliffe-Brown, who questioned Andaman Islanders who were sent to him from the local British gaol.) Such research is still carried out in modern institutional settings, where subordinates, be they prisoners, students, enlisted men, or mental patients, are brought to the office of the researcher for questioning about the customs and jargon of their fellows. Such fieldwork is characterized by the relatively high perceived power and authoritativeness of ethnographers, comparatively high control of the setting, high-to-medium control over contextual features, and medium-to-low control over interpersonal elements. Interaction is somewhat one-sided, flowing from investigators toward those studied. (Note that the perceived power of the fieldworker is being measured against the other varieties of fieldwork. If the two spectra of research relationships, between investigators and investigated and fieldworkers and informants, were superimposed, I suspect the verandah model would be located somewhere near survey research.)

Next on the spectrum of fieldwork relationships is the *noblesse oblige* model, exemplified by the fieldworker who moves into a substantial residence with a body of retainers, coming to play in local society the role of a wealthy patron. This role was perhaps easier to assume during the imperial era of the European presence, but it can still be played, and is, in fact, sometimes expected, by host peoples in many areas of the world. It works most easily when the fieldworker can establish a peer relationship with the local elite, and indeed in many such situations it is difficult for a relatively wealthy higher-status researcher not to be cast in such a role. (Thus, when I conducted fieldwork in a Jamaican farming village, the local inhabitants coached me and my children in the proper behavior for this role.) The fieldworker, here, has high-to-medium perceived power, some control of the research setting, no contextual control, and little control over research interaction, which flows in two directions.

In the next model, *going native,* the researcher tries in every conceivable fashion to adopt the way of life of the common people being studied: the fieldworker lives in their residences, eats their food, talks their language, and shares their lives. Such conduct is often difficult, because the researcher is attempting to learn the role of a local and responsible adult, itself a time-consuming task, while also conducting research and maintaining field notes. This role is handled most easily if the fieldworker is, or can be cast by those studied as a "native." (For example, when I conducted fieldwork in New York City on the contemporary American Women's Movement (Cassell, 1977) I was a native, studying other primarily white middle-class women like myself.) In this type of fieldwork, the investigator has little or no power, control of the setting, or control of contextual or interpersonal features.

In the next model, the *undercover agent,* the investigator seeks to expose the activities of persons who are for one reason or another concealing important parts of their lives. This infiltration is spoken of as "penetrating fronts" and " exposing the back-stage." (See Douglas, 1976, and Galliher, 1980, for two different rationales for carrying out covert participant observation.) Undercover agents, through deceit, obtain more power over those studied and more conceptual control, especially over interpersonal features, than is realized by the hosts. It is difficult to characterize the flow of interaction, since its course is blocked and distorted by deceit, which causes investigators to spend so much time and energy on "frontwork" that they tend to perceive those studied, and social life in general, in terms of deception and frontwork. (I believe that deceptive research is a special case that does not fit smoothly within the specturm derived from genuine relationships between investigators and subjects.)

On the far end of the spectrum is the *advocate* model of fieldwork. Many ethnographers study peoples who are economically or politically depressed and are moved to intervene to help people improve or transform their destinies. Advocacy can range from the liberal (or relatively conservative) approach known as "applied anthropology" to varieties of insurgency. Equally important, if not more so, advocates can range from those scarcely familiar with the hosts to those both familiar and deeply committed. Advocates wish to help those studied gain power; consequently, they frequently attempt to transfer to their hosts their own power and knowledge, or that of the group or milieu from which they come. Although they rarely control the research setting, advocates do in some ways influence the contexts of interaction by their definitions of the situations as those where their task is to aid or empower their hosts. Advocates do not control research interaction which flows freely in two directions, and, in fact, certain varieties of advocacy research are set up so that those who are studied help define contextual features and control the direction of interaction by determining the task and goals of research and helping to decide what methods will be used to achieve these (see Schensul, 1980, and Hessler, New & May, 1980, for descriptions of this kind of research).

Applying Kantian Ethics to Fieldwork

When considering the varieties of fieldwork, each with differing relations between researchers and researched, we see that different possibilities of harm and benefit are associated with each. Moreover, the potential harms of fieldwork typically are less immediate, measurable, serious, and predictable than those associated with other research modes.[3] Consequently, requiring a utilitarian risk-benefit assessment before research is conducted may do little to improve the ethical adequacy of research. Instead, fieldwork might be judged more appropriately in the context of respect for autonomy based on the fundamental principle stated by Kant, that persons be treated at all times as ends in themselves, never merely as means.

The concept of respect for autonomy is not a substitute for the avoidance of harms. Instead, it supplements utilitarian principles, in a situation where harms are relatively few and difficult to predict.

Wax, Chapter 2, argues that the categorical imperative is too individualistic an ethic to deal with the uniquely communal nature of fieldwork. I believe this objection can be surmounted, however, if researchers focus on respect for the autonomy of groups as well as that of individuals. Dworkin (1976) defines autonomy as authenticity plus independence. In following this definition, we can demand that fieldworkers respect and even attempt to augment the authenticity and independence of the communities they study.

In applying this principle, it becomes clear that certain extreme varieties of the verandah model of fieldwork might be considered questionable, even if subjects suffer little or no harm and the research benefits human knowledge. It is fatally easy, when conducting such research, for the investigator to treat subjects primarily as means rather than ends, and to destroy their independence through implicit or explicit coercion. Because of the asymmetry between informants and researchers, who control the research setting, and to some extent, the direction of interaction, a specific effort must be made to respect the autonomy of those studied and give them sufficient freedom so that they feel able to decline to enter the research sit-

---

[3] In thinking of harm, notorious cases that come to mind are "tearooms" (Humphreys, 1970) and Camelot. The first put subjects at risk, causing much comment and disapproval among social scientists, but apparently caused no harm. The second was canceled before it had any chance to put people at risk. In the controversial "Springdale" case, discussed by Johnson, Chapter 4, this volume, the greatest harm caused by violation of privacy appears to have been anger and hurt feelings. If there have been demonstrated instances where fieldwork caused more serious injury, they have not been cited in the literature, leading one to conclude that they have been successfully kept from the public eye.

uation or to leave it at any time. If the categorical imperative were applied to such fieldwork, certain situations might be judged in advance as too coercive. In such cases, it should be possible for fieldworkers to alter their research plans in order to minimize their perceived power and their control of the setting in which research is to take place. (Goffman, 1961, p. ix, for example, when studying a mental hospital, avoided sociable contact with the staff, and did not carry a key which in that setting served as a symbol of power and authority.)

When examining noblesse oblige fieldwork, or the going native model, incidents and relationships must be weighed on individual bases. In each case, however, the fact that an interaction or procedure might result in few harms would not be sufficient to have it judged ethically adequate. In making such judgments, it is more the quality of the interaction than the results that must be scrutinized.

In the undercover agent model of research, subjects are being used primarily as means rather than ends, even though there may be few harms if confidentiality is respected. In addition, in deceptive research the investigator presents an inauthentic self, making the research interaction inauthentic. Consequently, such research is doubly questionable. I am not implying that overt fieldwork proceeds wholly without deception on some ideal level of perfect truth. Fieldwork, like friendship, requires a number of social lies to keep interaction flowing fairly smoothly. Also, ethnographers frequently become honarary or symbolic members of the community, and friends with many of their hosts, who then tend to "forget" that they are being studied. It would be a rash investigator who, at a critical or confidential moment, said: "Wait a minute—don't forget you're being studied!" Fieldworkers who use friendships to obtain information without continually reminding informants what they are doing are, in a certain sense, deceiving them. So are researchers who agree with, or at least do not contradict, informants' remarks that they find unacceptable. Such "deceit" is probably necessary in fieldwork and in social life. I do not believe, however, that it violates the autonomy of those studied or treats them as means rather than ends. Participant observation conducted by an undercover agent does. Covert fieldwork also causes harm: it harms investigators, whose relations with those studied, and indeed whose very view of reality, are distorted by their own bad faith. I have pointed out that fieldwork is the only research method in which the interaction between investigators and subjects is included within the research paradigm. The interaction is the method; the ethnographer is the research instrument. Those who engage in deceptive research are using unreliable instruments, altering the course of research interaction, and obtaining distorted data. Consequently, I believe that deceptive fieldwork is unsound methodologically as well as morally. The argument has been advanced that certain information cannot be obtained except through deceit. Although this may be so, it is irrelevant. There is no principle holding that all information is equally necessary to science. For example, knowing just what goes on in brief homosexual encounters in public restrooms (Humphreys, 1970), or how couples use nude beaches to arrange sexual encounters (Douglas, 1976), is no more vital than much of the material found in The National Inquirer. If investigators must deceive to obtain such information, social science will survive without it. Proponents of deceptive research often argue that certain groups, such as the rich and powerful, or organized crime, can only be studied covertly. Some investigators, however, have managed with time and patience to study some such groups with relative openness (Chambliss, 1975; Klockars, 1974). (And, when studying an organization such as the Mafia, for example, one might well argue that honesty is not only the best but the healthiest policy.) Should investigators be convinced that it is essential to act as undercover agents in order to expose a particular variety of moral, political, or social chicanery, they can do so, as spies or investigative reporters, subject to the funding, ethical imperatives, and professional constraints that govern those occupations. But they should not be allowed to call themselves social scientists. (Interestingly, investigators whose most strongly oppose spying in the name of social science in Third World countries frequently espouse similar tactics when studying the rich and powerful in their own milieus. For a critique of this "two tier" morality, see Appell, 1980). Covert research is unfair to other investigators, causing hostility to social science and foreclosing future research when the deception is discovered, and it usually is discovered, if only when a study is published (Diener and Crandall, 1978, pp. 25-126). In addition, it may bias the findings: covert fieldworkers are so preoccupied with fooling others that they frequently perceive deceit or "frontwork" as the essence of the activity being observed. (For example, Hilbert, 1978, argues that covert research is the essence of participant observation because it teaches the researcher about the central fact of social life, which is "passing" or "impression management.")

Not only does covert research violate the autonomy of those studied, treating them as means to researchers' ends, it also carries a high potential for harm, since people may disclose damaging information when they do not know they are being studied. Therefore, undercover agent research may be considered unacceptable on utilitarian as well as Kantian grounds.

When the categorical imperative is applied to advocacy research, it becomes clear that there are certain varieties of advocacy in which subjects may be used primarily as means rather than ends. In such cases, fieldworkers are promoting predetermined goals for those studied, without examining indigenous values, goals, and lifeways. Thus, advocates whose fieldwork is really a species of revolutionary agitation may be violating the Kantian categorical imperative, if the host people are being used primarily as a means to gain the researchers' own revolutionary goals. Such fieldwork might be characterized as a kind of revolutionary "neocolonialism," in which researchers are convinced not only that they know more than their hosts about what will benefit the subjects, but also that it is worthwhile to risk the well-being of their hosts in order to chance the making of a revolution. (See Schlesier, 1979, and responses by Schlesier, 1980, Deloria, 1980, Demallie, 1980, Hill, 1980 , and Washburn, 1980, for an exchange of views on the fieldworker as activist and revolutionary catalyst.) The same critique applies to investigators who wish to keep their hosts "pure" or "untainted" by the modern world, even when those studied are anxious to obtain the techniques, ideas, and goods of that world. Because this posture regards only the values of the investigator, not the views of those studied, it treats people as means to alien ends and so violates their autonomy. Thus, even if one agrees with a particular fieldworker, in a particular effort to ameliorate or improve a group's situation, if the change is not desired by that group, then the effort is ethically questionable. The issue of whether a researcher should intervene when in the field has always been a difficult one, especially since there seems to be no sure way of calculating possible harms and benefits in advance. By concentrating on intent rather than results, the categorical imperative makes it easier to weigh such decisions: they are acceptable when people are treated as ends, not means, and their autonomy is respected. In contrast to research that treats people as means to researchers' ends are advocacy programs, in which investigators work closely with those studied, helping them determine the relevant problems, methods, and goals, and then working with them to achieve the goals (Hessler & New, 1972; Jacobs, 1974; Schensul, 1973). Here, fieldworkers are trying to enhance the autonomy of those studied, thereby treating people most fully as ends. Thus, we might consider such research a paradigm of the ideal relation between investigators and investigated.

To enforce the principle of respect for human autonomy, of using people primarily as ends rather than as means, research projects might be reviewed before investigators go into the field and again when they return. For example, a group of experienced fieldworkers could review ethnographic research plans before fieldwork is initiated. When particular techniques, such as verandah ethnography or undercover agent research appear questionable, the burden of proof would be on the fieldworker to convince colleagues that (1) this is the only possible way to carry out such an investigation, and (2) the research is worth doing. Fieldworkers might also undergo a debriefing when research is completed, where they are encouraged to examine the relationships established with those studied and discuss the ways in which the data will be presented. The discussions, occurring before and after research, should in themselves encourage reflection and a more informed attempt at conducting ethical fieldwork. The review committee might also employ sanctions, if necessary, including private and public censure and, in cases of flagrant abuse, refusal to allow publication of findings.

Analyzing Wrongs

In summary, current ethical prescriptions and regulations governing human research assume (1) that the relationship between researcher and researched is asymmetrical, (2) that harms and benefits are (a) relatively substantial, (b) at least partially measurable, and (c) occur as a direct result of the interaction between researcher and researched, and that (3) this research interaction, and consequently its harms and benefits, can be predicted in advance. When we examine the spectrum of research methods (from biomedical to psychological experimentation, to surveys, to fieldwork), it becomes clear that the closer we are to the pole of biomedical experimentation, the more valid are these assumptions. I have pointed out that at the opposite pole, of fieldwork, the relationship between researcher and researched is comparatively symmetrical; harms and benefits are relatively minimal, difficult to measure, and associated more with the manipulation of data than of people; and the course of interaction, and consequently harms and benefits, is unpredictable.

Accordingly, the application of ethical prescription and regulation based on these three assumptions may do little to improve the practices of fieldwork.

However, the fact that fieldworkers generally have little power to harm informants during research does not mean that they have no ability to wrong them. It is the process of wronging people, as opposed to harming them, that deserves attention, when discussing the ethics of conducting fieldwork.

People can be wronged without being harmed (May, 1978; MacIntyre, 1979): they can be treated solely as means to researchers' ends, their essential humanity can be ignored or discounted, their individual or group values can be denigrated or violated. The notion of wronging people follows naturally from the Kantian categorical imperative. This concept may well have influenced those who posed the Federal requirements for the informed consent of human subjects. I am not convinced, however, that obtaining informed consent solves the problem of wronging those studied, especially in the case of social science research. MacIntyre (1979) argues that the possibility and magnitude of harm are reduced as we move across the spectrum of research, from biomedical and psychological experimentation to surveys and, finally, fieldwork; at the same time, he contends, the possibility of wronging people is increased.

Of the behavioral and social research studies that have provoked dismay among critics, many have done so because they wronged rather than harmed the researched. When the morality of these studies is argued in terms of harms rather than wrongs, confusion results. For example, in Stanley Milgram's experiments on obedience to authority (1963, 1965) the evidence on whether subjects were harmed is equivocal: Milgram contends that subjects, when interviewed at a later date, claimed they were happy to have participated; moreover, respected and ethical social scientists have testified to the benefits to knowledge of Milgram's experiments (e.g., Kelman, 1979b). Nevertheless, when we hear of this and similar studies, many of us feel a sense of unease. Arguing in terms of harms versus benefits obfuscates the issues. When we think in terms of Milgram having wronged his subjects, by exposing them to a possibility of unwanted and unasked-for self-knowledge (which may or may not have harmed), the issue becomes clearer.

Again, a social scientist, who has published on ethics and is a member of a university IRB, told me how difficult it is to design survey questions to discover whether preadolescent girls had been exposed to incestuous advances from their fathers. "I've never heard of a question that harmed anyone," said the researcher to me. We are on less solid ground if we argue this on risk of harm weighed against possibility of benefit, the risk of disturbing the children against the possibility of learning how to idenfity and avoid such occurrences, than if we discuss it in terms of wronging them, violating the girls' privacy and autonomy, and treating them as means to the researcher's ends. I believe this is the type of wrong those who designed the human subject regulations meant when they spoke of psychological and social risks.

We find, however, that discussing the effects of such research in terms of psychic and social harms, and then weighing these against benefits leads to interminable and insoluble discussions of whether people were indeed exposed to harm, and whether such harms are worth the possible benefits of knowledge. One reason these discussions are so unsatisfying is that we are weighing apples against fish: as MacIntrye (1979) points out, although harms to interests can be weighed against benefits to interests, there is no way to balance wrongs against benefits to interests. MacIntyre also notes that people can be compensated for harms to their interests by being given benefits commensurate with the harm, but that compensation for a wrong makes no sense.

What are the wrongs associated with fieldwork? Deception, manipulation, and the unveiling of secrets come to mind.

Deception

In an earlier section, I discussed covert research, where the undercover agent wrongs the host people, by studying them without their knowledge and possibly against their will. Also mentioned was a "gray area," ranging in seriousness from small social lies, to implicit deception, to outright duplicity. Johnson, for example, in a book on conducting fieldwork (1976 pp. 95-99), has a section entitled "Using Reconstructions of One's Biography, " where he argues in effect that the most practical way to develop trust among those studied is by lying. The language is abstract and social-scientific, the advice (I believe), unethical: fieldworkers are counseled to alter their expressed beliefs and biographies to suit whatever audience they happen to be addressing. In my opinion, such deliberate duplicity wrongs those who are deceived.

Such biographical reconstructions are sins of "commission" rather than "omission": the researcher is deliberately falsifying information rather than holding back certain facts. Deliberate deception wrongs not only the researched, but other researchers as well, by creating a climate of mistrust (Bok, 1979, pp. 192-213) where people feel no qualms about lying to social scientists who, themselves, are perceived as liars. Bok (1979, p. 16) defines lying as "an intentionally deceptive message in the form of a statement."

Lying is defined by Bok as part of the larger category of deception, which underlines the fact that one can communicate a deceptive message without words. Thus, John Galliher (1980, p. 303) reports that when studying Mormons in Utah, he cut his hair, shaved his beard, and wore white shirts and a necktie; he felt this behavior was less than completely honest, although it resulted in a "zero rate of refusal from Mormons and several invitations to dinner and invitations to join their church." Did the researcher wrong those studied by altering his nonverbal presentation of self? I tend to feel he did not, that dressing so that one "fits in" might be classed as a variety of tact or politeness, despite the fact that Galliher, himself, seemed to think of it as a sort of hypocrisy. (This, of course, may be a generational difference: I was raised to think that dressing appropriately was good manners; Galliher clearly was not. This leads to an interesting issue: if the Mormon elders Galliher interviewed perceived appropriate dress as mannerly, was Galliher hypocritical to follow their standards rather than his own?) This example may seem trivial, but it is precisely in "trivial" everyday behaviors that a fieldworker may wrong the host people. One of the significant differences between fieldwork and other research techniques is that fieldwork generally takes place over a substantial period of time, interaction is the method, and the researcher is the instrument. As a result, the ethical dilemmas of fieldwork may be closer to the problems of daily life than those of other methods. In fieldwork, as in daily life, the line between politeness, on the one hand, and hypocrisy, on the other, may be a narrow one.

The line between truthfulness and aggression may also be narrow, and there are occasions when forcing the standards of the investigator on those studied, in the guise of "honesty," may be as much of an affront as purposeful duplicity. For example, when Melanie Dreher (1980) went to a Jamaican village to study the use of ganja (marijuana), she told the people she was interested in studying their way of life, which was true so far as it went. By the end of her time there, she reports, her study was an open secret among the villagers, and they themselves decided when to reveal and when to conceal her subject matter. In this case, complete openness at the beginning of her fieldwork would have endangered not only her study but her hosts. I tend to feel that openness, in a situation where the indigenous cultural rules dictated secrecy (the illegal use of ganga was an open secret which was discussed only among intimates) would not only have harmed those studied, but wronged them, by imposing on them alien standards of disclosure. (More ethically troublesome are situations where the concealment of significant information violates indigenous rules, e.g., the researcher, quoted by Glazer in Chapter 3, who neglected to tell the Arab villagers he studied that he was at that time affiliated with an Israeli university. Did he wrong them? Perhaps he did. Moreover, his actions may have exposed those studied to harm, if the interviews and the Israeli affiliation became public.) In contrast, Dreher's deception followed the local rules of disclosure and served to protect the people she studied.

This gives us two possible criteria for situations where deceptive behavior (as opposed to deceptive statements, or lies) might be acceptable: when the behavior follows local rules of propriety; and when it protects those studied from psychic, social, or legal harm. In other words, there may be situations where forcing the researcher's standards on others may both wrong and harm them. Thus, when I interviewed a fieldworker (Cassell 1978a, p. 81), who had promised to show his results to the administrators of an institution he studied, he said the administrators had made it very clear they did not want to see his findings; he also told me he knew his findings would disturb them. Nevertheless, the researcher, believing the violation of a promise was more important than the well-being of those studied, wished to show the unwanted and disturbing data to the administrators. "I don't feel professionally clean—for my own professional ethics," he said. This case illustrates the way in which a rigid and unthinking absolutism, a rote application of moral rules, may wrong those studied.

My interpretation of Kant's categorical imperative may well be idiosyncratic. One of the three formulations of the categorical imperative is that one should always act so that one's action could be construed as a universal law (1959, p. 39). Kant, himself, seems to have construed this universal law as an absolute prohibition against lying (see his article, reprinted in Bok, 1978, pp. 285-290). Kant would probably have prohibited every type of deception. My interpretation, based on a rather free reading of the second formulation of the categorical imperative, that people always be treated as ends, never merely as means (1959, p. 47), is that although deception may wrong people, there are times when aggressive, insensitive, and unnecessary truth telling may treat people as means to the truth-teller's ends, and thus wrong them.

Let me stress that, although I have discussed and reflected on the ethical problems of fieldwork for several years, I am no authority of formal ethics. Moreover, even acknowledged authorities disagree. A thoughtful reader's opinion on these, and similar issues, is as valid as mine, and can be bolstered by an impressive array of authorities.

The real point is that those who realize that their tactical decisions will have moral implications and who reflect about possible harms and wrongs beforehand are more likely to make sensitive and informed decisions during the course of research.

Manipulation

It was said that the situation of relative parity between fieldworkers and informants makes it easier for the researched as well as researchers to use psychic and social manipulation to achieve their ends. Is it immoral when those studied keep demanding goods in return for cooperation with the comparatively wealthy and well-equipped researcher? Few of us would believe so, although some might think the fieldworker unwise to keep acceding to escalating demands (see Chagnon's account, 1974, pp. 162-197, of fieldwork among the warlike and aggressive Yanomamo, where the demands for goods, and for submissive behavior by the anthropologist, became so extreme that the researcher's life was theatened and he had to leave the field).

Intuitively, it seems less ethical for the fieldworker to manipulate the norms of reciprocity in the other direction, so that the host people are pressured to give data they might prefer to withhold. Is it because our cultural norms prescribe a balanced reciprocity, unlike the one-upsmanship of the Yanomamo? (We are discussing norms, not behavior.) An amusing example of this contrast in norms is provided by the account of a young fieldworker (Glazer, 1972, pp. 88-96) who describes how he manipulated the norms of reciprocity, and his status as a comparatively well-heeled graduate student guest, to gain entry to a rare American Indian ceremony. He felt so guilty about this behavior that he concluded that "the anthropologist is a potent manipulator exploiting unsuspecting and naive subjects" (p. 94). I was present at a meeting where a researcher from another discipline, who has written extensively on ethical issues, denounced the shocking behavior of this fieldworker. Later, I discussed this account separately with three fieldworkers who had worked with American Indians; all found the story hilarious and were persuaded that the situation was a complete setup, where the naive researcher had been manipulated by his hosts to contribute to the ceremony!

Some accusations of manipulation are more serious. Members of Third World peoples frequently accuse fieldworkers of taking information from those they study and giving nothing in return, of serving as biased representatives of an imperialist power, and treating those studied as "primitives" who are somehow less than fully human (for example, see Chilungu, 1976). Proposed solutions range from declarations that only Third World researchers should study Third World peoples, to calls for greater sensitivity, to proposals that fieldworkers leave the academy and become revolutionaries (Diamond, 1974, p. 426). The issues are significant but, despite the fact that the problem is posed in terms of unethical or immoral researchers, the solutions are frequently political, involving adopting the political stance of the writer (which is most usually radical). Unfortunately, when the language of ethics is used for political disputes, where one's opponents are labeled immoral rather then mistaken, more heat than illumination is generated. (See Appell, 1980, 1978, and Wax & Cassell, 1979b, for discussions of some of these issues).

Manipulation of the researched by researchers can occur in a more immediate, and less politicized manner. For example, when researchers covertly studied a small flying saucer cult (Festinger, Riecken, and Schachter, 1956), whose members were waiting for the end of the world, they posed as fellow believers. The ratio of researcher-believers to true-believers was so high, however, that their participation wronged those studied not only by lying to them but also by providing false "evidence" to reinforce their beliefs (at the same time, altering the phenomena under investigation).

Transparency versus Secrecy

When discussing the wrongs, as opposed to harms, of fieldwork, MacIntyre (1979) stated that he believed the going native model of fieldwork was more dangerous than the verandah model, and possibly even more dangerous than the undercover agent. Following our own cultural values of transparency and disclosure, researchers may enter a group where secrecy and mystery are highly valued, and succeed in piercing the veil of secrecy to reveal their secrets. This, he stated, is an act of aggression, wronging those studied, if mystery is part of their culture, and they do not agree with our belief that understanding is a good in and of itself. Here the fieldworker is operating under false pretenses, even when the research role is disclosed, because those studied do not understand the investigator's undisclosed set of intentions.

As a member of the culture of science, where disclosure and understanding are highly valued, I find this accusation disturbing. Disturbing because it challenges my values as ethnocentric. Upon consideration, I realize they are. Although widespread, the belief that knowledge is a good, in and of itself, is probably unique to Western culture. Disturbing because, intuitively, MacIntyre's accusations have a ring of validity. Disturbing because if secrets are not revealed, perhaps fieldworkers are out of business.

Let us examine an example of secrets revealed: Frederik Barth (1975) studied the ritual knowledge of the Baktaman, a small isolated group in central New Guinea, whose ritual activity was based on a secret system of male initiations. The more sacred the information, the more secret it was, with fewer people sharing the sacred knowledge. The anthropologist ultimately managed to obtain detailed first-hand information on six of the seven degrees of male intitiation. His book includes photographs of sacred places, prohibited to noninitiates, with descriptions of the ceremonial meaning of each element, and descriptions of mortuary practices, taboos, sorcery, and the sacramental eating of human flesh. The author, who notes how the knowledge contained in these rituals is hedged by taboo and secrecy, and how their importance and validity are directly linked with the observation of secrecy (p. 217), states that the total corpus of knowledge upon which the book is based is stored only in the minds of the 183 members of the group (p. 255). Or was so stored, until collected, analyzed, and published by the anthropologist. As a ritual participant, Barth was told these secrets in trust and he says he did not fail in this trust while part of the group; he did tell the Baktaman that he would share this knowledge with others in his homeland who passed through "our" initiations, which was acceptable, but did not explain that the "initiates" would include women, which might not have been acceptable. He begs those few readers who might possibly come in contact with this small isolated group to be responsible and humane in their use of this secret knowledge (p.7).

Did Barth wrong the Baktaman by collecting, analyzing, and publishing their secrets? One cannot ask the 183 Baktaman. One cannot even ask their children, who may, while studying anthropology at the University of Papua, New Guinea, conceivably be embarassed by pictures of their parents and relatives wearing nothing but jewelry, a netbag, and an occasional scanty fiber skirt or penis shield. (A researcher reports that when a classic ethnographic film on New Guinea was shown to an educated Papua New Guinea audience, "one student angrily turned off the projector: 'What right does anyone have to record what we choose to forget." he inquired. Carpenter, 1972, p. 190.) Does one wait and ask the grandchildren or great-grandchildren, who may be grateful to have the forgotten knowledge of their fathers returned to them? Do they have the right to decide whether their forefathers were wronged?

In certain ways, it was easy for Barth to bypass his dilemma, because the secret belonged to 183 souls isolated in the midst of almost impassable countryside on the opposite edge of our universe, both geographically and culturally. (Perhaps this was the position of the first generation of researchers studying American Indians, who were isolated, hard to reach, and profoundly separated from the culture of the investigators.) But today no group stays isolated for long. The dilemma is the same, but more immediate, when those whose secrets were violated can read, write, and have access to the media to voice their complaints.

How does one weight a brilliant and illuminating analysis of cultural creativity, symbolism, ritual, and knowledge against wronging a small group of people who will probably never know they were wronged? The question, as Barth, himself, says in the preface to his book, is "vexing." Does it really matter that the Baktaman do not know they were wronged? What would anthropology, social science, and knowledge have lost if the book had not been written? As an anthropologist with an interest is ritual and symbolism, I find it difficult to say that the book should not have been written (or published). I have less difficulty, however, vetoing experiments, such as those on DNA, where I have no personal involvement. Perhaps such moral judgments must be made by people in other disciplines, who are not seduced by the beauty of specific kinds of knowledge.

Conclusions

We have come a long way from the tangible, measurable, and comparatively predictable harms of experimentation to the wrongs of fieldwork, and have arrived at no easy answers. Although the relatively symmetrical relationship between fieldworkers and informants, and the broad focus of research, probably reduce the magnitude and frequency of harms, these characteristics may facilitate wronging those studied.

Fieldworkers, then, have few grounds for sentiments of moral superiority. We are no better than other researchers, although perhaps more subtle in our ethical infringements, and harder to control.

What principles can researchers use to improve the ethical adequacy of fieldwork? I shall suggest three, based on reflection, avoidance, and a search for benefits.

My first proposal is perhaps less a principle than a practice, and of such simplicity, it may sound stupid: to reflect in advance on what may occur. Decisions that seem, and may even be presented in methods texts as, tactical are quite frequently moral as well. Thus, as noted, " reconstruction of one's biography," as suggested by one book on doing field research (Johnson, 1975), is not merely a method for gaining rappart, it is also a way of lying to people, and thus wronging them.

Second, we must make every possible effort to avoid both harming and wronging people. Although harms are difficult to predict, some can be foreseen and must be avoided. But, because utilitarian principles, which weigh possible harms against benefits, are not particularly effective for this genre of research, they must be supplemented by respect for the autonomy of those studied, and by the fieldworker's resolve to treat people as ends, rather then merely as means to the researcher's ends. The categorical imperative, then supplements rather than supplanting an avoidance of harms to those studied.

Since we cannot rely on results, which are unpredictable, we must rely upon our intention, neither to harm nor wrong those studied. One cannot give a list of recommended behaviors for every possible situation, which can be followed by rote like a recipe, at least, not without the risk or encouraging the mechanical behavior of the researcher (p. 19) whose own "professional ethics" were more important to him than were the people he studied. Vague sounding principles, however, can be helpful in concrete situations. Most important is the ability to recognize an ethical issue when it arises, so that one can make the correct decision. Much behavior which appears unethical results less from moral turpitude than from errors of classification: ethics are considered something large, important, and imponderable, "out there," while "right here" the researcher is engaged in making practical decisions about everyday matters.

Third, I believe we must actively attempt not only to avoid harms, but to benefit those studied, to augment, not merely respect, their autonomy. The anthropological principle of reciprocity, discussed by Wax and Glazer in Chapters 2 and

3, involves an obligation by the fieldworker to those studied. May (1980, p. 367) has used the concept of a covenent to characterize the special relationship between fieldworker and hosts. "A covenental ethics is responsive and reciprocal in character. It acknowledges a two-way process of giving and receiving." In return for their help, those studied must also be helped. In return for the benefits they confer upon the fieldworker, they too should be benefited.

One way to benefit the researched is through knowledge. Whether or not knowledge is a good in itself, it can surely be used to benefit those studied. Perhaps the fieldworker has an obligation to attempt to use the knowledge received from the host people to help them, or to help them decide what knowledge they need, how to get it, and what to do with it. Here, we have much to learn from the advocacy model of fieldwork, from the projects carried out by researchers such as Schensul (1980) and Hessler, New, and May (1980), where those studied were involved in designing projects and collecting and using data. In this type of research, the classic distinction between "pure" and "applied" research is blurred. Perhaps we can no longer afford such a distinction; when we separate knowledge for thinking from knowledge for using we may be wronging those from whom we received it.

If this is indeed so, and we owe some benefit, possibly associated with knowledge, to those who participate in our research, then the implications of this obligation extend beyond fieldwork, to every variety of research involving human beings. For a truly moral relationship between those who study and those who are studied, we must move beyond the avoidance of harm to an active search for reciprocal benefits.

Acknowledgments. This chapter was produced as part of the activities of the project on "Ethical Problems of Fieldwork," sponsored by Washington University, St. Louis, Missouri, and the Center for policy Research, New York City, and supported by the program in Ethics and Values in Science and Technology of the National Science Foundation.

References

Appell, G. N. Talking ethics: The uses of moral rhetoric and the function of ethical principles. *Social Problems*, 1980, *27* (3), 350-357.

Barth, F. *Ritual and knowledge among the Baktaman of New Guinea.* New Haven, Conn.: Yale University Press, 1975.

Bok, S. *Lying: Moral choice in public and private life.* New York: Vintage, 1978.

Carpenter, E. *Oh what a blow that phantom gave me!* New York: Holt, Rinehart and Winston, 1972.

Cassell, J. *A group called women: Sisterhood and symbolism in the feminist movement.* New York: David McKay (Longmans), 1977.

Cassell, J. *A fieldwork manual for studying desegregated schools.* Washington, D.C.: National Institute of Education, 1978. (a)

Cassell, J. Risk and benefit to subjects of fieldwork. *The American Sociologist*, 1978b, *13*, 144-152. (b)

Cassell, J. Ethical principles for conducting fieldwork. *American Anthropologist*, 1980, *82*(1), 28-41.

Cassell, J. Does risk-benefit analysis apply to moral evaluation of social science? In T. Beauchamp, L. Walters, & R. Faden (Eds.) *Ethical issues in social science research*. Baltimore, Md.: Johns Hopkins Press, 1982.

Cassell, J., & Wax M. L. (Eds.). Ethical problems of fieldwork. *Social Problems*, 1980, *27*(3).

Chagnon, N. A. *Studying the Yanomamo*. New York: Holt, Rinehart and Winston, 1974.

Chambliss, W. On the paucity of original research on organized crime: A footnote to Galliher and Cain. *The American Sociologist*, 1975, *10*, 36-39.

Chilungu, S. W. Issues in the ethics of research method: An interpretation of the Anglo-American perspective. *Current Anthropology*, 1976, *17*(3), 457-481.

Deloria, V., Jr. Schlesier, other anthropologists, and Wounded Knee. *American Anthropologist*, 1980, *82*, 560.

Demallie, R J. Comment on "Of Indians and anthropologists." *American Anthropologist*, 1980, *82*, 559-560.

Diamond, Stanley. Anthropology in question. In D. Hymes (Ed.), *Reinventing anthropology*. New York: Vintage, 1974.

Diener, E. & Crandall, R. *Ethics in social and behavioral research*. Chicago: University of Chicago Press, 1978.

Douglas, D. *Investigative social research*. Beverly Hills, Calif.: Sage, *Publishing*, 1976.

Dreher, M. Presentation given at a meeting on the Ethical Problems of Fieldwork, Wayzata, Minn., September 1980.

Dworkin, G. Autonomy and behavioral control. *The Hastings Center Report*, 1976, *6*(1), 23-28.

Engelhardt, H. T., Jr. Basic ethical principles in the conduct of biomedical and behavioral research involving human subjects. *The Belmont Report: Ethical principles and guidelines for the protection of human subjects of research* Vol. 1, Appendix, DHEW Publication No. (OS) 78-0013. Washington, D.C.: U.S. Government Printing Office, 1978.

Festinger, L., Riecken, H.W., & Schachter, S. *When prophecy fails*. Minneapolis: University of Minnesota Press, 1956.

Galliher, J. F. Social scientists' ethical responsibilities to superordinates: Looking upward meekly. *Social Problems*, 1980, *27*(3), 298-308.

Glazer, M. *The research adventure: Promise and problems of field work*. New York: Random House, 1972.

Goffman, E. *Asylums: Essays on the social situation of mental patients and other inmates*. New York: Doubleday Anchor, 1961.

Gray, B. H. *Human subjects in medical experimentation: A sociological study of the conduct and regulation of clinical research*. New York: Wiley, 1975.

Hessler, R. M., & New, P.K.-M. Toward a research commune? *Human Organization*, 1972, *31*, 449-451.

Hessler, R. M., New, P. K.-M., & May, J. T. Conflict, consensus and exchange. *Social Problems*, 1980, *27*(3), 320-329.

Hilbert, R. A. Learning from Agnes: Notes on covert participant observation. Paper presented at conference of the Association for Humanist Sociology, South Bend, Indiana, October 1978.

Hill, T. W. Grab the children and run: A comment on Schlesier's "Of Indians and Anthropologists." *American Anthropologist,* 1980, *82,* 557-558.

Humphreys, L. *Tearoom trade: Impersonal sex in public places.* Chicago: Aldine, 1970.

Jacobs, S.E. Doing it our way and mostly for our own. *Human Organization,* 1974, *33,* 380-382.

Johnson, J. M. *Doing field research.* New York: Free Press, 1975.

Kant, I. *Foundations of the metaphysics of morals.* Indianapolis: Bobbs-Merrill, 1959. (Originally published, 1785.)

Kelman, H. C. *A time to speak: On human values and social research.* San Francisco: Jossey Bass, 1968.

Kelman, H. C. The rights of the subject in social research: An analysis in terms of relative power and legitimacy. *American Psychologist,* 1972, *27,* 989-1016.

Kelman, H. C. Research, behavioral. In W. T. Reich (Ed.), *Encylopedia of bioethics* (Vol. 3). New York: Macmillan and Free Press, 1978.

Kelman, H. C. Remarks made at a conference on Ethical Issues in Social Science Research, at the Joseph and Rose Kennedy Institute of Ethics, Georgetown University, September 1979. (b)

Klockars, C. B. *The professional fence.* New York: Free Press, 1974.

MacIntyre, A. Comments at session on Informed Consent, Conference on Ethical Issues in Social Science Research, at the Joseph and Rose Kennedy Institute of Ethics. Georgetown University. September 1979.

May, W. F. Comments at session on Ethical Problems of Fieldwork, annual meeting of the American Anthropological Association, Los Angeles, November 1978.

May, W. F. Doing ethics: The bearing of ethical theories on fieldwork. *Social Problems,* 1980, *27*(3), 358-370.

Milgram, S. Behavioral study of obedience. *Journal of Abnormal and Social Psychology,* 1963, *67,* 371-378.

Milgram, S. 1965 Some conditions of obedience and disobedience to authority. *Human Relations,* 1965, *18,* 57-76.

Orne, M. T. On the social psychology of the psychological experiment: With particular reference to demand characteristics and their implications. *American Psychologist,* 1962, *17,* 776-783.

Orne, M. T., & Scheibe, K. E. Inadvertent termination of hypotized and simulating subjects. *International Journal of Clinical and Experimental Hypnosis,* 1964, *14,* 61-78.

Schensul, S. L. Action research: The applied anthropologist in a community mental health program. In A. Redfield (Ed.), *Anthropology beyond the university.* Athens, Georgia: Southern Anthropology Society, University of Georgia Press, 1973.

Schensul, S. L. Anthropological fieldwork and sociopolitical change. *Social Problems,* 1980, *27*(3), 309-319.

Schlesier, K. H. Of Indians and anthropologists. *American Anthropologist*, 1979, *81*, 325-330.

Schlesier, K. H. Reply to Deloria, DeMallie, Hill,and Washburn. *American Anthropologist*, 1980, *82*, 561-563.

Spradley, J. P. *The ethnographic interview*. New York: Holt, Rinehart, and Winston, 1979.

Washburn, W. E. "Of Indians and Anthropologists": A response to Karl Schlesier. *American Anthropologist*, 1980, *82*, 558-559.

Wax, M. L. On fieldworkers and those exposed to fieldwork: Federal regulations and moral issues. *Human Organization*, 1977, *36*, 321-328.

Wax, M. L. Once and future Merlins: The applied anthropologists of Camelot. *Human Organization*, 1978, *37*(4), 321-328.

Wax, M. L., & Cassell, J. (Eds.). *Federal regulations: Ethical issues and social research*. Boulder, Colo.: Westview Press, 1979. (a)

Wax, M., & Cassell, J. Fieldwork, ethics, and politics: The wider context. In M. L. Wax & J. Cassell (Eds.), *Federal regulations: Ethical issues and social research*. Boulder, Colo.: Westview Press, 1979. (b)

Wax, R. H. *Doing fieldwork: Warnings and advice*. Chicago: University of Chicago Press, 1971.

Chapter 2

Research Reciprocity Rather than Informed Consent in Fieldwork

Murray L. Wax

> Anthropological research does not have subjects. We work with informants in an atmosphere of trust and mutual respect. (Mead, 1969, p. 371)

With this emphatic characterization of her own research discipline, Margaret Mead discerned a sharp difference between the ethical problems of fieldwork and those peculiar to laboratory research, where, as she phrased it, human beings were

> reduced to the condition of powerlessness, stripped of their individual rights and dignities. (Mead, 1969, p. 367)

Some biomedical or psychological researchers might respond to Mead by claiming that they too work with informants in an atmosphere of trust and mutual respect; and conversely, some critics of fieldwork might contend that fieldworkers "have subjects" in the sense that their informants were subjected to the coercion of powerful investigators. In any case, however, the contrast between field and laboratory research styles is real and morally significant, whether or not it be taken as absolute or as established by disciplinary lines.

It is the ethical significance of the relationships within different styles of research which here concern us, and not whether disciplinary lines necessarily demarcate kinds of ethical issues in social sciences research. I argue that the analysis of the ethical problems generated by scientific investigation has been impoverished because of the insistence on regarding all research as if structured about the model of experimenter-subject. Enlarging the field of examination to include fieldwork, whether performed by anthropologists, economists, psychologists, political scientists, or sociologists, serves to enrich our understandings not only of the ethical problems of science, but also of the very ethical principles by which we hope to govern, not only scientific research, but also our daily activities.

By seeking to simplify the issues with universalistic formulations, both philosophers and bureaucratic regulators have muddied our discourse. As Cassell has argued (Chapter 1; 1978, 1980) the very use of the term "human subject" prejudges the nature of research since "subject" implies *subjection*. When the experimenter-subject dyad is regarded as paradigmatic and normative, then ethical analysis becomes impoverished, and those who wish to conduct ethically responsible research find themselves without guidance, while being themselves subjected to a regulatory process that may inflict a moral wrong on them.

I begin this chapter by examining the context in which fieldwork is done, elaborating on Cassell's (Chapter 1) characterization of how the relationship between fieldworker and informants (or hosts) differs from that of experimenter and subject. I then proceed to discuss the issue of informed consent versus concealment or deception as this tends to arise in fieldwork, and argue that the prescriptions developed by bioethicists and enunciated in the *Federal Register* do not contribute to resolving the ethical dilemmas that emerge in fieldwork. I then suggest an alternative approach to ethical evaluation that is rooted in the experiences of responsible fieldworkers.

Informed consent pertains to the initial contact between researcher and other. In most fieldwork, the researcher usually has little knowledge of how that contact will be experienced and has only hopes and fantasies as forecasts of the subsequent course of research. Almost invariably, the fieldworker has little or no power over the hosts and, frequently, it is they who are powerful, relative to the researcher. Rarely does there exist a suitable context for making a formal declaration or agreement such as is required by the Federal regulations. If field relations do develop satisfactorily they lead toward a condition of parity and reciprocity between the two parties. Like friendship, the relationship is complex and emergent and therefore difficult to confine with words or to judge by a simplistic ethical formula.

The Context of the Moral Challenge

The practice of fieldwork confronts the researcher with a series of serious moral challenges that are quite different from those inherent in other social science methods. At the simplest level, the challenge lies in the initiation of intimate contact with a community that may be culturally and ecologically alien, having norms, etiquette, techniques, and routines that are quite different from those that the researcher had previously encountered. Part of the literature of fieldwork is focused on the problem of trying socially and physically to survive, while coming to terms with communal practices that the researcher finds strange and perhaps repulsive or uplifting, and of how the orientation of the researcher may (or may not) be transformed. Thus, reflecting on her arrival among a small Indian band in a remote area of Peru, where the Amazon jungle is dense, Janet Siskind (1973, p. 5) comments: "The beginning of fieldwork is a terrifying period, when the problems of where to sleep, eat, and survive are overwhelming." More dramatic is the narrative of Napoleon Chagnon (1968, p. 5):

> I looked up and gasped when I saw a dozen burly, naked, filthy, hideous men staring down at us down the shafts of their drawn arrows! Immense wads of green tobacco were stuck between their lower teeth and lips making them look even more hideous, and strands of dark-green slime dripped or hung from their noses. My next discovery was that there were a dozen

or so vicious dogs snapping at my legs circling me as if I were going to be their next meal. I just stood there holding my notebook, helpless and pathetic.

But the moral challenge of fieldwork extends considerably beyond this initial crisis.

The dilemma of fieldworkers is that they must oscillate between being two persons: they arrive as members of the research communities of their native countries, and yet they wish to gain some acceptance as members of the community of their hosts. Within that acceptance, they wish to become involved with the intimate personal lives of persons to whom they are initially as strangers. Yet, they wish to become involved *in order that they may gather data*, which they will then transfer to their native institutions, to be refined into their contributions to the social-scientific enterprise. So, fieldworkers approach a community, seeking to live and work, and hoping to develop such intimacies as to be admitted into its privacies; yet, they wish to be able to convert their observations into data with the further hope that these data will become the basis of essays that will be adjudged as objective and allocated to a respectable place in the corpus of scholarly writings.

Not knowing their hosts, fieldworkers must inevitably approach them in the initial stages as a species of research objects, that is, subjects of the field investigation. Morally, this stance is uncomfortable because it seems a violation of the axiom of Kantian ethics that people are to be regarded as ends and never solely as means:

> I had visions of entering the village and seeing 125 social facts running about calling each other kinship terms and sharing food, each waiting and anxious to have me collect his genealogy. (Chagnon, 1968, p. 4)

> The self-seeking motive of obtaining a degree, the key to my profession, a rational motive in my society, led me to view the Sharanahua at times as those wonderful people who would help me to obtain my degree and to see myself as yet another foreign exploiter. (Siskind, 1973, p. 11)

The method of fieldwork constitutes a strategy that usually resolves this dilemma in a fashion that is useful, while being ethically responsible. But, it is important to note that the interaction between fieldworker and host peoples is reciprocal, so that the exploitative intent of the former is matched by that of the hosts, who are initially in a strong position to define the terms of interaction.

Many communities, tribal peoples typically, regard only their own folk as "human beings" and consider the rest of humanity as less than human or as prey. In many cases, the name used to denote one's own people is that also used to designate "human being." It is salutary to remind ourselves that hunting peoples usually regard other peoples as equivalent to the game that they snare and kill. As Nancy Lurie has explained,[1] the Plains Indians (of the eighteenth and nineteenth centuries) were oriented toward discovering herds of buffalo (bison) which they slaughtered

---

[1] This is implicit, but not forthrightly stated, in Lurie's wise analysis of "The Contemporary American Indian Scene" in Leacock in Lurie (1971, Chap. 14). The buffalo metaphor was used by her in personal conversation.

for their meat, hides, and other parts. When herds were encountered, there was prosperity; when they could not be found, there was hunger. These peoples, and some of their descendants, regarded strangers (and entities such as Federal programs) as if these also were buffalo, that is, potential sources of food, clothing, and wealth. From the viewpoint of such peoples, the intruding fieldworker is a potential game animal ("a buffalo"), and the problem is to discover how to utilize this stranger while minimizing any risk. For example, where fieldworkers have distinctive kinds of wealth, there may develop considerable rivalry within the host community as to who can be most successful in securing these, without suffering any consequences:

> Within a few days I was on my own, and before long the novelty of my medical help and my gifts of lines and hooks, as well as the initial excitement they had provoked, had worn off. My gift giving took on the status of a routine activity. In fact, I was treated as I deserved, as an inexhaustible provider. People approached me constantly; one had a headache, one had lost his fishing hook, one wanted this, one wanted that, endlessly. . . .

> The more I wanted to play a role, the more the Panare would attempt, and to a large extent successfully, to take advantage of it. They would test their power against mine. My goods and services were up for grabs.
> (Dumont, 1978, pp. 51-52)[2]

Openness, Deception, and Consent in Fieldwork

The regulatory system mandated by the Federal government lays great stress on the "informed consent" of the human subjects involved in the research. At first blush, this seems indeed to be a principle of such significance as to command our universal assent. Indeed, informed consent would seem implicit in the arguments of Immanuel Kant, who is one of the major authorities in modern Western ethical theory. Kant declares that we should treat other human beings as ends in themselves, and never solely as means to ends; or alternatively phrased, we should regard others as autonomous persons. This implies that we should neither deceive nor coerce research participants and it would appear that informed consent is a proper procedure for respecting their autonomy. But, when we turn to the actualities of field research, we may soon find ourselves conflicted when attempting to use informed consent procedures, and I propose to show how this may occur by providing a number of historical examples.

Most field research is performed among an exotic people, or more precisely (and less ethnocentrically), where fieldworker and host people are mutually alien with differing customs, it is impossible (inconceivable) for the research to proceed

---

[2] If goods can be secured with very little effort, then it is not only the Panare, but all other peoples who will try to get as much as they can, and often more than they want. This was demonstrated during the 1981 riots in Liverpool, Manchester, and London, England, when there emerged a bit of patriotic graffiti, "Loot British" (J, A. Barnes, personal communication, 1981).

covertly. The fieldworker's presence is conspicuous, even when attempting to participate or blend.

Some of the anthropological literature might deceive us on this point. For example, in his "Preface" to the *Argonauts of the Western Pacific* (Malinowski, 1922), Sir James Frazer stated (1922/1961, p. vii) that Bronislaw "Malinowski lived as a native among the natives for many months together." However, this characterization is so exaggerated as to be near ridiculous, and, Malinowski himself made no such claim. With his retinue of servants and his supply of trade goods, the fieldworking Malinowski of 1915-1918 did not live as a Trobriand native. Indeed, with his frail constitution, his hypochondria, and his intense focus on scholarship, he could not possibly have made a serious attempt to live in that fashion (M. L. Wax, 1972). From a careful reading of his diaries and his works, the reader obtains no evidence that Malinowski even wanted to live "as a native among the natives" but rather that his participation in their lives was occasional and pro forma.

On neither Malinowski's side nor that of the Trobriand natives was there any doubt as to his alien identity. Given that the natives were nonliterate and are now deceased and left no records on the matter, we can only guess as to what they thought of Malinowski and of his reasons for living among them. Had they turned for enlightenment to the European colonists, they might have found equal, possibly even greater, bewilderment concerning the ethnographic enterprise among persons denominated as "savages." So, for the moment we can say that the Trobrianders adapted themselves to a visiting alien, who was distinguished from his fellow Europeans by his sympathetic yet intrusive interest in the minutiae of their customs.

In contrast to Malinowski's overt research role, there was, a generation prior, some modest range of attempts at covert fieldwork by persons seeking to reform the workings of Western societies. These covert domestic researches provide the basis for a moral evaluation of covert practices, as well as illustrating the difficulties of assessing harms and benefits before the investigation is completed.

In 1888 a rich young Englishwoman assumed lower class garb in order to gain employment in a sweatshop. The episode was a modest part of the studies which she and her kinsman, Charles Booth, were conducting of poverty in London, but the episode was dramatized by both herself and the press. She was questioned about her observations by a Parliamentary Commission, and she claimed to have suffered severe pangs of conscience as she allowed it to be inferred that she had conducted her fieldwork for a number of weeks. However, a leading magazine published her observations under the title, "Pages of a Work-Girl's Diary" (Webb, 1888), and my own reading of these pages led me to conclude that she had spent but one day within the sweatshop.[3] Yet the length of time does not matter, for she had set an example, and she was to become a famous social researcher and reformer under the name of Beatrice Webb. She and her husband Sydney were to produce one of the first manuals on the conduct of social research (Webb & Webb, 1932), and it was influential.

---

[3] See also the account in Muggeridge and Adam (1968, pp. 112ff.).

I cannot say whether or not it was Beatrice's example that was influential, but two years later, in the summer of 1890, a German student of theology put aside his student's robes, dressed himself in humble clothing, and took a job as a factory laborer in order to discover for himself, not only the condition of the working classes, but the distinctive elements of what we would today term their subculture. The young man, Paul Göhre, felt it necessary to disguise his status as a student and his goal of research, and by carefully chosen falsehoods he succeeded in his aim. His fellow workers realized that by origins and training he was not one of them, but his incapacities and dedication aroused their sympathies and comradeship, so that they carried him along during the first difficult weeks of his effort.

Göhre published the results of his experiences, first, as essays in the journal, *Christliche Welt*, and then as a slender monograph (1895), which was "greeted by the wealth and culture of Germany like a revelation. As one of the most conservative newspapers of Germany put it, it was if someone had returned from the heart of Africa and described the ways of a strange and hitherto unknown nation" (Ely, 1895, p. viii).

Far more substantial than the fieldwork of either Paul Göhre or Beatrice Webb, and comparable rather to the survey of London conducted by Charles Booth and Webb (Booth, 1891, 1902-1903; Pfautz, 1967) was the project conducted in 1896-1898 to study "the actual condition of the colored people" in Philadelphia. The researcher was a recent Ph. D. from Harvard, William Edward Burghardt Dubois (1899/1967). Unhappily, he left us little in the way of narrative about his fieldwork during that study. A half-century later (1944, p. xix) he reminisced:

> In the fall of 1896, I went to the University of Pennsylvania as "Assistant Instructor" in Sociology. It all happened this way: Philadelphia, then and still one of the worst governed of American's badly governed cities, was having one of its periodic spasms of reform. A thorough study of causes was called for. Not but what the underlying cause of corruption was evident to most white Philadelphians: the corrupt semi-criminal vote of the Negro Seventh Ward. . . . With my bride of three months, I settled in one room over a cafeteria run by a College Settlement, in the worst part of the Seventh Ward. We lived there a year, in the midst of an atmosphere of dirt, drunkenness, poverty and crime. Murder sat on our doorsteps, police were our government, and philanthropy dropped in with periodic advice.

However, Dubois did not discuss how he, as a person so educated and erudite as compared with his neighbors, interacted with or was regarded by those who were the subjects of the study. Surely he was conspicuous, and his research interviews were communicated by his use of a formal schedule of inquiry.

By both fieldwork and survey techniques, DuBois was to continue his studies of Negro life, especially in the Deep South. But of more dramatic input within the academic world was the study of a southern community by Hortense Powdermaker, a white anthropologist from the border state of Maryland.

Powdermaker was among Malinowski's earliest students and had been a labor organizer. Like her mentor, she did fieldwork in the South Pacific, but after drafting that research report, Hortense Powdermaker decided in the 1930s to study

Negro life within a small town of the Deep South of the United States. Her researches could not be covert, for she was almost as conspicuously alien in rural Mississippi as she had been on the coasts of New Ireland. Moreover, the southern whites felt initially more threatened by her research efforts than did the Melanesian people. She soon realized that she could not study the blacks without studying the whites, but she felt that she could not be truthful about her aims with the latter, and so she practiced deceit and maintained part of her research effort as covert: "to all the whites I said I was studying Negro life; to the Negroes, I said I was studying the community—Negroes and whites" (1967, p. 146). In her autobiographical memoirs, she justified this verbal maneuver by the declaration: "That I was doing a social study would have been obvious to anyone, regardless of what I would have said" (1967, p. 146). She did mention her profession as an anthropologist, and adds, "I was more comfortable, and therefore more effective, in being as candid as circumstances permitted" (1967, p. 150).

Her deceit was with respect to the whites, who did not realize that she was observing and recording their lives as she participated with them: "Much of my data and understanding of the white people came from seemingly casual social participation with the middle-aged and older people in Indianola" (1967, p. 184). Toward the close of her study, her research interests in the white community became more explicit, as she conducted personal interviews with (white) planters and when she distributed 600 copies of a questionnaire via the major voluntary associations of the community. Since that instrument was designed to elicit white attitudes toward Negroes, the intent of her study must have become reasonably obvious to any thoughtful person. Nevertheless, we do not know what was the ultimate judgment of the various members of the community, especially after the publication of her monograph, *After Freedom* (1939).

Powdermaker had gone to rural Mississippi in 1932; four years later William Foote Whyte traveled the shorter distance from Harvard University to the area of Boston he called "Cornerville" and began his fieldwork. Having never conducted a field study, his ideas were vague, often grandiose, and impractical. In his 1955 "Appendix" to the second edition of *Street Corner Society*, he says that when he was introduced to Doc in February, 1937, he "went into a long explanation" which unfortunately he omitted from his field notes (1955, p. 291). Historically, it would have been nice to have a record of the conversation; but, ethically, I doubt that it matters, since the evidence well reveals how Whyte's conception of his study changed during the months of his fieldwork. He assumed that the local residents would wish to know about his project, and so he framed an explanation in terms of doing a "social history" of the community, except that this cumbersome recital fell flat. Finally, he found that the people of Cornerville "were developing their own explanation about me: I was writing a book about Cornerville. This might seem entirely too vague an explanation, and yet it sufficed" (1955, p. 300).

In an influential essay of 1940, Florence R. Kluckhohn singled out for discussion the research procedure that I have described as being utilized by various individuals since the turn of the century. Kluckhohn spoke of it as "the participant-observer technique in small communities" and illustrated it from her own experiences in rural New Mexico. The phrase "participant observation" had been used previously, and I find its earlier history to be murky, but her delineation and application of the phrase gave it an academic status which it had not previously enjoyed. Given the history we have here been outlining, it would have been possible for her to have characterized participant observation as either *covert*, or *overt*, or both. She chose to place the technique within a scientific framework which required it to be *covert*: "one's intentions cannot be disclosed" (1940, p. 333). From her own field experiences, the ethical limitations of this position were evident, because she confessed that the quality of her participation in communal life was "in most respects hypocritical" (1940, p. 341). She justified her own conduct on the grounds that race relations in rural New Mexico were inflamed, although one may note that this particularity would not have justified covert research in other localities.

An effective rejoinder to Kluckhohn's analysis is pragmatic and historical: scores of fieldworkers, from Malinowski and Mead to the present day, have proceeded openly, secured significant data, and written reports of scientific and practical consequence. It is little wonder that Mead, writing almost 30 years after Kluckhohn, could take for granted that the moral and methodological norm of her discipline was working "with informants in an atmosphere of trust and mutual respect."

On the other hand, our historical survey, even in its brevity and incompleteness, has indicated situations where covert research has seemed appropriate and has had benign consequences. Surely, it is (or was) of considerable importance to understand the workings of the sweatshop, and one of the most effective techniques for achieving an understanding is to go to work within one. In so doing the researcher was not acting illegally, but simply presented her or himself as a potential employee in a situation which for the management was routine.

This class of deceptive investigations has been generalized and extolled by social scientists, such as John Galliher (1980), and his argument is echoed by those who contend that researchers have been biased because they have studied "down" (the poor, the ethnics, the victims of imperialism), when they should have been studying "up" (namely, the elites, the powerful and wealthy).[4] From their point of view, the world contains numerous kinds of oppression, which should be described and analyzed by social scientists. Indeed, it is the unique ethical responsibility of social scientists to perform this function. Since these situations are characterized by oppression, usually masked by deception, and since overt entry by researchers into

---

[4] An ethnographic investigation may generate troublesome questions pertaining to consent and the political purposes for which the research may be used. For example, which authorities, and how constituted, should be regarded as having the right to allow (or deny) the entry of the fieldworkers into the geographic and social space of the community? When some factions are encouraging to the fieldworkers and others seek to be rid of them, how should this affect the conduct of the fieldworkers? Where there is exploitation and oppression of one group by another, either within the community or by exterior authorities upon the community, what are the responsibilities of the fieldworker, either initially and with regard to consent or later during the investigation? In bargaining with authorities for consent, what are proper and improper concessions with regard to the framing of the reports?

these situations would rarely be possible, and might be met by the construction of "potemkin villages" (i.e., special sites exhibiting social concern), then researchers are obligated to proceed covertly.

From this vantage point, if we examine the history of social research, then there is little question that positive social (and moral) benefits have derived from some kinds of covert research. Beatrice Potter Webb's examination of the interior of the "sweating trades" was an aspect of an overall examination of poverty, and that sequence of studies assisted the institution after the First World War of the British system of social welfare. The studies by Powdermaker and John Dollard (1937) helped to stimulate the overall assessment by Gunnar Myrdal (1944), and their findings were incorporated into his volume, *An American Dilemma*. In like manner, covert studies of police, mental institutions, and prisons, to mention but a few, have assisted both scientific and public understanding, and, in particular, have helped in such movements as the deinstitutionalizing of patients.

The point is that if we regard the focus of inquiry as an entire social situation, and if we take the elite (or the gatekeepers) on whom much of the research is focused to be but one element of the situation, then, on a utilitarian basis, we can contend the wrongs incurred by the practice of covert fieldwork may be far outweighed by the social benefit of exposure and analysis.

The "Consent Process" in the Community Study

These issues are clarified and elaborated by focusing further on a specific variety of ethnographic research, the community study. Scores of such studies have been conducted in all corners of the world, and some of the consequent reports have acquired great fame, e.g., see Johnson's description (Chapter 4) of the studies of "Springdale" and "Plainville." Some of the researchers have been single persons, some have been family units, and some have been teams of individuals unrelated except by professional status.

To be "a community" the entity must be discrete and bounded, have some degree of homogeneity (such as a common language, a shared moral code, and some central ceremonial life), as well as having some degree of autonomy and some system of internal social organization and political governance (Redfield, 1956). We may think here of a municipality in the United States or Europe, a village in India, or a tribal hamlet in traditional highland New Guinea. Where higher political authorities are involved, the fieldworkers will have had to present the project and solicit counsel and approval. Following this, once a community has been selected for consideration, the fieldworkers approach those persons who are regarded as authorities or influential, describe the nature of the projected study in a vocabulary appropriate to the situation, and solicit not merely consent but counsel, and positive assistance. For, conduct of a successful study requires not merely passive assent to the project, but the active cooperation of some of the members of the community. At minimum, the fieldworkers have to locate places of residence, and sources of food and supplies, as well as sites for scholarly work, including places to converse privately and to process and store field notes.

During the investigation, the fieldworkers will have innumerable occasions to describe the nature of their investigation, for, in most cases, the residents will be skeptical of the initial explanations and often will have devised their own interpretations of the enterprise on the basis of continued observations and shrewd speculations. Moreover, the fieldworkers may themselves easily become pawns in the factional struggles within and about the community, so that what is imputed of the enterprise may vary with the local political climate. Frequently, the presence of the fieldworkers will be condemned by some factions while being welcomed enthusiastically by others. Also, as the fieldworkers become increasingly knowledgeable about the community, the direction of their interests and the kinds of acceptance accorded by community members will continually be shifting. Thus, the fieldworkers cannot reasonably be expected to gain the same degree of "informed consent" of everyone in the community; and even within a particular bloc that consent will vary in scope even within different time periods.

The morality of the presence of the fieldworkers is determined less by the process of initial consent than by the interrelationships which the fieldworkers are able to construct with their hosts. Because they seek not merely consent but active cooperation, fieldworkers devote themselves to trying to serve and be of assistance. This is easiest to perform when the host people are poor or technologically underdeveloped, because then fieldworkers can provide medical services, or transportation (via an automobile), or firepower (rifles and ammunition), or the competencies of the educated in coping with alien bureaucratic forces. In this perspective, the fieldworkers are trying to establish networks of *reciprocal* exchange, in which the services they can offer then entitle them to secure information and assistance from among their hosts.

Because this kind of reciprocation is so natural and normal, and because fieldworkers can only proceed on the basis of acceptance by the local community, including the assistance of its members, there is in this phase of the research infrequent opportunity and less temptation for ethical wrongdoing. This does not mean that fieldworkers are morally superior beings, but only that in typical ethnography, they are placed in situations where their conduct is subject to intensive observation, monitoring, and communal control. An ethnographic investigation may wreak harm to the community studied, but, if this ensues, it is not likely to occur because of immoral behavior in the field but because of negligence in the framing of the published reports (see Johnson, Chapter 4).

To begin with, in many small towns (or residential communities), the fieldworker is conspicuously alien. In terms of dress, grooming, posture, dialect, and education, he or she is emphatically different from others, and his or her presence, as a person without the usual responsibilities of a mature adult, requires explanation. In many cases, an explanation in terms of research, e.g., writing a book about the town, or doing a history of the town, is more intelligible and appropriate than almost any other, and serves to legitimize a presence that might otherwise appear peculiar or dubious.

Second, normal residents cannot ask the same blunt and direct questions as can someone who has the public stature of a researcher. The former are restrained by the etiquette of civility; the latter can approach others with questionnaire schedule in hand and conduct a systematic interrogation, using the stance of a scholar in order to request enlightenment. Moreover, when the stranger is identified as a researcher, natives make it their business to instruct, even when the researcher is too ignorant or too courteous to inquire. Thus, when Powdermaker was leaving the village of Lesu in New Ireland, after completing her fieldwork, the *luluai* explained (1967, pp. 120-121) to a visitor from another village:

> You know when she came here, she was so dumb. She did not even know how to speak. She was like an infant. She knew nothing. But now, ah, all is changed. She speaks and she understands us; she knows our magic; she can dance with the women; she has learned our folk tales; she know how we garden and the different ways we fish; she has been to all our feasts; she knows about the *Malanggans*. . . . Ah, she knows much. Who is responsible? I am.

In most situations of disguised observation, such naivete as was evidenced by Powdermaker would have destroyed the disguise *and* prevented information gathering.

Finally, the researcher who conceals identity is constricted by the wearing of a mask. Over a period of weeks and months, not only does the facade become wearisome, it corrupts interpersonal sensitivities. In many cases, the finest insights of the fieldworker are developed from interaction within the self (cf. Devereux, 1967). This interaction is constricted and distorted when the researcher is preoccupied with sustaining a fraudulent presence. Indeed, the deceptive researcher seems to emerge from the field with a portrait of the hosts as engaged in deception (cf. Douglas, 1977). This situation may become even more complicated, if the entities being studied are organizationally so complex or of such size that the purported identity of the fieldworker cannot be systematically conveyed to all.

To urge upon fieldworkers that honesty, in the presentation of the self, is the best policy may seem ethically simplistic. However, the foregoing argument does not prohibit fieldworkers from acting on other and more purely ethical principles in deciding whether and how to be open about their inquiries, and in seeking informed consent.

The Relativity of "Informed"

Among those who have been analyzing the ethical issues in biomedical and behavioral research, there is consensus that consent should be "informed." Subjects should be informed as to what will be entailed in participating in the research project (and they should be in a position, sufficiently free and not subjected to coercion, that they may either give or withhold consent to their personal participation). However, what fieldworkers have repeatedly observed is that those who may become the researched, namely, the host population, seldom focus their attentions on the goals and formal design of the project and mostly direct themselves to assessing (1) the sponsorship of the researcher, (2) the character and disposition of the researcher, and (3) the immediate utility and direct benefit of project activities in their own lives.

Powdermaker was able to commence her researches in the Mississippi town of Indianola only because she was able to establish a linkage with the distinguished literary figure who was locally regarded as an aristocrat. Presumably, he sponsored her because he recognized her as a fellow member of the academy, and his status was such that his endorsement prevailed over the xenophobia of many of the town's influential white citizens. In the case of blacks, a rumor soon spread that she herself was really a Negro, passing for white in order to study the whites. She preferred to deny the rumor (1967, p. 148) but, knowing such populations, I wonder whether the local Negroes believed her denial.

In Whyte's case there was parallel sponsorship by "Doc," the leader of a group of "cornerboys." As time went on, Whyte tried to explain his research endeavors, but, as he discovered:

> I found that my acceptance in the district depended more on the personal relationships I developed than upon any explanation I might give. Whether it was a good thing to write a book about Cornerville depended entirely on people's opinions of me personally. If I was all right, then my project was all right; if I was no good, then no amount of explanation could convince them that the book was a good idea. (1955, p. 300)

Research Reciprocities

We began this chapter by citing Margaret Mead's description of anthropological research as working with informants in "an atmosphere of trust and mutual respect," yet our subsequent discussion revealed a set of ethical dilemmas, as we tried to integrate the experience of ethical fieldwork with the injunction that researchers must always seek the informed consent of their subjects. How is it possible to reconcile Mead's roseate description with these dilemmas?

Informed consent is both too much and too little to require in fieldwork and therefore often irrelevant to the ethical assessment of fieldwork. On the one hand, informed consent is *too much* in situations where conduct and information are public, so that the field researcher seems to exhibit a troublesome case of overscrupulousness in requesting formal and explicit consent to observe that which is intended to be observed and appreciated. Formal and explicit informed consent also appears overscrupulous and disruptive in the case of many of the casual conversations that are intrinsic to good fieldwork, where respondents (informants) are equal partners to the interchange, under no duress to participate, and free either to express themselves or to withdraw into silence. On the other hand, informed consent is *too little* because fieldworkers so often require much more than consent; they need active assistance from their hosts, including a level of research cooperation that frequently amounts to colleagueship. Indeed one genre of research report is the narrative of the relationship with a person who played so integral and collaborative a role in the field as to merit the title of research associate (Casagrande,

1960). Informed consent is a troublesome misconstrual of these field relationships because the field process is progressive and relationships are continually being renegotiated, so that, if the research is going well, the fieldworker is admitted to successively deeper levels of responsibility together with being required to share communal intimacies (e.g., by being invited to participate in "secret" ceremonials). To ask initially or formally for consent to be admitted to that level of intimacy would be to affront the sensibilities (and autonomy) of the hosts, who need the opportunity of getting to know the fieldworkers, in order to assess the field-workers' responses to obligations, and to judge when they would be sufficiently mature to be asked to assume higher levels of responsibility and adulthood.

The foregoing requires further analysis that is grounded in the empirical actuali-ties of field experience. While there have been several flurries of exchanges concern-ing disguised participant observation, which signifies that the researcher did not obtain informed consent, the ethical level of discussion has remained fixated on concepts and issues deriving from the biomedical model. Among the better of such discussions is that of O'Connor (1979, pp. 225-258) and of Diener and Crandall (1978, Chap. 7):

> Since disguised and nondisguised participation studies range along a con-
> tinuum, there is no absolute cutoff where they definitely become unethi-
> cal. Nor is there agreement among social scientists about whether disguised
> participant observation is justified. Erikson (1967), Jorgenson (1971), and
> Davis (1961) have argued that disguised participation is unethical, whereas
> Denzin (1968), Roth (1962), and Galliher (1973) defend the strategy.
> (Diener & Crandall, 1978, p. 125)

My contention is that this kind of argument is misdirected, and that an entirely different category of relationship underlies good field experiences, and that this is manifest in the dictum of Mead. What fieldworkers hope to do (whether consciously or not) is to enter into the networks of reciprocity of the host community; and, it is by entering into those networks that hosts and fieldworkers recognize each other as fellow, moral human beings, and enforce on each other the adherence to a suit-able set of moral norms. Indeed, it is the very process of entering that relationship that arouses in fieldworkers both the sensitivity to understand the human events they seek to understand, and the sensitivity to understand what it means to be ethical in the particular fieldwork role, as Glazer explains in Chapter 3.

Whether it be the Sharanahua (Siskind), the Panare (Dumont), the Trobriand Islanders (Malinowski), the tribal peoples of New Guinea (Mead), the Boston corner boys (Whyte), or the groupings within the Mississippi town of "Indianola" (Powder-maker), the fieldworker's functioning rests on a moral foundation of reciprocity. Among sociologists and social anthropologists, Mauss (1925) was the earliest to analyze the role of reciprocity, although it was perceived as early as Simmel (1908/ 1950), and it continues to be reemphasized by scholars as diverse as Gouldner (1960) and Lévi-Strauss (1949), while R. H. Wax (1952, 1971) directed early attention to its role in fieldwork. Among political philosophers, Emmet (1974) has commenced the analysis of its comparative role, noting its appearance within Hel-lenic philosophy in the Greek word, *dike*, often translated as "justice."

The societal workings of reciprocity may be dramatically visible to us in societies such as those of the Trobriand Islanders, where men labor in their gardens to feed the families of their sisters, while themselves being fed with the produce raised by the brothers of their wives (Malinowski, 1929; Weiner, 1976). But the nonexploitative character of reciprocity is perhaps more graphically illustrated for us in the account of Dumont (given earlier in this chapter), where he complains of the lack of reciprocity, of how the Panare exploited his willingness to distribute fishhooks and medication. Only when giving is reciprocal does it establish the participants as peers and fellow human beings.

Emmet (1974, p. 74) thinks of Kant as the "paradigm philosopher" of the morality based on reciprocity, but she also recognizes that he "brings in some actual notions of right and wrong taken out of the *mores* of the Protestant Christianity in which he was brought up." As an anthropologist, I would also have to add that his ethical theory communicates an imperfect notion of the organic reality of community (or society), so that the reader is left with a view of an aggregate of autonomous individuals, rather than of a social fabric. Moreover, as MacIntyre (1966) has perceived, by denying the relevance of the natural inclinations of the actor and emphasizing the formal notions of duty of the autonomous and individuated person, Kant renders morality so abstract as to be void of meaning and therefore it may be filled with any content. In contrast, here I hope to provide such content by referring to the networks of reciprocity of the host community.

Contrary to Florence Kluckhohn, the implicit basis of participant observation is the notion of *parity*, that is, researcher and hosts have become peers of one another (Wax & Wax, 1980). Between peers, communication can be open, direct, and informative in a fashion that is not possible where there is relative ranking. Participation by the researcher in the activities of the host community is more than an attempt at acquiring "*Verstehende*" insight (or empathy); it is symbolic of the parity among the parties to the field investigation. Where there is parity and reciprocity, the ethical quality of the relationships has progressed far beyond the requirements of "informed consent."

References

Booth, C. *Labour and life of the people*. London, William and Norgate, 1891.

Booth, C. *Life and labour of the people in London*. London, Macmillan, 1902-1903.

Casagrande, J. *In the company of man: Twenty portraits by anthropologists*. New York: Harper & Row, 1960.

Cassell, J. Risk and benefit to subjects of fieldwork. *The American Sociologist*, 1978, *13*, 134-143.

Cassell, J. Ethical principles for conducting fieldwork. *American Anthropologist*, 1980, *82*, 28-41.

Chagnon, N. *Yanomamo: The fierce people*. New York: Holt, Rinehart and Winston, 1968.

Davis, F. Comment on "initial interaction of newcomers in Alcoholics Anonymous." *Social Problems*, 1961, *8*, 364-365.

Denzin, N. On the ethics of disguised observation. *Social Problems*, 1968, *15*, 502-506.

Devereux, G. *From anxiety to method in the behavioral sciences.* New York: Humanities, 1967.

Diener, E., & Crandall, R. *Ethics in social and behavioral research.* Chicago: University of Chicago Press, 1978.

Dollard, J. *Caste and class in a southern town.* New Haven, Conn.: Yale University Press, 1937.

Douglas, J. *Investigative social research.* Beverly Hills, Calif.: Sage, 1977.

DuBois, W. E. B. *The Philadelphia Negro: A social study.* New York: Schocken, 1899/1967.

DuBois, W. E. B. My evolving program for Negro freedom. In R. E. Logan (Ed.), *What the Negro wants.* Chapel Hill: University of North Carolina Press, 1944.

Dumont, J.-P. *The headman and I: Ambiguity and ambivalence in the fieldworking experience.* Austin: University of Texas Press, 1978.

Ely, R. T. Prefatory note, pp. vii-viii, in Göhre (1895).

Emmett, D. Three strands in morality. In Mackenzie, M. J. M. *Political questions: Essays in honour of M. J. M. Mackenzie.* Manchester, England: Manchester University Press, 1974.

Erikson, K. T. A comment on disguised observation in sociology. *Social Problems*, 1967, *14*, 366-373.

Galliher, J. F. The protection of human subjects: A reexamination of the professional code of ethics. *American Sociologists*, 1973, *8*, 93-100.

Galliher, J. F. Looking upward meekly. *Social Problems*, 1980, *27*, 298-308.

Göhre, P. *Three months in a workshop: A practical study* (A. B. Carr, trans.). London: Swann Sonnenschein, 1895.

Gouldner, A. W. The norm of reciprocity: A preliminary statement. *American Sociological Review*, 1960, *25*, 161-178.

Jorgenson, J. On ethics and anthropology. *Current Anthropology*, 1971, *12*, 231-234.

Kluckhohn, F. The participant-observer technique in small communities. *American Journal of Sociology*, 1940, *46*, 331-343.

Leacock, E. B., & Lurie, N. O. (Eds.). *North American Indians in historical perspective.* New York: Random House, 1971.

Lévi-Strauss, C. *Les structures élémentaires de la parenté.* Paris: Presses Universitaires, 1949.

MacIntyre, A. *A short history of ethics.* New York: MacMillan, 1966.

Malinowski, B. *Argonauts of the Western Pacific.* New York: Dutton, 1922/1961.

Malinowski, B. *The sexual life of savages in North-western Melanesia.* New York: Harvest, 1929.

Mauss, M. *Essai sur le don, forme achäique de l'échange.* Trans. by I. Cunnison as *The gift: Forms and functions of exchange in Archaic societies.* New York: Norton, 1925/1967.

Mead, M. Research with human beings: A model derived from anthropological field practice. *Daedelus*, 1969, *98*, 361-386.

Muggeridge, K., & Adam, R. *Beatrice Webb: A life, 1858-1943*. New York: Knopf, 1968.

Myrdal, G. et al. *An American dilemma*. New York: Harper& Row, 1944.

O'Connor, F. W. The ethical demands of the Belmont Report. In C. B. Klockars & F. W. O'Connor (Eds.), *Deviance and decency: The ethics of research with human subjects*. Beverly Hills, Calif.: Sage, 1979.

Pfautz, H. (Ed.). *Charles Booth on the city*. Chicago: University of Chicago Press, 1967.

Powdermaker, H. *After freedom: A cultural study of the Deep South*. New York: Viking, 1939.

Powdermaker, H. *Stranger and friend: The way of an anthropologist*. New York: Norton, 1967/1976.

Redfield, R. *The Little Community*. Chicago: University of Chicago Press, 1956.

Roth, J. Comments on secret observation. *Social Problems*, 1962, *9*, 283-284.

Simmel, G. Exkurs über Treue und Dankbarkeit (Note on Faithfulness and Gratitude). In K. H. Wolff (trans.), *Sociology of Georg Simmel*. Glencoe, Ill.: Free Press, 1950. (Originally published in *Soziologie, Untersuchungen über die Formen der Vergessellschaftung (Sociology, studies of the forms of sociation)*).

Siskind, J. *To hunt in the morning*. New York: Oxford University Press, 1973.

Wax, M. L. Tenting with Malinowski. *American Sociological Review*, 1972, *37*, 1-13.

Wax, M. L., & Wax, R. H. Fieldwork and the research process. *Anthropology and Education Quarterly*, 1980, *11*, 29-37.

Wax, R. H. Reciprocity as a field technique. *Human Organization*, 1952, *11*, 34-37.

Wax, R. H. *Doing fieldwork: Warnings and advice*. Chicago: University of Chicago Press, 1971.

Webb, B. Pages from a work-girl's diary. *Nineteenth Century*, 1888.

Webb, S., & Webb, B. P. *Methods of social study*. New York: Longman's Green, 1932.

Weiner, A. B. *Women of value, men of renown: New perspectives on Trobriand exchange*. Austin: University of Texas Press, 1976.

Whyte, W. F. *Street corner society: The social structure of an Italian slum*. (2nd ed. with appendix on fieldwork). Chicago: University of Chicago Press, 1955.

Chapter 3

The Threat of the Stranger: Vulnerability, Reciprocity, and Fieldwork

Myron Glazer

In the summer of 1977 while revising a fieldwork course, I decided it would be enlightening to invite a group of researchers to discuss their experiences. I also wanted to record their words so that students could review and have access to them in future semesters. Tom O'Connell, Director of our Electronics Department, suggested videotaping. He had the expertise and the equipment. I approached researchers from Smith, from nearby Amherst and Hampshire Colleges and the University of Massachusetts. Later colleagues from Harvard, Yale, and the University of Pennsylvania visited. The project became an interschool endeavor.

Several related themes emerged from the interviews and became the focal points of class discussion: the motivations of researchers in pursuing their studies, their ability to gain acceptance from local populations, the ethical tensions inherent in the effort to probe behind the scenes of social life, and the researchers' responsibility to their respondents or informants both during the fieldwork and after its completion.

Central to many of these questions was the vulnerability of both respondents and researchers. An analysis of the fieldwork relationship underscored why some form of reciprocity between the parties was essential to vitiate the fear of harm to those under study and to researchers themselves (Glazer, 1972). The discussions by Martha Fowlkes and Joel Migdal, which follow, reveal that the vulnerability of those interviewed can be generated by the exposure of sensitive personal material or by the discussion of community issues in a highly political environment. The investigator's task was to create a relationship that would enhance trust (Gusfield, 1955). This process entailed listening sympathetically or required the researcher to provide a funnel to the outside world for a political cause. Conversely, rejection resulted when the situation was too threatening and the researcher's project was not considered to be worth the risk. One fieldworker had such an experience recently when a number of Spaniards, who had been associated with the Anarchist Movement 40 years earlier, refused to reveal their past associations to her.[1] They still

---

[1] Conversations with Martha Ackelsberg in spring, 1980.

feared harassment despite the recent change in government and nothing she said to express her sympathy with them could overcome their fears which had developed over a lifetime of political repression. Only when she developed a network of supporters did she win cooperation from those who needed to be reassured that other Spaniards knew her and could vouch for her political reliability.

In sum, all of our visitors revealed how reciprocity, the exchange of favors and commitments, the building of a sense of mutual identification and feeling of community, became a central theme in their research encounters. For some, reciprocity was immediately evident in their involvement and contribution to the lives of those under study. For others, reciprocity was less direct and was to be acted out in the later production of a research document which would cast favorable light on the challenges and struggles of informants and respondents. In each situation, the research relationship would not have developed without such explicit agreements. Instead, the researchers would have been quickly dispatched as uninvited guests who were, at a minimum, a nuisance and, at worst, a direct danger to the well-being of those who were asked to provide information. The precise nature of the reciprocal relationships will be presented as each interview unfolds.

In the course of the interviews we also explored other types of fieldwork encounters that were upsetting because the researchers had to deal with their own attitudes toward pain, suffering, and loss. In such cases investigators had to ponder whether they were capable of remaining sufficiently analytic to complete the project. Kai Erikson's discussion of his experience with survivors of a devastating flood demonstrated how the researcher's intellectual acumen and emotional fortitude were put to a special test when he also had to serve as an advocate in a court of law.

In the face of the most severe crises, illness and death, researchers, in fact, questioned the very meaning and worth of the whole research enterprise. Did it serve any useful purpose? Renée Fox described how her intense involvement with patients threatened to overshadow her commitment to research. It became apparent that researchers frequently draw on the encouragement and support of respondents and informants in such moments of indecision and despair. Reciprocity, which is essential to completion of the research project, is clearly a two-way process.

Our visitors' statements, then, highlighted a number of dilemmas which seemed to challenge most fieldworkers. An analysis of them points to a set of principles that serves as a major focus of our discussion: the respondents' right of refusal; the necessity of the researchers' maintaining fidelity in the light of promises made; the requirement to serve as an advocate for those who have suffered grievous losses; and the appropriateness of compassion when studying those who are facing death.

The Pain of Words and the Right of Refusal

In the mid-1970s, Martha Fowlkes, then a graduate student at the University of Massachusetts, conducted a study on the wives of professional men (Fowlkes, 1980). From her own experiences in combining professional and family life, she had observed the apparent advantage of her male peers. Their wives took care of the children and maintained the household, and often served as research assistants, typing field notes, papers, and even interviewing respondents. After a careful reading of the literature on the professions, Fowlkes decided to investigate whether successful careers were so structured that they required the services of an auxiliary person. She designed a project with a sample of 20 physicians and 20 university professors and decided to interview their wives on questions concerning the men's careers and the nature of the women's supporting roles. While some women accepted her readily, others initially resisted talking about their relationships with their husbands. Fowlkes described how reciprocity, respectful sensitivity to the feelings of a respondent, enabled the respondent to benefit from an interview in which all of the early indicators pointed toward an unsuccessful encounter.

> Interestingly enough, you get a sort of wariness at the beginning and a distrust. One woman in particular was very suspicious on the phone and said, "I don't know why you would want to talk to me anyway—well—all right you can come." We set the time and when I got there, I faced one of those anxieties that every interviewer has. She had forgotten that I was coming; she had a child home sick, and she had an appointment scheduled in 45 minutes.
>
> I thought, all right, we'll pare this one down and I will get the absolute basics of what I need about how the career and the marriage unfolded. She really had her guard up at the beginning and gave a lot of very stock kinds of answers: "Everything's in place. He's very successful. We are very happy. . . ."
>
> What I often did when this kind of resistance came up was to try to make it more and more gratifying in a personal way to the woman. I moved into different areas and she talked more about herself. Well, she got so interested that she canceled the babysitter, decided to stay home ostensibly because her child was sick, talked for another two hours and then when I turned the tape recorder off let out a whole lot of stuff about incredible career crises that had come up, how unhappy she had been, how strained the marriage had been, and where she saw this thing resolving itself. At that point I put the tape recorder back on and she ended up by saying "Well, this is really like having my own private psychiatrist."
> Sometimes you'll hear on the front end, when the relationship is still very tenuous, "No, I don't want to talk to you" and it's partly because it is painful, but it is also because there is no trust. (Videotaped Interview, October 27, 1977)

Martha Fowlkes makes clear that initial resistance in an interview situation can be triggered by a person's sense that the stranger coming to her door may infringe on her privacy by asking personal questions. The very act of such questioning can also raise emotional material which can threaten the individual's sense that her life, however troubled, is at least under control. To deal with the threat and overcome the emergent sense of vulnerability, it is easiest to reject the stranger. It is not coincidental that the image of the "psychiatrist" was raised by the woman. For, in the successful psychiatric relationship, there is an attempt to create an ambience that assures the patient that anything can be said; judgment is suspended, and the therapist will not retreat from the patient's expression of hostile feelings or the report of conflict-laden relationships. Such a relationship places a special set of demands on the researcher.

During Martha Fowlkes' class visit a student asked how she reacted when she had raised questions that were painful to the respondent. The student wondered whether Fowlkes stepped back or kept "pressing." Fowlkes responded:

> It's partly the norms of the 1970s that make us very conscious about whether we are nice guys or whether we are hurting other people, and I think one can go so far to protect the feelings of others that one implicitly insults the person being interviewed. People don't say anything in an interview situation that they don't want to say. At least that's been my experience. If the interview is painful, it is painful because the life lived has been painful, not because I evoked intensive, personal, private feelings. If it was painful, the woman made it so herself through her own need to do so and I would let that come out, but I would not usually probe in any great detail.
>
> These were interviews that could be fairly impersonal if you wanted them to be. I have very indirect ways of asking personal questions. For example, I did feel it somehow necessary to see whether these professional involvements in any way put special kinds of temptations in the way of the men. Or whether in any way the women felt that because their husbands had chosen certain careers that the marriages were vulnerable. I don't really like asking people directly, "Well, have you ever had an affair? Has your husband?" So I would say "You know, it's funny—other people tell me or I have read that sometimes being a doctor is a male role in a world full of women and that it must be very sexually tempting. Have you ever heard anything like that?"
>
> You leave room for a number of different kinds of responses and she can say one of three things. "Absolutely and let me tell you what happened to me," or you can get some kind of nervous laughter, "Well, I know that happens a lot to other people, but not to me," at which point I would let that drop because it was how she wanted to answer. Or, she would come out with a very strong statement of "That is not a problem in my life," and would then elaborate on the quality of her marriage relationship which would make me feel fairly certain that at least if her husband was having an affair she didn't know.
>
> Respondents and interviewees have their own reasons for wanting to be interviewed. For example, they may have an emotional need to express some very intense, private, painful feelings in an arena which is utterly safe. It's like talking to a stranger on a plane. . . . You are never going to see that person again. These interviews were confidential. They knew that. Their names would never be used. Women would ask me, especially the doctors' wives, "I understand you interviewed my friend so and so." I would reply, "Well, I really can't say. If somebody wants to tell you she was interviewed, she can tell you."
>
> Fieldwork is a two-way process and to get so hung up on whether your are hurting these people is to forget there is another grown-up there with a right of consent, and with her own ability to set limits and say, "I'm sorry; that's too painful." (Videotaped Interview, October 27, 1977)

Fowlkes' analysis is founded on the existence of certain principles of research ethics that protect the respondent (Galliher, 1973). The researcher gives the respondent an assurance of confidentiality, an assurance that the researcher can be trusted to protect the respondent's anonymity before potentially interested outsiders. This verbal contract insulates the relationship, and protects the respondent from exposure and the researcher from charges of exploitation.

Despite the assurance of confidentiality, some social scientists would challenge Fowlkes' statement that respondents never say more in an interview than intended. The very attention and intimacy engendered by the research encounter encourages respondents to speak more openly than they normally would. It is debatable how much control respondents have over what they say or what use is made of their material after it is put into the researcher's hands. A skilled interviewer can elicit personal information effectively and easily uncover material which respondents might prefer had remained unexposed.

Willard Gaylin, a psychiatrist as well as a practiced researcher, is among those who disagree with Fowlkes' position. He argues that respondents are vulnerable and that the interviewer must be particularly sensitive to their needs.[2] His sense of respondent's vulnerability is exemplified in his own research experience with imprisoned draft resisters. In 1967, Gaylin was approached by two worried fathers whose sons had refused to consider army induction and were planning to declare themselves as resisters to the Vietnam War. The men asked Gaylin whether it would be preferable for their sons to go to prison or to leave the country. Although Gaylin's previous writing had included work on psychiatry and the law, he found that he was at a loss to respond intelligently to the query. He had never been in a prison and had no idea of the impact on its inmates. In the ensuing years Gaylin studied imprisoned war resisters and wrote a compelling book detailing the consequences of incarceration for the young resisters and the nature of prisons in a society concerned with social justice (Gaylin, 1970).

To pursue the investigation, Gaylin obtained the permission of the Bureau of Prisons and the cooperation of prison administrators of two institutions. Most important, he convinced the young resisters that they could trust him, that his questions would not endanger them, and that his writings would provide a fair assessment of the fate of resisters during an unpopular war. Initially, men did not entirely accept Gaylin without checking him out through the "grapevine." However, their greatest hesitancies were put to rest by his obvious concern, and by his willingness to listen during hour-long sessions which spanned a period of months. The men desperately needed to feel that they were not forgotten by the outside world and that they continued to have some links to those beyond the prison gates. They were not threatened by Gaylin's use of a nondirective interviewing technique which enabled them to speak freely rather than in direct response to specific questions.

Gaylin recognized that he had assumed a heavy responsibility when he sought out these prisoners for careful and detailed probing of their background and

---

[2] Hastings Center Seminar, June 19, 1979.

experiences. Throughout his discussions with the men Gaylin remembered that he was there in the service of his research and not in response to a request for therapy. Because his interview was likely to evoke trauma, he was careful to monitor the pain engendered by their responses and to make sure that he provided encouragement in their struggle to maintain their own sense of self and dignity. This was best exemplified by his willingness to make follow-up visits despite the great distance of the prison from his own home, and by his increasing awareness of the cost of imprisonment on these "gentle felons." Despite these cautions Gaylin, like Fowlkes and other researchers, could not guarantee that his queries had not opened new wounds or caused old ones to come to the surface. He could only proceed with the care engendered by long years of psychiatric training and practice.

Whether interviewing people in their well-appointed living rooms or in stifling prison closets, the researcher seeks information by presenting an aura of concern that may disarm even the most suspicious respondents. Researchers hope that such an attitude will alert those under study that the researcher identifies with their difficulties and can be trusted not to exploit them in the cause of the research. Such bonds of reciprocity do not prevent pain, however, or reduce the obligation of the researcher to support the respondent in dealing constructively with unresolved feelings. For example, Brian Miller (Miller & Humphreys, 1980) has described how emotionally painful his interviews with gay fathers proved to be for those men, many of whom broke into tears. Their sharing of their secret with the researcher, who is inside the gay community, opened severe wounds. However, the bonds of reciprocity both enabled the men to draw on Miller's support, and also gave Miller a view of their lives far more detailed than that normally offered to the researcher. Many follow-up letters and conversations were required to bring the reciprocal relationship to an equitable and logical stopping point.

Miller's experiences underscore the care with which a researcher must approach the uncovering of personal material. It is our obligation to decide what material it is ethical for us to elicit, under what circumstances, and with what safeguards. Such an obligation should be examined long before the researcher moves out into the field and the examination of these questions should be part of the early training of all fieldworkers. Teachers and students alike might pose the simple question: How sensitive am I to the pain of words? How aware am I of the problematic outcome of probing, as the uninvited guest who will normally leave after one visit, never to be seen again?

The answers to these questions are complex. Yet one rule may be underscored: Despite fieldworkers' enthusiasm and commitment to their research, they must provide respondents with the opportunity to refuse to participate. It is essential for investigators such as Fowlkes, Gaylin, and Miller to provide a comfortable atmosphere in which their respondents may discuss personal feelings, but it is inappropriate to define those with information as adversaries whose resistance to disclosing personal information may be overcome, as some researchers have done (Johnson, 1975; Douglas, 1976). From the adversarial perspective, those who do not wish to cooperate must be manipulated, or the researchers must regard themselves as failures. The adversarial stance is a poor one to live by and to pass on to our students.

While we are committed to our work and usually believe in its significance, others may view our intentions with suspicion and our intensity with caution. There is a vast ethical difference between encouraging participation, and viewing refusers as recalcitrant, resistant, or paranoid. In the final analysis, despite our oft implicitly proclaimed value superiority, our desire to know is no more moral than our respondents' occasional commitment to keep us out of their lives. We should be sensitive to the legitimacy of noncooperation.

Certainly, as has been pointed out by Murray Wax in his brief history of fieldwork (Chapter 2), there are many instances in which researchers have proceeded with subterfuge or deception to gain information which powerful figures might otherwise have denied them. Our values as people of humane conscience might support such actions. Yet it is essential that we separate scientific principles from political, social, and economic commitments. From the latter perspective we may applaud those who surreptitiously enter factories to learn of working conditions or who penetrate the frontiers of totalitarian societies to uncover social injustice. Yet we should admit that these are political decisions that can be defended as such rather than claiming that we are motivated only by scholarly values that are more elevated than those of our adversaries who want to keep us out.

The Fear of Retaliation and the Problem of Fidelity

The issue of vulnerability becomes even more explosive in a highly politicized environment where providing information can have serious and sometimes unforeseen consequences. When prospective respondents feel vulnerable to violent retribution for speaking to researchers, researchers will be rejected until they are labeled as nonthreatening outsiders by all concerned. Prior to the October 1973 Middle East War, Joel Migdal, then a faculty member at Tel Aviv University, initiated a study of Palestinians living on the West Bank of the Jordan River. His previous research had focused on social change in peasant communities (Migdal, 1974) and after interviewing peasants in Mexico, Spain, and India, Migdal decided to study the economic and social impact of the Israeli occupation. Although he was an American who had no official connection with the Israeli government or military, he soon found that any identification whatsoever with Israeli authorities would preclude his acceptance when conducting research in the occupied territories.

> I wasn't sure what was going on in people's minds and what kinds of fears they had. I knew the situation was a tense one but I really didn't have a good image of the kinds of things that they were concerned about. There were several instances right at the beginning that helped clarify these. They were very painful for me and painful for the people who were being interviewed.

> In one case an Arab was hitchhiking in his village and we gave him a ride from one side of the village to the next. I mentioned to him that I was doing a research project and I asked him if he cared to be interviewed. His response initially was what everybody else's response was. He was very

pleased to be selected. I started off with simple biographical questions. How old are you? Have you always lived in this village? and similar things. After two or three questions his level of anxiety went up precipitously. He began to look around outside the car, and it became very obvious to my associate and me what was going through his head. . . . He was afraid of what other people in the village were thinking seeing him talking to a non-Arab. Who was he talking to? What kind of information was he conveying? In the middle of the interview, he bolted from the car and simply ran. Just took off and ran.

A second instance occurred in a coffee house where we interviewed the owner. We had a very congenial conversation with him—these interviews were rather long, lasting sometimes up to several hours—and at the end of the interview he said, "My God, I'm in here alone talking to you. People know I'm talking to you and they don't know what I'm saying. There are agents all over the place. Either you can use this material against me by bringing it to the authorities and having me arrested or people could suspect me of being an agent."

Everyone is being suspected of being an agent. The situation is one where you cannot trust your neighbor. The Israelies have paid off numerous people in the villages, or at least there is a perception that they have. I had to devise a method that would put people in a position where they would not feel I was an agent and where they could be sure that they would not be suspected of being agents.

I presented myself as an American academic. I did not tell them about my Tel Aviv affiliation. They grasped the notion of my being an American. They said, "Oh, an American writer. The American people are being fooled by Nixon. The American people are basically good. You will be our conduit to the American people. You will tell our story." My response was a halfhearted attempt to tell them that academics are only read by very, very small numbers. They weren't listening when I said that.

As far as saving them from suspicion by others, this was a more complex issue and this also worked itself out by a sort of serendipity. When I indicated to them that I wanted to interview them, they said, "Okay, fine, but you can't interview me yet. First you must come to my home, sit in my courtyard and my house, you must drink tea or coffee with me."

Their friends and neighbors and relatives gathered there. My initial attempt was to do what every good social scientist should do—to get the respondents alone, so they would not be influenced by this larger audience. However, by being interviewed in front of their friends, relatives, and neighbors, they were able to protect themselves. Everybody knew that they were not agents. The informants' responses were completely aboveboard. They felt comfortable with the situation and they provided the kinds of data that were needed for the study. (Videotaped Interview, March 1978)

The challenge of doing research in a situation of military occupation is particularly acute. The feeling of danger expressed by several of Migdal's respondents was based on an assessment that they were caught between Palestinian groups determined to oppose the Israeli occupation and the power of the Israeli authorities. Too close identification with either group might prove costly and certainly not worth the effort of speaking to an unknown American. Unlike the people Fowlkes, Gaylin, and Miller spoke to, the threat of the stranger came not from the raising of delicate personal issues but from the fear of direct retaliation of armed groups capable of inflicting awesome revenge. Only as Migdal's project was interpreted as directly beneficial to the villagers was he provided entree.

As in all such cases, my class debated whether Migdal should have withheld his Tel Aviv University affiliation from the villagers. The interviews provided unusual insights into life in an occupied territory since they set the stage for the expression of intergenerational conflict in which young people criticized their elders' acquiescence in the face of Israeli authority. However, we questioned the extent to which Migdal may have exacerbated tensions in these Palestinian villages.

The class also considered whether Migdal's report could satisfy the Palestinians' desire to have *their* story told to the world. As the publication of his book was imminent, Migdal became increasingly skeptical about the possibility of reciprocity.[3] He recalled being in a village near Ramallah. It was his first visit to a Palestinian community and he knew of its existence through an anthropological account. When Migdal mentioned this, the village Mukhtar (head) began a lengthy diatribe against the author of that account, a Palestinian social scientist who had lived in the village years before. The mukhtar was incensed by what he considered to be an unfair description of how the village treated its women. Obviously, Migdal noted, any critical commentary was totally unacceptable. As he wrote about the West Bank villages, Migdal had to bear this dilemma in mind. While he carefully analyzed village life and attitudes, he clearly presented the villagers' complaints of continued Israeli control of captured territories and the personal hardships resulting from the government's unwillingness to allow people to return to the villages if they had not physically resided there in 1967, when the Israelis took over (Migdal, 1980). In Migdal's teaching, public talks, and writing, he has advocated the importance of confronting the grievances that the Palestinians expressed to him. Yet, from Migdal's perspective, a scholar who does not also write about internal conflict, cleavage, and power relationships is not worth his salt. Astute fieldworkers know this from the beginning and thus their implicit contract with respondents and informants presents an ethical dilemma. The latter expect that researchers will write a sympathetic and positive account. Investigators, on the contrary, know full well that their work will only be successful if they are analytic and critical. The social, geographical, and spatial distances that exist at the time of the writing make this divergence ever more pronounced.

Migdal's experiences represent a prime instance of the limits of reciprocity. As a sophisticated researcher, his report could not completely fulfill the Palestinians' desire that he present their case to the American people. His account was drawn through the lens of political science and his knowledge of Israeli society and politics. Here resides the tension when the researcher promises that his document will serve

---

[3] Conversations with Joel Migdal in winter 1979, spring 1980.

partisan purposes. The promise is made in the context of the guest relationship but must be severely tempered in an academic environment with competing values, norms, and world views. While it is always tempting for researchers to commit themselves in advance, it is a path fraught with difficulty and likely to leave respondents disillusioned and researchers suffering from well-earned feelings of guilt. In recognition of the researcher's special role and the concurrent legitimacy of respondents' expectations, we should underscore the researcher's interest, commitment to listen, and yet independence in the analysis of the data and the writing of the report.

Migdal's reflections thus highlight an additional principle of responsible behavior in field relations: do not promise more than you can give and do live up to promises which are made. The issue of promises became paramount in the late 1960s and early 1970s as fieldworkers engaged in research overseas or on minorities within the United States and were accused of "academic imperialism." Too many researchers, it was charged, "mined data," packed them within their briefcases, and disappeared behind academic walls despite their commitments to informants and respondents. The material facilitated their own careers and contributed to burgeoning academic disciplines. But what of those studied? In what ways, if any, did they benefit? In response to this alleged exploitation, demands were made that researchers provide information to studied peoples and that whenever possible researchers train local people in research techniques.

For some researchers these accusations, demands, and challenges resulted in a determined effort to fulfill promises. For example, as a young fieldworker in an Indian village, Gerald Berreman had been able to convince his suspicious hosts that cooperation would bring recognition from the outside world. While it is difficult to measure the impact of Berreman's years of subsequent research and writing, he was recently awarded an honorary degree by his Indian colleagues in recognition of his scholarship on their nation. Berreman had written extensively about India and had also participated actively in public debates about the legitimacy of U.S. military sponsorship of research in India and elsewhere in the Third World. This is a noteworthy instance in which the achievement of reciprocity, of promises fulfilled, was provided public recognition.[4]

The Plight of Survivors and the Promise of Advocacy

In February of 1972 a dam holding mine wastes collapsed, pouring millions of gallons of water and debris on an unsuspecting population of miners and their families. In the deluge, 125 men, women, and children perished, and communities were destroyed all along the Buffalo Creek area of West Virginia. Many survivors lost their loved ones and were uprooted and placed in mobile homes by HUD with little consideration to past social relationships which had been the foundation of their existence. Law suits were instituted against the mining company which had built the dam and which had been responsible for its maintenance. Lawyers, medical person-

---

[4] Correspondence and personal conversation with Gerald Berreman in spring 1980.

nel, and psychologists became part of a team assisting the residents in their legal battles. Kai Erikson was asked to recommend a graduate student to study the impact of the disaster from a sociological perspective. Erikson traveled to Buffalo Creek and his visit had such an impact on him that he undertook the research himself (Erikson, 1976).

Although he had the unusual advantage of identification with a law firm representing the local inhabitants, Erikson too had to prove that he deserved cooperation. During his first days he realized that wearing a suit and beard put him at a disadvantage. He shaved and changed his dress. Erikson also learned how threatening a careless phrase could be.

> The very first day I went to a gas station, which is the nearest thing to a streetcorner at Buffalo Creek. I just stood there as people came in and out. I didn't know this at the time, but looking back on it I would describe myself as somebody trying very hard to be acceptable in their terms but long before I knew what their terms were. So I would engage in conversations which I thought were kind of shrewd mountain talk but which were really just New Haven versions of shrewd mountain talk.

> This guy comes limping in that first day, an old wizened, tough looking miner, and he greeted me cordially because that is the way in those parts. I looked out the window at the sky and gathering clouds. "Hm, it's coming up a storm." (I had learned that expression.) It was the dumbest thing I could possibly do because I should have known (it takes a while to find these things out) you just don't talk about storms on Buffalo Creek. It isn't a casual piece of conversation. A storm is what kills you. A storm is what you live in fear of. He just turned on his heel and limped out of there. So I think the first three or four days were punctuated by a lot of interactions like that where I wondered what on earth I was doing down there and why. I must have had a graduate student that could have done better than that. (Videotaped Interview, November 1977)

Erikson is unusually honest and insightful in speaking of his blunders in establishing rapport with the people of Buffalo Creek who had suffered grievously from mine officials' carelessness for their personal safety. His initial efforts revealed the continued impact of the disaster. Since Erikson was known as a representative of the law firm, his position as a stranger could be mitigated. Yet the local people still had to determine whether they could trust him with the task at hand. Was he an appropriate advocate for their cause?

> And then you get tested a lot and I took it at first to be a question of whether I was man enough. But it really wasn't. I think people were just trying to figure out what kind of creature I was, because I was as far out of their experience as they were out of mine.

> It must have been in the first two or three days. I called somebody and went to see him at his house. It was early evening and they had come out of the mines, but the sun was still up and there were three or four men sitting around a pickup truck that had failed. It looked to me that it had failed at least 20 years ago. It was sitting there up on blocks. They were

hunched down sitting on their heels and just staring at the truck. I don't know a thing about auto mechanics, but I walked up there with a tape recorder and carried all my awkwardnesses with me.

So I hunched down on my heels, which is a position I can only maintain for only about 45 seconds without excruciating pain, and the conversation went on at least a half hour about what they are going to do about repairing this pickup truck. Clearly I was being tested to see if I was the kind of person who could fix the truck. It would have been very good for me if I had, but I wasn't and it turned out that didn't matter. I was the kind of person who could sit on my heels for a while and *talk* about fixing up a truck. I was being gently initiated into a slower rhythm of mountain life. When we finally got finished talking about the truck, the guys said, "What do you want to know?" and I sort of looked helplessly at my tape recorder (it needed to be plugged in) and looked helplessly at them. I wanted them recorded.

But they knew that and they were waiting to see how I responded; whether I could slow down enough just to pick up the very slow cadence of what would be a talk. So it went on for hours after that. I ran out of tape long before we were done talking.

But it takes a long time to appreciate that, for me, coming out of the north. (Videotaped Interview, November 1977)

Erikson's challenge lay in becoming sensitive to ways of the mountain people and in coming to terms with their loss and its impact on him. He had come to study the miners, their families, their community, and to be their advocate when called upon. To accomplish this he had to be close enough to these people to become sufficiently intertwined in their lives, to record their feelings and thoughts, and to be able to portray them so that a court could understand the magnitude of their trauma. Yet he could not become emotionally one of them for fear of failing at the moment of the crucial test.

I stayed in a town 30 miles away, partly because there was no place to stay in Buffalo Creek. The first time I went down, I went into one of those trailers and spent the night there. That was about 4 minutes sleep and that was the end of that trailer. But I found I had to get out, as did the psychiatrist and the lawyers. It was plain too depressing. After a while if you stayed there for 24 straight hours, you were going to be a survivor yourself —at least for somebody with my temperament who gets so caught up with what they are saying.

So I would get up early in the morning, have a huge breakfast in Logan which is the county seat 30 miles away and then stay in Buffalo Creek until about midnight. That was as much as I could do. And 4 or 5 days of that was as much as I could do, without really getting the feeling that I was losing my purchase as a sociologist. That obviously separated me from the community.

At the end, when it was all over, the people there understood. They used language which was typical of their world but by this time knew what it would mean in my world, and as I left would say, "You're in now—you're a member of the family—you are part of the community." I would say, which was by that time quite true, "Well, this isn't my home but it sure is my second home." Which I felt then and I feel now.

So, it was the best thing I think that could happen to a visiting social scientist. A special status was invented for me which gave me the privileges of membership, but none of the obligations that go with it. (Videotaped Interview, November 1977)

Erikson's reactions can be contrasted to the fieldworker who lives among people, learns their ways, becomes part of their culture, and rejects the researcher's requirement to report back to a scientific community. The possibility of "going native" has long intrigued students of the research adventure (Gronewold, 1972). Fieldworkers among survivors may be inundated by feelings of sympathy and identification. These can diminish the possibility of writing about the profound loss which has been engraved in the countenance of one's new community.

For Erikson the task was complex; he had to become close to the people to feel their individual pain and communal loss without becoming overwhelmed by their grief. His book and oral statement show his uncommon ability to present the intensity of their tragedy. Erikson immerses the reader in the survivors' accounts so that only the most unfeeling can remain unmoved. To achieve this a researcher must become deeply involved with his material and allow it to absorb him while remaining emotionally vital enough to step back and perceive the contours of the data. It is a rigorous affective exercise demanding emotional reserves and critical perceptiveness.

It is precisely these qualities which people like Terrence De Pres have drawn upon in their reading of the records of concentration camps, visiting the sites, and holding lengthy interviews with former inmates (De Pres, 1976). Like Erikson, De Pres does not turn away but rather forces himself and his readers to confront the reality with all its horror and brutality. He neither plunges into deep despair, nor does his portrait of struggle suffer from false detachment. His connection and his bond with the survivors give vibrancy to their words. In works like those of Erikson and De Press, the writers' strength enables the reader to navigate the most painful passages. These recorders are completing a mission that renders their work immediate and searing. The obligation is to those who have perished and to those who have survived and serve as witnesses to the millions who know little of the holocaust.

Erikson met the challenge and his document was no dispassionate legal brief to be filed in a court's caverns. His was a living testimony passed on to those inside and outside of the academy. Erikson had also to remain faithful to his original charge to serve as a witness in a legal action against the coal company. This posed an additional complication. The test of the expert witness is severe and success is only partially dependent on accumulated knowledge. The courtroom setting can be intimidating. In the cross examination, any weakness can be magnified. The task of the opposing attorney is to expose and highlight any unexamined assumptions that might pass unnoticed in ordinary academic discourse. Erikson had to be prepared for such a challenge by monitoring his own reactions. He was deeply affected by the continued suffering of the Buffalo Creek residents. His own emotional vulnerability now became an active ingredient to be monitored. Yet he used his involvement and commitment to write a powerful account of people struggling to make sense of a tragedy that had destroyed so much of their lives.

Unlike Fowlkes and Migdal, Erikson had a special obligation to the people of Buffalo Creek and reciprocity had to be enacted in the concrete document and testimony in support of their cause. In his class visit he expressed his unease at the prospect of a court appearance as a "hired gun" who would help the flood victims gain justice. Could he contribute to their cause in court as well as he could with the written word? He felt relieved and "slept better" when the case was settled and he was not required to testify. Yet, he had been ready to appear to argue that the destruction of community at Buffalo Creek had had a major negative impact on the peoples' recovery from the disastrous flood. Only a small percentage of researchers are ever called on to reciprocate in such a direct and public manner. Their research agreements do not usually call for such a commitment. Nonetheless, reciprocity does at times demand that researchers put themselves and their professional reputations on the line (Laue, 1978).

The principles of reciprocity, then, include a third item that goes beyond recognition of the right of refusal, or fulfillment of obligations concerning the written report. Often, researchers commit themselves to reciprocate in a direct and concrete manner. Whereas Erikson's commitment was institutionalized by his contract with a law firm, other researchers have informally promised to represent their informants. Elliot Liebow (1967) and Carol Stack (1974), when studying a black ghetto, and Pierre van den Berghe (1967), when studying the apartheid system in South Africa, implicitly promised to carry the message of injustice to all who would listen.

As social scientists rather than journalists, the challenge of finding an appropriate public forum may be particularly difficult. Joel Migdal correctly indicated to the Palestinians that academics are read by only a handful of their colleagues. Moreover, the fieldworker who takes to the printed page of a national or local newspaper, or who appears on the airwaves, may quickly be defined by colleagues as a "publicity hound." Nevertheless, when promises have been made, it is the researchers' responsibility to "go public" despite the implied or explicit critique of those who are fearful of contaminating the purity of academic discourse.

The Face of Death and the Call of Compassion

As a graduate student, Renée Fox studied interaction in a clinical and experimental hospital ward. Despite her status as an outsider and a social scientist, she quickly found that both the physicians and patients accepted her readily. The physicians, challenged by the tasks of treating and studying seriously ill men, were willing to have an observer on the ward who might provide them with additional insights into their own roles and the characteristics of ward life. The patients defined Fox neither as a member of the staff nor as an outsider who had come to look at them through a lens. Observing her limp, they learned of her past hospitalization for polio and accepted her as a former patient who had come to live and work among them. Their sense of her own past suffering created an immediate bond. She played the role of participant observer who made the daily rounds with physicians, overheard their informal banter, spent hours in the company of the patients and assisted them by carrying trays, fixing beds, and becoming an active member of the ward (Fox, 1959).

From those earliest experiences, confirmed by subsequent years of fieldwork both in the United States and abroad, Fox reflected on the peculiar challenges of participant observation. Researchers become close to the people they are studying and yet they must complete the task of making careful and sustained observations. This tension leads to a subtle transformation. Some of these may be troubling but others provide an insight into those under study and into the researcher herself.

> The fieldwork experience deeply affects and deeply modifies one, so that the researcher is changed every time by virtue of the piece of fieldwork. As Bill Whyte reported in that famous appendix to *Street Corner Society*, one day you may find yourself voting three times in an election, and you say, "How is this possible? What has happend to me? Why am I doing this? I believe that people should vote only once in an election, and what's more this behavior may even have no instrumental rationality whatsoever. You don't need to ingratiate yourself with Doc and Chick by showing them you don't cringe at the thought of putting in two phony votes out of three." It's simply that you have been so transformed by this intensive relationship, that you have begun to behave like the people in it.

> Something like that happened to me on Ward F-Second when I was doing a study which later became *Experiment Perilous*. One day when I went to somebody's house for dinner, I made a very startling kind of black joke in a setting where it seemed to me totally inappropriate. As a matter of fact, I had never heard myself make that kind of joke before, whether it was inappropriate or appropriate. The next morning when I went back on Ward F-Second to begin my daily rounds of participant observation I noticed I was doing it all the time. I noticed that patients and the doctors were doing it all the time. In a very interesting kind of way I discovered a phenomenon that was one of the most important things to study on that ward by virtue of the fact that I had been taught to do this by the men of the ward.

> There was the patient on the Ward who was one of the leaders of the patient community who later described to me what I looked like when I first appeared. "You look as if you would bust out crying any minute," he said to me. "And so we took you in hand and we taught you how to deal with the situation," which is exactly what they did when new patients came, of course.

> I never knew how to do that before and I learned it deeply and well and I owe to those men a resource of life and in the face of death I would never have had if I hadn't come to live with them for a while—gallows humor, blasphemous hilarity. I thought that a sense of humor was pleasant, decorative, nice if you had it, not serious if you didn't have it. I had no understanding of the vitality of that kind of humor, of the existential meaning of the way that in the face of the deepest, most tragic aspects of life, how much like a prayer that is. (Videotaped Interview, March 10, 1979)

Renée Fox's words reveal what can be learned by close relationships with those she hoped to understand. That very closeness derived from her empathetic understanding of their fate and their sense of her past vulnerability and current unease. As a young fieldworker in the world of the sick, her past had been re-kindled. It showed in her gait and face. The researcher became no threat. She had known their suffering which was in some ways akin to hers. She needed acceptance, teaching, and a place among them. Her exchange for their acceptance was the indication that she had taken on the ways of these people who desperately needed acknowledgement of their continuing worth and vitality. She had experienced a significant resocialization process of a kind that often occurs to field workers (R. H. Wax, 1971). The challenge for Fox lay in not reacting with total submersion.

> Fieldwork allows and obliges you to tap into what I keep referring to as some very fundamental aspects of the human condition. These are the kinds of things that people don't share blithely with others. Suffering, joy, secret hopes and desires and disappointments, births, deaths, mortalities, some of the problems of meaning.

> Some of the crises of fieldwork, as a matter of fact, have to do with what you are going to even record in your field notes. That was one of my problems on Ward F-Second when Paul O'Brien died. Was I going to write that down in my notebook? Was I going to be at his death? He wanted me there, so I was there, like any human being. I was witness to his death.

> Was I going to go home that night and write it up in my notes because this was a nice juicy day in the field? Boy, what a scoop. I could write up in detail how Paul O'Brien died. And then, even if you put it in your notebook, because you assume the act of writing is very important, do you write it up for other people to read it? Do you put it in the dissertation? Do you put it in a book? (Videotaped Interview, March 10, 1979)

Fox answered all of these queries in the affirmative. From her perspective she was obliged to record all that occurred. Yet the death of Paul O'Brien deeply affected her. For a time she considered terminating the research. Surely, she felt, a sociological treatise was an ineffective way to present the men's struggle against illness. A novel might be a more dramatic vehicle and would be unencumbered by sociological concepts.

As expressed clearly by both Fox and Erikson, the stranger who stays beyond a visit or two may be provided entree and becomes an insider by careful tutoring in appropriate behavior and attitudes. The stranger learns what people say and how they act when questions are not asked and observation is unsuspected. Coaching gives the astute observer skills in knowing what to ask and what cannot be put into words.

This process of resocialization is invaluable but potentially costly as it can lead to complete absorption whereby the fieldworker becomes a full-fledged member of the community (Wood, 1934; Reiss, 1968). Erikson knew his own limits and tried to maintain clear barriers. In Fox's first experience as a young researcher, involvement took her to the brink of abandoning her study. That act would have broken the agreement with the men of Ward F-Second. Fox's implicit understanding with them centered on her willingness to experience their fate, record it, and put its events on paper. The bonds of reciprocity required her to control her own feelings and maintain her belief in the utility of her research. Her challenge lay in feeling a sense of deep loss but not permitting it to undermine her commitment. Ultimately, the completion of her research was the clearest tribute to the patients and the lasting acknowledgement of their trust.

My students and I have wondered about the researchers' feelings when faced with the death of those whose lives they have come to record. How do fieldworkers confirm the significance of their efforts? Are they burdened by guilt feelings that another's tragedy is dramatic data for their analysis? Fox believed in the importance of sociological studies for understanding illness and personal courage in the context of modern medical practice. She was also buoyed up by her active involvement in the patients' struggles. She did not play the role of the emotionally detached interviewer or the passive observer. Throughout her study, she lent a helping hand and was defined by doctors and patients as having an important mission, a long range goal, and an immediacy of purpose, which was portrayed in Paul O'Brien's request that she be with him on the day of his death. The definition of others gave additional meaning to her presence. She was the involved participant who observed and analyzed, but whose strength and support came from the men who wanted her there, saw her rightful place, and provided legitimacy in the face of the ultimate question concerning the significance of her work.

Fox's experiences are confirmed by another young researcher who wrote about *The Private World of Dying Children* some twenty years later. Myra Bluebond-Langner (1978) needed the cooperation of physicians and parents. But the most important acceptance came from the children themselves who tested her interest and personal strength and found her worthy. She was the anthropologist who stayed with them, played games, and helped out when other staff members were too occupied. The children defined her as the "big-kid" who studied them, was devoted to them, and over whose time they had some control. She proved that despite their anger, shouting, even hitting, she would not desert them. Unlike doctors, nurses, and social workers, she was there only for them. This definition gave her access and allowed the children to ask questions and tell her things they might not share with their parents or other members of the staff. She was different and that very difference enabled her to understand and accommodate the very special needs of each child. She was available and had been taught by staff, parents, and children the culture of the hospital ward. She became an integral member with a unique role. Her lengthy stay provided the opportunity to carry her knowledge and growing sensitivity from one child to another. As she became more attuned to the ways of the hospital she was increasingly understanding of what new patients and their parents were experiencing.

Bluebond-Langner shared their games and laughter, but she was never able to escape the shadow of their illness and the knowledge that despite all the new drugs, they were marked to die from leukemia. Their fate was inescapable and gave a sense of urgency to the research. It also raised profound questions for her to consider.

Anger quickly replaces these thoughts and feelings. Why this child? What did he do? Why can't something be done? The anger builds and is often directed at strangers, people too busy to know that a child is living with dying. I walk through the toy section of a large department store, crowded with Christmas shoppers, full of Christmas cheer. While two ladies argue about the best style bike for a nine-year-old boy, I try to find a toy for Jack that will not remind him of the bike he can no longer ride and may never see again. Another woman is pushing ahead in line so she can be home in time to help her grandchildren decorate the tree. I muse to myself. I am in a hurry too. I promised Andy an angel for his tree, and I am spurred by a different urgency.

The anger soars. It wells up into an indictment of this country for its priorities on spending. It is thrown up to a God I am not quite sure exists, but who deserves to be blamed just the same. I have to blame someone, something; how can I explain to myself the death of a child? I must do something, and what can I or anyone else do? Dr. Abrams said to the residents, "What makes you think that your medicine is any more powerful than that novena?"

The feeling of omnipotence is overwhelming. But the rage has passed. No one heard me. I really did not say or do anything. I am tired. Guilt always seems to follow the rage and anger. I can walk out of the hospital, I can leave it all behind, I can intellectualize it all, I can even profit from it. For out of this experience will come a dissertation, perhaps even a Ph. D. I will become an anthropologist. But these children will *not* become.

They have done for me in so many ways, but I wonder what I have done for them. It was always so hard to do something for them. How we all talked about the Marias who right up until the end asked to be taken to the bathroom, about the Jeffreys who shouted us out of their rooms, and about the Seths who would not let us in; all because they knew when we could not take it. . . .

My feelings vacillate from day to day. If I had it to do again, would I? I have changed since the time I did the study. I am older, married, and have experienced the deaths of some of my closest friends and relative. When I did the research, I had not had these experiences; my "innocence" was in many ways essential to my doing the study as I did and accomplishing what I did. I am haunted by another question: How many were helped and how many were hurt by my study? When one does such research, contributions to science are not sufficient justification, in my view. I have failed unless this study contributes to the memory of the children, to those who cared for them, and to children who still must suffer. (Bluebond-Langner, 1978, pp. 254-255)

Bluebond-Langner forces us to consider yet another aspect of our indebtedness to others. Her research is part of a mission to preserve the memory of the children's battle with forces destined to take their lives. She was not content to accept easy assurances that her caring and presence had reciprocated for their acceptance. Is there any exchange which can compensate for the trust of a dying child? Perhaps she raises in poignant form the query that must press all fieldworkers: Have I been sufficiently resourceful in exchanging favors, gifts, and affection with those who have permitted me to know them? Perhaps it must suffice to raise the query and to contemplate often the various forms of reciprocity and the limitations and tensions associated with them.

The answer has led some researchers to modify their goals and to write accounts which come closer to capturing the struggles of those under study. Willard Gaylin records that his initial goal in studying war resisters had been the writing of a research report for a professional journal. The outcome would surely have been a sophisticated and yet technical analysis of the mens' backgrounds and how this led them to a decision of conscientious objection. As Gaylin came to know the resisters he deemed it far more important to write a volume that would be accessible beyond a professional audience and would highlight the dehabilitating impact of incarceration. Few readers of Gaylin's account can leave its pages unmoved by his sensitive portrayal of the men and by his call to examine our assumptions of war and peace, prison and its utility, and the power of the state to decide the fate of generation after generation.

It is now standard in various social science communities to emphasize the significance of detachment and dispassionate analysis in approaching and presenting scientific data. A review of the researchers' remarks presented to our class and a perusal of many other fieldwork accounts lend a weighty challenge to this conventional wisdom (R. H. Wax, 1971). Rather than celebrate the requirement of distance, it seems advisable to highlight another reality that characterizes many fieldwork relationships. Compassionate analysis suggests the desirability of researchers becoming closely attuned to the feelings and world views of those they are studying, of identifying with these, and of attempting to experience the emotional vibrations and the intellectual perspectives associated with them. Concurrently, in accordance with the mission of the scientific observer, it is also necessary to analyze the content and derivation of these perspectives. It is a trying but reachable goal as portrayed in the work of many of those who have contributed to these pages.

The possibility of employing compassionate analysis will often depend on the nature of the populations studied, the researchers' emotional and intellectual orientations, and their definition of the appropriate functions of academic discipline. While compassionate analysis cannot be applied in all cases, it is a legitimate method and one that has often provided insights unreachable by other approaches as the work of Bluebond-Langner, Erikson, Fowlkes, Fox, and Gaylin so clearly and powerfully exemplify.

A Word of Summary and Acknowledgment

The material presented in these pages provides a set of working principles to be considered, debated, modified, and expanded. Each states a clear challenge to those who contemplate fieldwork. Surely the requirements of reciprocity demand an ongoing and careful assessment of our right to acquire information held by others whether in their thoughts, emotions, file cabinets, or wall safes. The right that others have to reject us places a special burden on us to think seriously of the goals and requirements of our research. The message is simple: it will always be necessary to defend our values and research procedures against the resistance and critique of those who may want to reject our appeal for assistance.

Where the research does proceed, fieldworkers must carefully consider promises made in return for information and assistance. It is inadvisable for a researcher to make promises and agreements whose consummation is clearly open to doubt. It has long been part of our procedure to assure respondents and informants that the research product can assist them in some direct way. I sense that we have often made promises that were unnecessarily broad and all encompassing and that assistance and cooperation are usually forthcoming when we are perceived as trustworthy and competent. There are situations, however, where researchers have lived and worked among those who are clearly disadvantaged and exploited and whose cause can benefit from the pen and voice of a knowledgeable outsider. In such situations the requirements of reciprocity demand that the fieldworker assume the responsibility for advocating greater public concern or particular ameliorative actions. When this has occurred in the past, the involved researchers, at least in my view, have an aura of legitimacy which derives from their scholarly observations and humane concern for the well-being of those they have come to know in the process of their investigation.

Finally, it is not infrequent for researchers to work among those who have suffered some personal or communal loss. Here, intellectual perceptiveness must be matched by the researcher's emotional strength. An understanding of others requires that the investigator share their vulnerability and pain, experience their moments of despondency and gloom, and yet remain committed to telling their story and dissecting its component parts. Such is the challenge of compassionate analysis.

In essence, reciprocity requires the careful formulation of agreements, the willingness to exchange goods and favors for information, the understanding that others may both assist us and attempt to use us for their own gains, the likelihood that we will be expected to serve as advocates and thus go beyond the requirements of putting our thoughts down on the printed page, and the necessity to share both the joy and fun and the pain and loss of those we hope to understand.

The ethical and emotional requirements of field research add a substantial burden to those who are formally trained in the intellectual traditions of their discipline. Remarkably, thousands of researchers have been able to combine these diverse requirements. Their written accounts and the statements of those whom we have interviewed reveal, however, that this does not occur easily, that the problems are many, and that the rewards, while existent, require a continual assessment of what we are about.

Acknowledgments usually occur in the footnotes to papers at their inception, but the requirements of reciprocity demand that this conclusion highlight my indebtedness to the many researchers who have visited and spoken in detail about their experiences.[5] A review of their videotapes pointed to the centrality of vulnerability and reciprocity in most research relationships and these themes permeate this presentation. Their experiences can serve as a clear reference in preparing our students for the privilege of studying the lives of others and in reminding all of us of the mutual dangers and opportunities inherent in the coming of the stranger.

Acknowledgments. This chapter is an expanded version of an article published in *The Hastings Center Report*, October 1980. Sections from this report are reprinted with permission of the Hastings Center. © 1980 Institute of Society, Ethics and the Life Sciences, 360 Broadway, Hastings-on-Hudson, N.Y. 10706.

I am deeply indebted to Thomas F. O'Connell for his colleagueship in the videotaping project. Jennifer McGowan provided essential assistance and Norma Lepine typed the interview transcripts and the manuscript. Warm thanks go to all of them. I must also toast three others who have stood as severe critics and dedicated friends: Penina Migdal Glazer, Gail Levy Perlman, and Michael S. Perlman.

References

Bluebond-Langner, M. *The Private World of Dying Children*. Princeton, N.J.: Princeton University Press, 1978.

De Pres, T. *The survivor*. New York: Oxford University Press, 1976.

Douglas, J. D. *Investigative social research*. Beverly Hills, Calif.: Sage, 1976.

Erikson, K. T. *Everything in its path*. New York: Simon and Schuster, 1976.

Fowlkes, M. *Behind every successful man: The wives of medicine and academe*. New York: Columbia University Press, 1980.

Fox, R. C. *Experiment perilous*. Glencoe: Free Press, 1959.

Galliher, J. F. The protection of human subjects: A reexamination of the Professional Code of Ethics. *The American Sociologist*, 1973, *8*, 93-100.

Gaylin, W. *In the service of their country/war resisters in prison*. New York: Viking, 1970.

Glazer, M. *The research adventure: Promises and problems of fieldwork*. New York: Random House, 1972.

Gronewold, S. Did Frank Hamilton Cushing go native? In S. T. Kinball & J. B. Watson (Eds.), *Crossing cultural boundaries: The anthropological experience*. San Francisco: Chandler, 1972.

Gusfield, J. R. Field work reciprocities in studying a social movement. *Human Organization*, 1955, *14*(3), 29-33.

---

[5] Kim Townsend (Amherst College); Marjorie Swett (Boston, Massachusetts); John Boettiger, Penina M. Glazer, Gloria Foseph, Miriam Slater, Barbara Yngvesson (Hampshire College); Laurel Sorenson (Hampshire Gazette); Martha Fowlkes, Gerald Schamess, William Van Voris (Smith College); Michael Lewis, Stephen Markson, David Schimmel (University of Massachusetts, Amherst); Renée Fox (University of Pennsylvania); Joel S. Migdal (University of Washington, Seattle); Kai Erikson (Yale University).

Johnson, J. M. *Doing field research*. New York: Free Press, 1975.

Laue, J. H. Advocacy and sociology. In G. H. Weber & G. J. McCall (Eds.), *Social scientists as advocates*. Beverly Hills: Sage, 1978.

Liebow, E. *Tally's corner*. Boston: Little, Brown, 1967.

Migdal, J. S. *Peasants, politics, and revolution: Pressures toward political and social change in the Third World*. Princeton, N.J.: Princeton University Press, 1974.

Migdal, J. S., et al. *Palestinian society and politics*. Princeton, N.J.: Princeton University Press, 1980.

Miller, B., & Humphreys, L. Keeping in touch. In W. B. Shaffer, R. A. Stebbins, & A. Turowitz (Eds.), *Fieldwork experience*. New York: St. Martin's, 1980.

Reiss, A. J., Jr. Stuff and nonsense about social surveys and observations. In H. S. Becker et al. (Eds.), *Institutions and the person*. Chicago: Aldine, 1968.

Stack, C. B. *All our kin*. New York: Harper & Row, 1974.

van den Berghe, P. L. Research in South Africa: The story of my experiences with tyranny. In G. Sjoberg (Ed.), *Ethics, politics and social research*. Cambridge, MA: Schenkman, 1967.

Wax, R. H. *Doing fieldwork*. Chicago: University of Chicago Press, 1971.

Wood, M. M. *The stranger*. New York: Columbia University Press, 1934.

Chapter 4

Risks in the Publication of Fieldwork

Carole Gaar Johnson

In Chapter 1, Joan Cassell indicates that risk and benefit may occur at two different times in fieldwork, during interaction and after the data become public. She sees the latter time as the one posing the greater possibility of risk. There are many examples to support this contention. In Chapters 2 and 3 Murray Wax and Myron Glazer have considered some of the risks connected with interaction. This chapter is devoted to the examination of some risks arising from publication and some approaches to minimizing these risks.

This chapter is deliberately limited to the consideration of community studies, a form of fieldwork in which one might not even recognize that ethical problems concerning publication are present. Specific problems raised by the studies of the communities Plainville and Springdale are described to provide concrete examples of ethical problems connected with the publication of fieldwork. Some of the problems considered include (1) the "upset" of persons (able to identify themselves in a report) at the way they are portrayed; (2) the subjecting of individuals to unwanted publicity; (3) hazards of disclosing data about identifiable individuals or groups to others who have the power to use that information for exploitative purposes; (4) problems of depicting peoples in a way that is embarrassing to the larger group to which they belong; and (5) harm done to science, scientific opportunities, and to individual scientists. A sample of the questions asked and answered are: (1) What obligation does the author of a community study have to the people of the community he studies, particularly when it comes to the publication of his findings? (2) What is morally wrong with making public unflattering information that most of the members of a community already know? Is there some moral norm that scientists could take as their guide in publishing such information?

The discussion then generalizes to issues beyond those explicitly raised in the Plainville and Springdale studies. Then, summarizing the issues and recommendations offered in the first two parts of the chapter, guidelines for the "ethical proofreading" of fieldwork manuscripts are presented. Finally, since there has been little prior investigation of the efficacy of various approaches to reducing risks connected with the publication of fieldwork, some ideas and suggestions for future research along these lines are offered.

The special problems of subpoena of data and of protecting the anonymity of respondents even from the investigator are discussed by Knerr (Chapter 9, companion volume) and by Boruch and Cecil (Chapter 10, companion volume), respectively, and are not considered here. Also, omitted from this chapter is a discussion of the ethics of disseminating fieldwork performed among groups engaged in politically sensitive or illegal behavior. For discussions of the ethics of fieldwork on deviant and illegal behavior see *Deviance and Decency* (Klockars & O'Connor, 1979); and for a discussion concerning research on politically sensitive entities (e.g., Camelot and tearoom trade) see *The Practice of Social Research* (Babbie, 1979). A third sector of fieldwork that raises ethical problems concerning publication, but that is omitted here, is fieldwork done within corporate settings, and fieldwork done "for hire," e.g., contract research involving impact studies; this topic has been ably discussed in *Contracting for Knowledge* (Orlans, 1973).

Lessons in the Ethics of Publishing Fieldwork Exemplified by the Studies of Springdale and Plainville

Excellent examples of harmful and constructive reporting of community studies can be found in the studies that have been performed on Springdale and Plainville. As an analysis of these publications reveals, it is possible to deal with the problems of publication in ways that minimize the potential wrongs and harms of public disclosure, and yet to create a report that is respectful and beneficial to those studied.

Springdale and Plainville are fictitious names of actual towns studied by fieldworkers during the middle of this century. Some of the publications that resulted from these studies are noteworthy both because they were important pieces of research and because they were written with little awareness of the harm that could and did occur to those studied as a direct result of publication. The publications include those of Carl Withers who published *Plainville U.S.A.*, under the pseudonym of James West (1945); the book *Psychological Frontiers of Society*, published by Abram Kardiner, based in part on West's data; and the book *Small Town in Mass Society*, by Arthur Vidich and Joseph Bensman (1958), which was based on a Cornell University field study of a small New York town referred to as Springdale. A publication that exemplifies ethical decision making in which sensitive issues are discussed in a manner that is respectful of and instructive to the persons studied is *Plainville Fifteen Years Later* by Art Gallaher (1961).

In discussing Springdale and Plainville the focus is on the communities' reactions to the books published about them, possible reasons concerning such reactions, and suggestions to researchers as to how negative reactions on the part of subjects might be minimized. No apparent harm occurred during the research of Springdale and Plainville; in both cases harm occurred after publication. Anonymity was violated; individuals and groups were subjected to unwelcome publicity; and members of both communities were upset at the portrayal of themselves and their communities.

Demonstrably the works under discussion have been of value to the disciplines of sociology and anthropology and now with the passage of time to allied fields such as history and American Studies. The benefits overshadow any negative aspects. However, with more care and diligence, the same care and diligence used by Gallaher when he wrote and published his study, Vidich and West (Withers) could have minimized the negative reactions of those studied.

The purpose of using these publications as examples is not to criticize Vidich and West, nor to praise Gallaher. Vidich and West were, in a sense, pioneers of community studies of this nature and Gallaher's care and diligence resulted from his knowledge of the criticisms levied against West by the Plainville community.

Plainville

The study of Plainville done by anthropologist Carl Withers was based on materials he gathered between June 1939 and August 1940 and July and August 1941 (West, 1945, p. vii). The research was published under the pseudonym of James West to help preserve the anonymity of persons involved in the study. Withers will be referred to as West throughout the rest of this discussion. West's work was one part of a research project on acculturation financed by the Social Science Research Council of Columbia University, and directed by Ralph Linton, Chairman of the Department of Anthropology at Columbia. Plainville is located in the rolling prairies of the Midwest, and, at the time of the study the town had a population of 275, while its county had a population of 6,500. Plainville served as the main local trading center and social center for the 200 farms surrounding it (West, 1945, p. 2). West's study was an

> attempt to learn specifically and in detail how one relatively isolated and still "backward" American farming community reacts to the constant strain of traits and influences pouring into it from cities and from more "modern" farming communities (West, 1945, p. vii).

Housing was a problem for West. Initially he lived with the county agent. In November 1939 he began residing in a furnished apartment in a business building formerly occupied by the undertaker. Finally in April of 1940, West was able to rent a house where he remained until the study was complete.

Another difficulty for West was gaining acceptance in the community. "The first reaction of the community to 'being studied' was one of suspicion, great restraint, and even resentment, which no amount of verbal explanation of what I was doing and why I was doing it was able to allay" (West, 1945, p. ix). West was initially thought to be a detective or "federal man" in disguise (West, 1945, p. ix). As Glazer notes in Chapter 3, an important first step for the researcher is to dissociate himself in the minds of his subjects from threatening identities. Several weeks after his arrival, West accomplished such dissociation by having printed in the Plainville weekly paper a column describing his research intentions and thanking people for their cooperation to date. Tensions lessened and his research endeavor was facilitated.

West used personal interviews, participant observation, and documents to obtain his data. He talked at least briefly with about half the adults who traded mainly at

Plainville. "Formal interviews were held with more than fifty people, totalling from two hours to several hundred hours each" (West, 1945, p. xiii). He obtained eight life histories, of 30,000 to 75,000 words each. He utilized records in the county courthouse, the local AAA, FSA, Social Security, and the local weekly newspaper.

In 1945 West published his book *Plainville U.S.A.* which discussed in depth the social structure of Plainville including everything from "loafing and gossip groups" to technology and occupations (West, 1945, pp. 99-106; 8-30). West changed all place names and personal names including his own "because every serious informant requested, and was promised, the protection of complete anonymity" (West, 1945, p. xv). Despite such precautions, the identity of Plainville was discovered.

Enough descriptive information of Plainville is given at the beginning of the book that it is recognizable to anyone familiar with the area. There is also enough information that anyone who is not familiar with Plainville and the surrounding area, with a little investigation, can locate Plainville. Below is a sample of that revealing information:

> Plainville is a small town in the central part of the United States of America. The town is here called Plainville because it rests near the edge of a little prairie. . . . The Plainville prairie is about eighteen miles long and four or five miles wide, and like other smaller prairies in the region it is hemmed in irregularly on both sides by timbered or brush-covered strings of hills that run generally north and south. These hills are too small to be called 'mountains'. The 'real hills', or mountains, are southward, nearly a hundred miles. . . . Both geographically and culturally, Plainville is in the region which has been labeled the North-South Border, a long belt extending from eastern Kentucky past the Ozark country, and lying everywhere just north of the mountains. . . . Plainville is near the geographical center of Woodland County, which serves an area slightly over 400 square miles. . . . The present population of Plainville is 275. That of the county seat, Discovery, five miles east, is 250. . . . Stanton, eleven miles west, has 450 inhabitants. . . . But Plainvillers also 'go outside' nowadays. They go to 'X', a county seat of 1,000 inhabitants, situated thirty miles north of Plainville. . . . They go still more often to 'Y', another county seat about the same distance south. . . The population of 'Y' is 2,600. . . . For really important purchases, entertainment, or medical care, Plainvillers often travel to Largetown, a regional metropolis of 60,000 people, in the hills seventy miles south; or even to Metropolis itself, an important Midwestern city with a population of nearly half a million. Metropolis is northward, 135 miles. (West, 1945, pp. 1-5)

An actual map outlining the above appears on page twelve of the book.

Concerning the community's reaction to the book, West believed that with the exception of the mail carrier, whose social rise he had described, most Plainvillers had taken his book "with relative composure" (Gallaher, 1964, p. 286). However, Art Gallaher, another anthropologist, upon entering Plainville 15 years later to do a restudy detected "certain anxieties regarding West's work" (Gallaher, 1964, p. 287). Plainvillers had thought that West was a historian or that he was going to do a history of Plainville. They knew he was an anthropologist, but they did not know what that meant. Thus, they felt deceived (Gallaher, personal communication, 1979). Gallaher was told that "a great number of people were mightily upset." Criticism seemed to focus on West's handling of the data. Some upper class people felt he had painted "an incomplete picture of their community." Some felt West had

> exaggerated their poverty and their backwardness. They saw the book as an effort to single them out as a unique entity. . . they believed the author too closely identified too many people in it. (Gallaher, 1964, p. 292)

Gallaher even found that the local library's copy of the book had the real names of individuals penciled in beside the pseudonyms. Many of West's critics felt that he had betrayed them because the book was not to their liking, and they regretted that they had cooperated. Most did feel, however, that the analysis was essentially correct—it just did not "go far enough" (Gallaher, 1964, p. 292).

Individuals felt that West pointed out the negative, but did not point out the positive, too (Gallaher, personal communication, 1980). I have chosen one description in the book that might illustrate the above. Concerning bathing, West states:

> Lacking bathrooms, people bathe infrequently. . . . The stated ideal of cleanliness is 'a bath once a week.' Many women bathe weekly, if no more than a sponge bath, and most of them keep their babies and small children fairly clean; but among men no particular value is attached to cleanliness. Many men are said to go through the whole winter without a bath. Women consider most men to be 'dirty as animals,' this criticism applying not only to their 'dread of washwater' but to their use of pipes, chewing tobacco, and cigarettes, their spitting, and so forth. (West, 1945, p. 36)

West seems to have lacked the qualities of sympathy and reciprocity described by Glazer. Perhaps West failed to see how he would have behaved under the same circumstances. Perhaps, even though he originally came from a rural area, West looked with urban perspective at how people conducted themselves, and not from the broader perspective of how people cope with available resources. Perhaps scientists sometimes forget that less educated individuals can still be intelligent, perceptive, and sensitive.

In contrast to West's value laden and unempathic description, Gallaher describes the plumbing conditions in terms of objective data, and gives the reasons underlying the scarcity of modern bathrooms, as follows:

> West reports that there were three modern bathrooms in Plainville in 1940. By 1955 there were twenty-five in the village, exclusive of highway service stations, with about the same number in farm homes. Many families who feel they cannot afford modern bathrooms install running water for kitchen use, and some anticipate the future by setting aside a room, or planning to add one someday, for an indoor bath. . . .
>
> The cost of buying and installing fixtures, particularly septic tanks (professional servicing of these is an added cost), and, in most cases, of drilling a deeper well to provide water, deters many who want modern bathrooms. This is particularly true now (1954-55) because of the drought. (Gallaher, 1961, p. 96)

West used words that were offensive and not objective. For example, West used the term "hillbilly" and wrote of "people who lived like animals." Gallaher, instead, referred to people "from the hills." Gallaher states:

> Plainvillers do not use labels with sufficient consistency, applied to a specific group of people, to warrant their use for descriptive or classificatory purposes. It is true that the terms 'good' or 'bad', 'better', 'honest', 'average', and on occasion 'lower element' or 'high-' or 'low-class', are used by some people when speaking of certain families or individuals. However, consistency is not such that particular terms denoting inferior or superior are associated with a specific group.

> Particular attention was paid to the term 'people who live like animals'. I found this term voluntarily used by only one elderly man, who, when pressed to identify specific families in the category, either could not or would not do so. . . . I cannot agree with his choice of the label 'people who live like animals' for those on the absolute bottom of the prestige system. My data does not reveal consistent application of the label; therefore, considering the extreme semantic implications possible from such a descriptive phrase, I believe it a poor choice. (Gallaher, 1961, pp. 192 & 224)

The manner in which West wrote about the communities could have made the inhabitants feel that they were singled out. Gallaher avoided this by generalizing first and then writing of the specifics. As an illustration, Gallaher begins his discussion on status as follows: "All societies classify their component members according to the roles they play and according to certain ascribed qualities and personal achievements" (1961, p. 194). He continues for several pages discussing status as it applied to mankind in general, before providing examples of status hierarchies in Plainville.

West used the mail carrier as an example of an individual who managed to move into a higher social rank (West, 1945, p. 137). This discussion angered the mail carrier and in a letter to Gallaher, West admitted that he had erred. A hypothetical example would have served West's purpose without offending anyone in the community. Gallaher, in giving examples, disguised the identities by changing such characteristics as age and sex.

Since West's study, Plainville has been plagued with requests from students and others desiring further information on Plainville.

> Requests for information from students doing term papers in college and university classes were received by superintendents of the Plainville schools, the county superintendent, vocational agriculture teachers, extension agents, other county officials, and one such request that came to my attention was addressed merely to the mayor. A number of these queries sought to establish rapport by indicating that their desire for information was prompted by doubts about West's material, especially his depiction of the community as so backward. (Gallaher, 1964, p. 293)

The superintendent of schools gave Gallaher while he was in Plainville two or three such letters to answer. Also, Gallaher found that students from St. Louis would frequently stop in Plainville for gasoline and talk about the book.

Gallaher himself restudied and resided in Plainville from August 1954 to August 1955. His book *Plainville Fifteen Years Later* is an analysis of the economic, social, and cultural changes during that time. The research methods used, which were much like the ones used by West, were analysis of documentary data, participant observation, and interviews (Gallaher, 1961, p. 6). Gallaher and his wife rented an apartment in Plainville. They, like West, had some trouble finding a place to stay; they could not move into their apartment immediately and actually left town for two weeks after their initial arrival.

As far as Gallaher could tell, Plainvillers did not react negatively to his book.

> If there is hostility. . . it must be confined to a small number, and so far has remained latent. A number of people have indicated that they agree with my findings, that they feel I presented an honest picture, but it 'still hurts to see things so carefully laid out.' (Gallaher, 1964, pp. 302-303)

After writing his book, Gallaher mailed ten to twelve copies to Plainville requesting that they be circulated. Gallaher received no negative feedback from readers. He has returned to Plainville a number of times since the publication of his book and again has received no negative responses. He has also written people in the community and none of them has written or spoken to him negatively about the book (Gallaher, personal communication, 1980). He reports that some individuals actually found the book boring; others were disappointed that they could not identify people in the book (Gallaher, personal communication, 1979).

One might wonder why there were no criticisms of the book particularly since scientists have pointed out that it is often impossible not to cause minimal discomfort in writing truthfully about communities. However, subjects may be more understanding and less critical when researchers are as tactful as Gallaher. Gallaher had a "Note to Plainvillers" at the beginning of his book. There, he states in part:

> I wish to thank all of you who gave of your time, effort, and cooperation in the interest of the research reported in this book. . . .
>
> I do not have to tell you that life in a small community under study is not the same as before a researcher arrives. . . . It is understandable that you sometimes regret, certainly always find it difficult to accept, the relatively dispassionate, detached image of your community painted by one like myself who is not a permanent part of it. . . .
>
> I am sure that some of you are not going to like the conclusions I have drawn about Plainville, but I believe you are aware that no analysis of community life can be completely pleasing and still be honest. Furthermore, I believe you will understand that nothing I have written is intended to cast ridicule on your community or anyone in it. In fact, I have the greatest respect for you. . . . (Gallaher, 1961, pp. xiii-xiv)

It would be difficult to be highly critical after reading such a note. Gallaher also thought it helpful to instruct the community so that they might understand what he was doing as an anthropologist. He "broke down the stereotyped image of anthropologists by talking about the variety of anthropologists and the many things they do" (Gallaher, 1964, p. 295). Perhaps this also eased tension and skepticism.

One other publication resulted from West's study: Abram Kardiner's (1945) *The Psychological Frontiers of Society*. Kardiner wrote in considerable detail about three different cultures describing the basic personality types of each. One of these cultures was that of Plainville. Kardiner's hypothesis was that basic personality types exist due to acculturation, and that deviations are due to culturally atypical experiences in early life.

Kardiner obtained his materials on Plainville from West. Abram Kardiner held a seminar at Columbia University, and James West was a student in that seminar. All materials presented in Kardiner's book were originally presented and discussed in the seminar. As Kardiner states in his preface:

> To Mr. James West I am deeply grateful for presenting his excellent materi-
> al on Plainville at the Seminar, for permitting its use in this book, and for
> writing the section which bears his name. I am additionally indebted to
> him for generously lending me the life histories which he took in the field
> and upon which my chapter on the personalities of Plainville is based
> (Kardiner, 1945, p. xxi)

West's four life histories loaned to Kardiner contained very sensitive information, i.e., sexual histories of informants including specifics such as when the informant first masturbated or had sexual intercourse. These histories gave adequate detail so that not only could each individual be identified but Plainville could also be identi-fied. (Fortunately, Kardiner's book is not thought known to Plainvillers.)

More specifically, Chapter X of Kardiner's book is titled "Plainville, U.S.A." by James West and has the following footnote:

> The data for this partial description of a rural community were collected
> in 1939-1940 on funds provided by the Social Science Research Council of
> Columbia University. . . . The materials collected have since been analyzed
> more fully and published separately (in *Plainville, U.S.A.*, Columbia Uni-
> versity Press, 1945). (Kardiner, 1945, p. 259).

This chapter contains the same description of Plainville (cited earlier) that the book *Plainville, U.S.A.* contains, i.e., information that is sufficient for Plainville to be identified.

Chapter XII, written by Kardiner, is titled "The Personalities of Plainville." James L., the first individual described, "was born at Plainville in 1897, the oldest of four brothers" (Kardiner, 1945, p. 379). He enlisted in the army in 1916 (p. 389). Here alone is enough information for the local people of Plainville to identify James L. The account goes on to relate personal facts about James such as the fol-lowing: His first wife was not a virgin. He started masturbating at age eleven or twelve. "He was troubled all his life by fears that his penis was too small" (p. 384). His second wife was frigid.

The above raises the question, "What were West's and Kardiner's responsibilities for protecting the privacy of Plainvillers? Current thinking on this issue is that researchers are accountable to their subjects both when publishing materials and when permitting other use to be made of their data. This is not to say that appro-priate secondary use of data is not highly desirable from scientific, practical, and ethical perspectives (see Campbell and Cecil, Chapter 5), but it is to say that researchers are accountable to their subjects when permitting other use of their data. For example, Lewis Terman carefully guarded the confidentiality of the information he gained through his study of young geniuses, and named in his will the social scientists (Pauline and Robert Sears) to whom these confidential data were entrusted upon his death.

By today's standards, West was responsible for the data given to Abram Kardiner and later used in Kardiner's book. That material was highly personal and sensitive; people could have been identified. A great deal of harm to the persons described in Kardiner's book could have occurred. Had Plainvillers become aware of Kardiner's book, West would have been responsible for such harm.

West thought that he had protected his subjects by changing all names including his own. He did not see the publication of Kardiner's book as jeopardizing anyone. But, had West realized that his subjects' true identities could have been discovered, what should he have done? To prevent such harm without preventing the publication of Kardiner's ideas, West could have stipulated, in a legally enforceable contract with Kardiner, the conditions of anonymity under which Kardiner could use the data.

Other issues brought to mind by the case of West and Kardiner are the relationships of students to professors and the influence that that relationship may have on publication activities. Who is responsible for the publication errors or indiscretions of a student? Might West or any other student feel compelled to provide his raw data to a professor? Might students feel unable to ask and demand greater protection for their information from a professor? Because ethical issues in social science research were not an issue in the 1940s and 1950s as they are today, Kardiner's and West's mistakes are understandable although not acceptable. Today, however, the responsibility for ethical research including publication and uses made of the data clearly and compellingly rests with the individual doing the research. A student's responsibility is to the research and thus to the subjects of that research. A professor's responsibility is both to teach students effectively and appropriately, e.g., to sensitize the student to ethical problems and dilemmas, and to also set an appropriate example of research behavior. Kardiner's use of West's potentially identifiable data clearly violates both of these requirements.

Thus, the case of Plainville begins to raise a number of questions concerning research and its publication. The difficulty of keeping a community and its people anonymous becomes clear here. This example illustrates some of the ways in which subjects may be wronged or harmed such as the "upset" of persons able to identify themselves in a report at the way they are portrayed and the subjecting of individuals to unwanted publicity. This case also raises questions concerning the use of secondary data, and the student/professor relationship when it pertains to publication. Springdale, another community study, raises some of these same questions, but, in addition, it brings to the fore such questions as, what is morally wrong with making public unflattering information that most of the members of a community already know? Is there some moral norm that scientists could take as their guide in publishing such information?

Springdale

The data used by Vidich and Bensman (1958) in *Small Town in Mass Society: Class, Power and Religion in a Rural Community* were a by-product of a larger research project called "Cornell Studies in Social Growth," carried out at Cornell University in the Department of Child Development and Family Relations under the direction of Urie Bronfenbrenner, a social psychologist. The data were based on a small New York town given the fictitious name of "Springdale." Vidich was the field director of the project, and spent two and one-half years living in Springdale. Vidich began work on the book after leaving Cornell. Joseph Bensman, who had not been involved in the project itself, collaborated with Vidich in the writing of a book on Springdale (Whyte, 1955, p. 1).

> Springdale is located in upper New York state about twenty-five miles from three different commercial-industrial centers, medium in size, in a region that is ordinarily regarded as primarily agricultural (Vidich & Bensman, 1958, p. 3)

At the time of the study, Springdale village had a population of approximately 1,000; and Springdale township had a population of around 3,000 (Vidich & Bensman, 1958, p. 15).

Vidich and Bensman's book was

> an attempt to explore the foundations of social life in a community which lacks the power to control the institutions that regulate and determine its existence. (Ridich & Bensman, 1958, p. vii).

Among other things the authors discussed in detail the local political life.

Prior to the publication of Vidich and Bensman's book, the manuscript was reviewed by the project director, Urie Bronfenbrenner. Bronfenbrenner objected to the fact that individuals within the book, although given fictitious names, were identifiable within Springdale. He also believed that "certain individuals were described in ways which could be damaging to them." An editorial statement by William Foote Whyte gave the following example:

> One member of invisible government, in agreement with the principal's educational policy, has remarked that "He's a little too inhuman—has never got into anything in the town. He's good for Springdale until he gets things straightened out. Then we'll have to get rid of him." (Whyte, 1958, p. 1)

Bronfenbrenner agreed that he would not object to Vidich using other project data in his book only after Vidich stated, "Whenever possible I will delete the material you consider objectionable." "However, a comparison of the book with Bronfenbrenner's written objections indicates that, in most cases, changes were not made" (Whyte, 1958, p. 1).

Following the publication of Vidich and Bensman's book, an editorial article appeared in *Human Organization* (Whyte, 1958) entitled "Freedom and Responsibility in Research: The "Springdale Case." In the article there was a quote from a Springdale newspaper:

The people of the village (Springdale) waited quite a while to get even with Art Vidich, who wrote a Peyton Place-type book about their town recently.

The featured float of the annual Fourth of July parade followed an authentic copy of the jacket of the book, *Small Town in Mass Society*, done largescale by Mrs. Beverly Robinson. Following the book cover came residents of (Springdale) riding masked in cars labeled with the fictitious names given them in the book.

But the pay-off was the final scene, a manure-spreader filled with very rich barnyard fertilizer, over which was bending an effigy of "The Author."

The people of Springdale must have felt that they had been betrayed much as Plainvillers had expressed to Gallaher their sense of betrayal by West. They had been promised anonymity and that promise had not been kept. This raises sharply the ethical question: What obligation to pursue anonymity does the author of a community study have to the people of the community he studies, particularly when it comes to publication of his findings?

Concerning anonymity Vidich had stated the following:

All personal names throughout the text are fictitious. Although this may not hide personal identities from those who are familiar with Springdale, our material could not be meaningfully presented without reference to individuals. Since political affairs are public in the broadest sense of the term, our procedure of using names and reports of official meetings is necessary. (Vidich & Bensman, 1958, p. 111)

However, before the Springdale project even began, the people were assured by project personnel that no individuals would be identified in printed reports (Whyte, 1958, p. 1). In fact, a code of ethics, Principles of Professional Ethics: Cornell Studies in Social Growth, had been devised for the project. These principles had been established prior to Vidich's hiring. The code states:

The first (purpose) is to safeguard the integrity and welfare of those who serve as subjects for or who may be affected by the research study. . . . The social scientist views people as individuals, not as subjects to be exploited. Specifically, he takes every precaution to preserve the security and privacy of the individuals and groups under study. . . . All data from the field are regarded as confidential and every precaution is taken to insure the anonymity of individuals and groups. . . . (Bell & Bronfenbrenner, 1959, pp. 49-52)

Robert Risley, in writing about the responsibility of project staff to the project director, states:

. . . if an individual in charge of a project has arrived at some understanding on these points (anonymity and confidentiality) in a given situation, those working with him are bound by the understanding as much as he. . . .

As a corollary of this point, it seems to me that individuals who are hired to work on a project are not free to use data obtained from the project for their own purposes. Essentially, my position would be that the material accumulated by individuals assigned to the project belongs to the project. Consequently, no use should be made of data which a staff member of a project obtains, except in a situation in which the staff member has received authorization for its use from the individual heading the project.

I realize that my line of reasoning obviously will cause problems for junior members on the projects and might well be viewed as interfering with the freedom of a researcher. As the editor so well points out, however, 'this freedom like other freedoms is balanced by responsibility.' (Vidich, Bensman, Risley, Ries, & Becker, 1958-1958, p. 5)

In addition to questioning the violation of anonymity, Whyte also questioned the actual "tone" of the book. He criticized Vidich's use of the term "invisible government." "The words themselves suggest an illegitimate form of activity, a conspiracy to gain and hold power." One could even question the accuracy of that expression: was the government actually invisible to the people of Springdale? Perhaps, "informal government" would have conveyed much of Vidich's meaning in sociological terms and yet would not have been so upsetting. Vidich used words that were offensive and not objective, as did West. If they had been more careful in their choice of words, if they had chosen inoffensive yet effective words, perhaps their books would not have caused such negative reactions. Earl Bell states in this regard:

Personally, I have come to the conclusion that responsibility to the community does not conflict with the responsibility to science. As a matter of fact, I have found frequently that attempting to state material coolly and objectively, rather than in terms of personalities and anecdotes, sharpens my understanding of sociological processes. (Bell & Bronfenbrenner, 1959, p. 49)

Two subsequent issues of *Human Organization* contained responses to the editor by Vidich and Bensman, and five other social scientists. Vidich and Bensman stated that the editor's

phrasing of the issues was too narrow, in that it was limited to the social and public relations problems of social science investigation. It failed to consider any of the problems related to the purposes of inquiry and to the scientific problems which social inquiry presumes to state and solve. (Vidich et al., 1958-1959, p. 2)

In response to the community's reaction, they stated:

Negative reaction to community and organizational research is only hard when results describe articulate, powerful, and respected individuals and organizations. We believe there would have been no objection to our study if it had been limited to the shack people. (Vidich et al., 1958-1959, p. 4)

Here it seems that Vidich confuses the ethical issue in question. The question is not whether the people researched object to the published material about them. The question is whether a disclosure is respectful and constructive.

Apart from the use of unflattering stereotypes, one might ask what is morally wrong with publishing unflattering information that most of the members of a community already know? Is there some moral norm that scientists should take as their guide in publishing such information? Vidich's own study gives insightful material on this very question. One of the questions raised in Vidich's study was, "is there a difference between 'public knowledge' which circulates from mouth to mouth in the village and the same stories which appear in print" (Whyte, 1958, pp. 1-2).

> The etiquette of gossip which makes possible the public suppression of the negative and competitive aspects of life has its counterpart in the etiquette of public conversation which always emphasizes the positive. There are thus two channels of communication that serve quite different purposes. In public conversation one hears comments only on the good things about people. . . . More than this, the level of public conversation always focuses on the collective success of its members. People comment on the success of a charitable drive. . . failures occur, when the play 'was a flop', as of course must happen from time to time, one senses what is almost a communal conspiracy against any further public mention of it. . . . At the public level all types of success are given public recognition while failure is treated with silence. (Vidich, 1958, pp. 44-45)

It appears that Vidich in his publication grossly violated "the etiquette of gossip."

Concerning confidentiality Howard S. Becker and Robert Risley pointed out the importance of establishing a clear understanding between the researcher and the subjects of all matters pertaining to publication and confidentiality. Risley writes:

> It may well be, on occasion, that, at an early stage of a project, there is a temptation to provide greater assurances concerning anonymity than are justified in view of any use of data in published form. Sometimes this is done in order to 'get in,' with the thought that, once in, matters can be resolved later. It seems to me that this is not appropriate and if, in a given situation, agreements cannot be arrived at which are satisfactory to the researcher and to those individuals within the situation which is to be studied, research opportunities must be sought elsewhere. (Vidich et al., 1958-1959, p. 5)

Beyond Plainville and Springdale

To this point ethical issues discussed have been ones raised by the studies of Plainville and Springdale. The discussion now branches out to consider additional ethical issues not explicitly raised in connection with Plainville and Springdale. These include the overall scientific responsibility of fieldworkers, social needs versus group rights in the balancing of risk against potential benefit, consent to risk violation of confidentiality, and publication of secrets.

Scientific Responsibility

Fichter and Kolb (1953) in their article "Ethical Limitations on Sociological Reporting" discuss the researchers' responsibilities to six entities: sponsors, funding agencies, publishers, other scientists, society, and subjects. To these authors there exists a dichotomy: researchers' responsibilities to subjects conflict with the responsibilities to all others. However, this perspective seems one sided. If research and its publication affects one group, it affects all. If a researcher upsets or angers a community, there is possible destruction of a research site, thus, harm to other scientists. If such research results in negative publicity, other potential research sites may be "destroyed."

Fichter and Kolb failed to mention the seventh entity to whom the researcher is responsible: the researcher himself. Recall the embarrassment suffered and mentioned by Vidich and Bensman (Vidich et al., 1958-1959). They paid a heavy price for their contribution to science. In considering publication, the researcher might remember that negative reactions will be directed toward him not only by the subjects, but also possibly by other scientists.

Recently, William Partridge (1979, p. 239), reflecting the now broadened awareness of these issues, summed up the ultimate responsibilities of scientists quite nicely:

> Our central concern as scientists is that our procedures and the uses to which the results are put will add constructively to knowledge but will not be harmful for the subjects of the study, the agency or foundation sponsoring the research, or our professional colleagues. Our central concern as humanists is that the scientific aims, procedures, and results of our work not harm our subjects, but enhance their human potential.

Here, all seven "obligations" are aligned; any conflicts among them dissolve using Partridge's overarching criterion of constructiveness.

Fichter and Kolb cite factors for the researcher to think about when considering the publication of a particular study. Three of these factors are relevant to the discussion here:

1. The nature and extent of possible harm or wrong to persons by the publication of data concerning their behavior. For example, how would the individual written about in Vidich's book have felt when he read, "He's a little too inhuman—has never got into anything in the town. He's good for Springdale until he gets things straightened out. Then we'll have to get rid of him"? Might reading it affect this man's behavior in relation to Springdale? Would Springdale have been adversely affected in some manner as a consequence?

2. The degree to which subjects are members of the same moral community as the author and the typical American citizen. Organized crime would be an example of a group whose members are not of the same moral community as most tax paying, law abiding citizens. Thus, where a researcher would not publish certain information about individuals or groups within his own moral community, he would more likely be justified in publishing that information if it pertained to a group outside of his moral community.

3. Social need versus group right (Fichter & Kolb, 1953, pp. 547-550). In the case of most community studies, the subjects would be of the same moral community. When the same moral community is involved, social need must then somehow outweigh the group's rights in order to justify the setting aside of the group's rights. Rainwater and Pittman (1967, pp. 365-366) appear to view the study of persons acting on behalf of the public as an example of social need being greater than group rights:

> . . . sociologists have the right (and perhaps also the obligation) to study publicly accountable behavior. By publicly accountable behavior we do not simply mean the behavior of public officials . . . but also the behavior of any individual as he goes about performing public or secondary roles for which he is socially accountable. . . . One of the functions of our discipline, along with those of political science, history, economics, journalism, and intellectual pursuits generally, is to further public accountability in a society whose complexity makes it easier for people to avoid their responsibilities.

From this position, Vidich behaved responsibly in publishing a book in which he revealed questionable political activities; moreover, as a result of publication, some political ways were changed in Springdale. However, in the book that Vidich and Bensman actually wrote, it is the manner in which they exposed the townspeople of Springdale that is objectionable and ethically questionable.

Consent to Risk Violation of Confidentiality

The issues raised here go beyond anonymity, however. There is no way that a scientist can ensure that the identity of a community studied will remain secret. There are too many different ways in which the identity of a community can purposefully or accidentally be discovered. This is particularly true when a researcher has to rely on other human beings to keep the identity of a community secret; inevitably one of these individuals, perhaps one of the subjects, will leak the identity. No doubt, the people of Plainville and Springdale, for example, played a part in spreading the true identity of their towns.

The ethical dissemination of a case study or a community study is problematic in other ways as well. When field or organizational research is funded and sponsored by public agencies or private industries, it becomes difficult for scientists to control the use of their data. The problem of ownership and use of data also arises when the research is done by more than one scientist. There are bound to be differences in opinion as to what is or is not ethically acceptable use of the data. In such cases, the scientist's "ability to ensure confidentiality to the subjects of research, or even to anticipate when, where, or for what purposes confidentiality may be compromised" is limited (Chambers & Wolfe, 1978, p. 2). When total confidentiality or anonymity cannot be guaranteed, the issue becomes, in part, one of on-going communication and agreement (or informed consent) between the investigator and the research participants.

In discussing confidentiality and large scale field or organizational research, Chambers states:

> It becomes impossible to report effectively on agency operations and policies without identifying key individuals.
>
> Where appropriate, it should be the responsibility of both those who manage such experiments and those who do the actual data collection to make it clear to research subjects that certain levels of confidentiality cannot be insured. The implications should also be made clear. In the AAE (administrative agency experiment) the principal aim was to evaluate various aspects of an experimental program. The job performance of particular individuals was of only minor concern. The consequences, however, of publishing data which might reflect on the job performance of individuals go beyond the intent of any experiment. Research subjects should be forewarned that material relating to their job performance might eventually come into the hands of individuals who have a significant influence on their careers. This forewarning might make aspects of the fieldworker's task more difficult, but the implications of doing otherwise are far worse. In many cases, the actual gain in rapport might work to the researcher's advantage. People often appreciate being dealt with 'on the level,' and they sometimes respond in kind. (Chambers, 1977, p. 265)

When considering the risks of publication and communicating those ideas candidly to prospective participants, the scientist should aknowledge beneficial as well as wrongful uses that may be made of the findings. In Chapter 4, other volume, Mirvis and Seashore make this similar point and indicate effective means of establishing and maintaining such communication on a continuing basis. As Herbert Kelman (1968, pp. 9 & 23) states:

> On the one hand, there is the danger that the findings of social science research may be used for the suppression of human freedom and the dehumanization of social life. On the other hand, there is the potential that social science knowledge may contribute to the advancement of human welfare, the rationality of social decisions, and the achievement of constructive social change. . . the man engaged in 'basic' research . . . must consider the relative probabilities . . . that this knowledge will be used to enhance or to restrict people's freedom of choice.

Publication of Secrets

J. A. Barnes concerns as to publication are slightly different: "With publication we run the risk of making public that which our informants would prefer to keep secret" (Barnes, 1970, p. 246). He asks, "if we protect our informants, is it right to expose the myths of their institutions?" (p. 247). He suggests:

> One way of controlling the effect of publication is to make sure that those affected agree to what is being said about them. The number of people who may possibly be affected by the publication of the results of a social inquiry is immense, and if the ethnographer tried to get unanimity he

would certainly publish nothing. In practical terms all that can be done is to clear the manuscript with those most closely concerned. (p. 245)

Another ethical aspect of publishing concerns the sensitivity of the information to be disseminated. The more sensitive and private the information, the greater the potential to harm others. Sex, criminal activities, family, and/or marital problems are all examples. Barnes states:

> Some of the actions he (the fieldworker) has to describe and analyze are bound to be dispicable, immoral, illegal or reprehensible, and most of the people concerned will prefer to keep them unheralded and unsung. (p. 247)

Cassell suggests that:

> A more appropriate ethical framework for judging fieldwork might be constructed upon respect for the autonomy of individuals and groups based on the fundamental principle that persons always be treated as ends in themselves, never merely as means—the Kantian categorical imperative. (Cassell, chapter 1)

This general ethical framework is applicable to the publication of research.

Guidelines for "Ethical Proofreading" of Fieldwork Manuscripts

Instead of a summary, a list of guidelines is offered for the "ethical proofreading" of fieldwork manuscripts prior to their publication. By evaluating manuscripts as directed by these guidelines, the author is in a better position to make changes that would diminish potential harm to subjects.

1. Assume that both the identities of the location studied and the identities of individuals will be discovered. What would the consequences of this discovery be to the community? To the individuals? What would the consequences be both within the community and outside the community? Do you believe that the importance of what you have revealed in your publication is great enough to warrant these consequences? Could you, yourself, live with these consequences should they occur?

2. Look at the words used in your manuscript. Are they judgmental or descriptive? How accurate are the descriptions of the phenomena observed? A judgment, for example, would be to say that a community is backward. A description might be to say that 10% of the adult population can neither read nor write. The latter is preferable both scientifically and ethically.

If you are inclined to leave judgmental statements in your manuscript, be clear about your purpose in doing so. If you choose to take a chance of offending someone, know the reason why and be sure the reason is valid and warranted.

3. Where appropriate in describing private or unflattering characteristics, consider generalizing first and then giving specifics, as Gallaher did when writing about status. This tends to make research participants feel less singled out. It also adds to the educational value of the writing.

4. Published data may affect the community studied and similar communities in a general way even though the identities of the community and individuals may

remain unknown. In the case of West's book on Plainville, for example, people were described as backward. Some people were said to live like animals. Some men were said to be as dirty as animals. West also related that many people from Plainville left the community to seek employment in the cities. What if such descriptive information about rural communities affected individuals' opportunities for employment due to the creation of negative stereotypes about people from rural areas? Therefore, ask yourself how your information might be used in a positive way? In a negative way? And again ask if the revelations are worth the possible consequences.

5. Will your research site be usable again or have you destroyed this site for other researchers? Have you destroyed other similar sites? Is such destruction worth the information obtained and disseminated?

6. What was your perspective toward subjects? What were your biases? How did your perspective and biases, both positive and negative, affect the way you viewed your subjects and wrote about them? Where was it difficult to maintain objectivity in your writings? Have you done what you could to increase objectivity? Do your writings honestly acknowledge your biases to the reader?

7. In what ways can research participants be educated about the role of fieldworkers and the nature of objective reporting of fieldwork? Gallaher's note to Plainvillers at the beginning of his book is not feasible in all cases, but it may be advisable to caution your subjects at various stages of the research that it is not easy to read about oneself as one is described by another.

8. When conducting research within a larger project, know the expectations of other project members concerning what each member will be permitted to publish both in the short and long run, i.e., are there any limitations? If not, what limits ought ethically to be imposed? Who will have the final say about publication? Who will own the data? Who will have access to the data and on what terms? What will happen to the data after publication? Most important, see that agreements are set forth in writing in a legally enforceable contract.

9. Have several people do "ethical proofreading" of your manuscript. One or two of those people might be your subjects. They should read it for accuracy and should provide any general feedback they are inclined to offer. One or two of your colleagues should also read the manuscript. Preferably those colleagues should not be ones who are particularly supportive or sympathetic to your research but colleagues who can be constructively critical.

These guidelines are offered as a means for refining the writing of fieldwork manuscripts, making them more scientifically and ethically sound. The purpose of these guidelines is to increase any writer's awareness of what he or she is writing, why he or she is writing it, and what might be the consequences of what is written and published.

Directions for Future Research on the Ethics of Publishing Fieldwork

Virtually no research has been done on the effects of the publication of field research on the lives of those described therein or similar others. Below are some suggested research approaches. This list of suggestions is hardly exhaustive. I hope it will stimulate readers to think further along these lines and to initiate original inquiry.

1. What harm or good has been done as a result of fieldwork and other social science publications? To whom did the harm or good occur? How did it occur? One useful approach to answering such questions would be to enter any research site from which data have been gathered and published, and find out what people regard as the result of the study and publication. How much good or harm occurred from the research only? How much occurred due to publication only? Have the subjects read the publication? Have there been changes within the community as a result of the publication? Has the research site received outside attention due to publication? If so, what were the consequences?

2. Have relationships between people been adversely or positively affected because individuals played the role of informants? Has published information caused informants to be ostracized, for example? One might obtain a list of informants from colleagues and interview them as to their experience since publication.

3. How do people react when they read about themselves? To learn about such reactions, for example, I might have a colleague disseminate to funeral directors a fieldwork report I wrote about funeral directors (Johnson, 1979). That paper could be given to the funeral directors whom I interviewed and to an equal number not interviewed. The introduction and wording of the paper might be varied experimentally to test ideas such as those set forth in this paper. Among funeral directors whom I interviewed, I might have systematically varied my introduction along lines similar to Gallaher. Another group of individuals who are not funeral directors might also be given the paper. Through such systematic control of treatment and subject variables, one could examine the main and interaction effects on readers' reactions of reading about oneself, about one's own group, or of reading about others; and the effects of wording of the paper (e.g., objective versus judgmental; prefacing unflattering specific descriptions with a detailed general discussion of the phenomena or not) and effects of specific fieldworker behaviors (e.g., explaining the roles of fieldworkers, warning informants about the unpleasantness of objective descriptions of one's community).

4. A review of the literature and interviews of investigators concerning the consequences of publication needs to be conducted. For example, William Foote Whyte (1955) talks about his return trip to Cornerville; that trip revealed that Doc had difficulties reading and accepting what Whyte had written about him although it was true. A follow-up interview of Whyte concerning his perception of the consequences of his work would enrich today's understanding of the consequences of published information. Similar literature reviews and interviews concerning the work of other community fieldworkers may provide a rich compendium of insights about the ethics of publishing fieldwork.

5. The graduate and undergraduate educational system in the social sciences needs to be examined to determine if and how ethical issues in fieldwork are or might be taught and whether there are effective ways to sensitize students to the effects of their writing about others.

In conclusion, it is obvious that the writing of the fieldwork report is a necessary step in the production of useful knowledge about communities. What is not obvious is how to maximize the usefulness of such knowledge, and how to minimize its possible harms. This chapter and the current state of the art leave much for social scientists to learn about the ethics of publishing fieldwork on communities.

Reference Notes

1. Gallaher, Art. Personal Communication, 1979.
2. Gallaher, Art. Personal Communication, 1980.

References

Babbie, E. R. *The practice of social research.* Calif: Wadsworth, 1979.
Barnes, J. A. Some ethical problems in modern fieldwork. In W. J. Filstead (Ed.), *Qualitative methodology: Firsthand involvement with the social world.* Chicago: Markham, 1970.
Bell, E. H., & Bronfenbrenner, U. Freedom and responsibility in research: Comments. *Human Organization*, 1959, *18*, 49-52.
Chambers, E. Working for the man: The anthropologist in policy-relevant research. *Human Organization*, 1977, *36*(3), 258-267.
Chambers, E. & Wolfe, A. W. Legal and ethical problems in client-oriented field research. A paper prepared for presentation in a symposium, Ethical Problems of Fieldwork, at the 1978 Annual Meetings of the American Anthropological Association.
Fichter, J., & Kolb, W. Ethical limitations on sociological reporting. *American Sociological Review*, 1953, *18*, 544-550.
Gallaher, A. *Plainville fifteen years later.* New York: Columbia University Press, 1961.
Gallaher, A. Plainville: The twice-studied town. In A. Vidich, J. Bensman, & N. Stein (Eds.), *Reflections on community studies.* New York: Wiley, 1964.
Johnson, C. G. Occupational self image and the funeral director. Unpublished paper, 1979.
Kardiner, A. *The psychological frontiers of society.* New York: Columbia University Press, 1945.
Kelman, H. C. *A time to speak: On human values and social research.* San Francisco: Jossey-Bass, 1968.
Klockars, C. B., & O'Connor, F. W. (Eds.). *Deviance and decency: The ethics of research with human subjects.* Beverly Hills, Calif.: Sage, 1979.
Orlans, H. *Contracting for knowledge.* San Francisco: Jossey-Bass, 1973.
Partridge, W. Epilogue: Ethical Dilemmas. In W. L. Partridge & S. T. Kimball (Eds.), *The craft of community study: Fieldwork dialogues.* Florida: University of Florida Social Sciences Monograph Number 65, 1979.
Rainwater, L., & Pittman, D. Ethical problems in studying a politically sensitive and deviant community. *Social Problems*, 1967, *14*, 357-366.
Vidich, A., & Bensman, J. *Small town in mass society: Class, power and religion in a rural community.* Princeton, N.J.: Princeton University Press, 1958.

Vidich, A., Bensman, J., Risley, R., Ries, R. E., & Becker, H. S. Freedom and responsibility in research: Comments. *Human Organization*, 1958-1959, *17*, 2-6.

West, J. *Plainville U.S.A.* New York: Columbia University Press, 1945.

Whyte, W. F. *Street corner society: The social structure of an Italian slum.* Chicago: University of Chicago Press, 1955.

Part II

The Roles of Social Scientists in Research Regulation and in Giving Social Science to Society via the Mass Media

The embracing of alternative methodologies or models in social science opens up many possible kinds of relationships for scientists not only with research participants, but with other sectors of society as well. The humanist who takes science seriously (or the scientist who takes humanistic concerns seriously) has many perspectives and relationships to consider but not many role models or much formal knowledge to guide these relationships. The chapters in this part are intended to provide some role models and formal knowledge to guide social scientists in various research related relationships. It is intended to challenge social scientists to draw creatively from various models of social science when shaping their relationship with the larger world to which the social science relates.

When the National Commission for the Protection of Human Subjects of Biomedical and Behavioral Research began to gather information and formulate positions, few social scientists stepped forth to testify, and even fewer offered constructive testimony. Among those who testified, many objected to restrictions on the conduct of science, and some testified about specific wrongs that had been committed in the name of science. However, few combined rigor and humanistic perception to create useful new ideas for the Commission to consider. One particularly creative contributive was that of Donald T. Campbell and Joe Shelby Cecil, which is presented in Chapter 5, in revised form.

In their testimony, Campbell and Cecil deal with the issue of evaluation research in the public sector, an issue that raises many interesting ethical problems. In today's highly technological and information oriented society, public policy makers and other decision makers who have the power to create social programs attempt to base their decisions on the soundest evidence available. Yet, program evaluation often generates conflict between the needs of society for information and the interests of individuals in maintaining their privacy and well-being. Moreover, risks to those who are on the periphery of the study and who are in control groups may also arise. What are these risks? How are they to be balanced against the benefits of research to determine what is ethically justifiable? Can the requirement of informed consent be met in evaluation research?

Campbell and Cecil prepared a summary of ethical problems in evaluation research and a set of recommendations for its regulation. Both are psychologists and evaluators; Campbell has pioneered in experimental field methodology and Cecil is a lawyer. They raise and examine a range of problems including the problem of selecting the appropriate review panel for nationwide research, conflicts of interest between the rights of privacy of the subjects of evaluation research and the interests of government in auditing and reanalyzing the results of public programs, and the rights of the poor to be protected from harm resulting from participation in social experiments.

Part of Campbell and Cecil's summary and recommendations is presented in Chapter 5. The magnitude and seriousness of potential ethical problems in program evaluation are impressive and the need for regulation of this research is evident. The difficulty of formulating entirely fair and constructive regulations is also evident: protecting vulnerable populations sometimes seems incompatible with performing evaluation research at all. Consequently, there is tremendous disagreement within the scientific community as to how or whether humanistic and scientific concerns are to be balanced. In an attempt to arrive at the most judicious formulation of recommendations, Campbell and Cecil polled many investigators, public advocates, and others qualified to advise. But while extensive consultation is crucial in order to understand the issues and evaluate tentative regulations, consultation and carefully reasoned regulations cannot guarantee that conflicts of interest between need for information and the rights of individuals can be resolved satisfactorily.

To illustrate the difficulty of arriving at satisfactory solutions to these conflicts, two critiques of the Campbell and Cecil chapter are offered in appendices to Chapter 5. Ernest R. House, specialist in the evaluation of educational programs, offers cogent criticisms to the effect that the Campbell and Cecil recommendations pay too little attention to the needs of the individuals for freedom from data collection programs that may jeopardize their social, political, or economic well-being. While agreeing in principle with most of the recommendations, House raises frightening examples of possible abuses of individual rights and freedoms that remain possible within the guidelines that Campbell and Cecil have offered. He is particularly wary of the recommendation that data not containing unique identifiers be made available for analysis without the informed consent of the subjects. He argues that the issue is not simply one of privacy. Rather, the possession of information about others implies a power relationship, giving to the one who possesses the information power over the lives of others. House argues, therefore, that people from whom data are collected have a right to know the purposes for which the data will be collected and the right to veto. Thus, House, presents a humanist critique.

In contrast, Norman M. Bradburn, a survey researcher, expresses concern that the recommendations of Campbell and Cecil place so many restrictions on the investigation that it may become impractical or impossible to conduct valid evaluation research in many cases. Bradburn is concerned that attempts to place the review process in the hands of a governmental agency will result in a rigid, cumbersome, and time-consuming process of review that will create more problems than it will solve. In addition, he poses persuasive arguments against requiring that consent be obtained from subjects to use existing records concerning them.

The tension is evident between the scientific and humanist views that must be brought to bear on a project such as that of Campbell and Cecil. We see that without some ability to flexibly employ the four methodologies described by Mitroff and Kilmann (in Chapter 1, companion volume), one could neither devise useful guidelines nor stand the heat that arises from doing so.

In Chapter 6, we observe the efforts of another partnership between social psychologist and lawyer in pursuit of better regulation of social science research. Elizabeth and Tony Tanke provide a description and analysis of actual and ideal functioning of the Institutional Review Board (IRB). They begin by tracing the steps involved in the review of proposals; they discuss the jurisdiction of the IRB, problems in identification of risk to subject interests, and the role of the IRB in the management of risk and in the weighing of risks against benefits. They then analyze the interaction between the IRB and the research community and identify problems that have stood in the way of effective communication and education. Finally, they recommend ways of facilitating effective review. Since the effective assessment of research risk requires consultation with others whose viewpoint and expertise are different from one's own, we see that the properly constituted, well-run IRB offers an impressive array of expertise to the investigator and is a nearly perfect mechanism for recognizing the interests of subjects as well as of science. The tasks of developing maximally constructive, easily interpreted guidelines for IRBs, and of administering them effectively, are thus of great importance. One is struck by how qualified social scientists are to study these matters, but how few have risen to the challenge.

Finally, in Chapter 7, S. Holly Stocking and Sharon L. Dunwoody explore a largely neglected matter, namely, use of the mass media to give the layman knowledge of social science. In 1969, George Miller urged psychologists to "give psychology away." He argued that the most valuable product of the social sciences is knowledge that is clearly and responsibly communicated to the layman so that all individuals may use it to improve and transform their lives as they see fit. However, social scientists know that there are risks to themselves, to science, and to society, connected with their use of the mass media, and have largely avoided mass media dissemination of their work.

Stocking and Dunwoody point out that benefits as well as pitfalls are connected with the use of mass media by scientists, and that scientists who understand how science news is gathered and used by media professionals are in the best position to reap benefits and avoid pitfalls. Stocking and Dunwoody review empirical research on how journalists are trained, how they select scientific news, the accuracy of their reporting, the perception within the sciences of scientists who "go public," and the effects of mass media dissemination on policy making and science. There is little empirical research on these topics, since there is not yet even agreement within the mainstream of social science that it is appropriate for social scientists to "go public." But within the limits of existing empirical data and reasonable speculation, Stocking and Dunwoody offer suggestions to social scientists on ways to improve their communication with journalists, and increase their chances of achieving useful and accurate mass media reporting of their work.

These three chapters exemplify potentially useful relationships social scientists may cultivate with nonscientific sectors of society, and ethical issues likely to arise in those dual roles. In each of those roles, the scientist is expected to serve the values of science and the values of some other institution, as well. For example, Campbell and Cecil set out to serve science, regulators of research, and the participants in public policy research; the scientist/IRB member is expected to serve science, the research institution, and human subjects; and the scientist-in-the-media is expected to provide objective, balanced scientific information, but to do it simply and in a way that makes "good news."

As social scientists seek to serve society responsibly, other roles such as these continue to arise. For example, in 1981, a six person subcommittee of the American Association of University Professors considered the likely impact of the 1981 Federal Regulations of Human Research on the academic freedom of faculty members engaged in research (Thompson et al., 1981); their role was more than that of scientists, for they were commissioned to formulate recommendations that consider the legitimate interests of society as well. There are many other dual roles of this kind that the scientist with a social conscience may be motivated, but unprepared, to fulfill responsibly. The scientist who takes the role of social advocate is expected to be objective and truthful, yet to gerrymander evidence to make a political point effectively. Can one do both? If so, how? The scientist who seeks to influence public policy, to teach science effectively, or to serve as an organizational development specialist confronts similar role conflicts. Perhaps no one is better equipped than social scientists, themselves, to study and analyze these complex scientific roles and to determine how to fulfill them responsibly.

Reference

Thompson, J. J., et al. Regulations governing research on human subjects. *Academe*, 1981, *67*(6), 358-370.

Chapter 5

A Proposed System of Regulation for the Protection of Participants in Low-Risk Areas of Applied Social Research

Donald T. Campbell and Joe Shelby Cecil

This chapter offers a series of proposed regulations for areas of applied social research that have little risk for the research participants. Such areas include program evaluation, social experimentation, social indicators research, survey research, secondary analysis of research data, and statistical analysis of administrative records.[1] These areas of research, which we will refer to collectively as "program

---

[1] There is enough ambiguity and technical terminology in these areas to call for some definition of major terms:

Program Evaluation: Assembly of evidence bearing on the effectiveness and side effects of ameliorative programs, social innovations, etc. These programs have usually been initiated by governmental agencies.

Social Indicators: Statistical summaries, often in time-series form, bearing on the well-being of the nation or smaller social units. Social indicators may be viewed in contrast to more common economic indicators. Many social indicators are generated from statistical summaries of administrative records. Others, such as indicators based on the Census, are produced by institutionalized survey procedures. Increasing attention is being given to "subjective" social indicators, in which representative samples of the public report on their "happiness" or satisfaction with various aspects of their lives in public opinion surveys.

Social Experimentation: This will be narrowly defined to refer to an experimental form of policy research or program evaluation, experiments carried out in social (as opposed to laboratory) settings evaluating governmental or other social interventions. (This definition excludes experiments in public settings to test scientific theories.)

Respondents: Participants, interviewees, anthropological "informants," the persons whose responses are recorded, the "subjects" of research, etc. Many social scientists prefer the terms "respondent" or "participant" to the term "subject," since the term "subject" has been associated with an exploitative attitude. While "respondent" seems to us the most appropriate general term for participants in social research, the report of the Commission used "subjects" throughout.

evaluation," have been free of publicized abuses, and relatively free of regulation common to other areas of biomedical and behavioral research.

Although recent federal regulations have moved away from requiring institutional review of these areas of social research (DHHS, 1981), we believe that the nature of the data collection process in these areas results in risks to the research participants that require the measure of protection suggested by our proposed regulations. While the participants in such research clearly have rights and interests that may be violated, the nature of these risks is somewhat unique. Rarely will a risk to physical health be involved. Indeed, the participants in the experimental group often receive an apparent boon, such that the rights of the participants in the control group often may be the greater problem. The more frequent danger in program evaluation is the risk that sensitive research data will be misused. Such data may be subpoenaed by prosecutors searching for evidence of crimes, or become a source of malicious gossip or blackmail. Federally funded program evaluations frequently require audit,

---

Statistical Data: The Privacy Act of 1974 uses this term to refer to information collected originally for research rather than administrative purposes. This use will be avoided here in favor of the more general term, "research data."

Statistical Analysis, Statistical Product, and *Statistic*: These terms refer to summary indices no longer containing individually identifiable data, based on either research data or administrative records. Means, standard deviations, correlation coefficients, *t* ratios, *F* ratios, probability levels, etc., exemplify statistical products. Frequency counts and percentages usually qualify as statistical products precluding individual identification, but not if the identities of individuals can be deduced through association of research data with public records.

Administrative Records: This term refers to data collected originally for bureaucratic purposes rather than research purposes. School grades, achievement test scores, earnings subject to withholding tax, unemployment insurance payments, days hospitalized, incidence of serum hepatitis, and auto insurance claims all represent administrative records that can be of great value in program evaluation if they are used in ways safeguarding individual privacy.

Record, File, Data Bank: These are terms used for collections of data on individuals, either administrative or research data.

Reanalysis and *Data Analysis by Outsiders*: These terms refer to the use of research data or administrative records for purposes other than were originally understood by the respondents, and by persons other than the regular custodians of the data.

File Merging: This refers to combining individual data from two files containing data about the same respondents, so that one or both of the files, or a third file, ends up containing individually identified data originating in another file. Unified data banks involve file merging.

File Linkage: This refers to the linking of data from two or more files so that statistical products are generated involving data from both files. File merging is the most complete form of file linkage, and where permissible, the most statistically efficient. It is important to note, however, that there are restricted forms of file linkage that do not involve file merger, and where no individually identified data are transferred from any file to any other (e.g., the "mutually insulated" file linkage.)

verification, and reanalysis. These activities may preclude a promise of complete confidentiality to the respondents and increase the risk that the information they provide will be used for purposes other than those initially intended. However, if respondents are fully informed of these risks, the quality of the research data may be diminished. From these few examples it is apparent that these areas of social research present a different set of problems from those encountered in medical and laboratory research.

Some background on the development of this chapter is in order. In the fall of 1975, Campbell was asked to prepare a paper concerning protection of participants in program evaluations for the National Commission for the Protection of Human Subjects of Biomedical and Behavioral Research (the Commission). This invitation was no doubt motivated by an interest in having a paper prepared by someone clearly identified with program evaluation research. Campbell had been a member of the Social Science Research Council's Committee on Social Experimentation, which produced a short chapter on "Human Values and Social Experimentation" (Riecken et al., 1974, pp. 245-269), and on the National Academy of Science/ National Research Council Committee on Federal Agency Evaluation Research, which addressed these issues in a report entitled, *Protecting Individual Privacy in Evaluation Research* (Rivlin et al., 1975). Campbell had also authored one of the few published defenses of deception in social psychology laboratory research, and had recommended against informed consent or debriefing where the experimental treatments fall within the normal range of public communications (Campbell, 1969). However, he had later argued that for public policy research, the voting booth rather than the experimental laboratory was the appropriate model, and that the informed consent and opportunity for participant access to the research findings should be required (Campbell, 1971a, 1971b). Cecil brought to the collaboration training in both law and program evaluation, and an interest in procedures for protecting privacy while permitting research in data archives (Boruch & Cecil, 1979; Boruch & Cecil, in press; Cecil, 1978; Cecil & Griffin, 1981). A major interest in accepting the invitation to prepare the background paper was a desire to propose a regulatory scheme that permits the use of administrative records for program evaluation while protecting the privacy interests of the individuals (Boruch & Cecil, 1979; Campbell, Boruch, Schwartz & Steinberg, 1977; Schwartz & Orleans, 1967).

In January 1976 a draft of proposed regulations was distributed to some 400 persons for comment, the names coming from various lists we obtained of committees, symposia, and conferences on the topics of ethics, privacy, confidentiality, rights of subjects, etc., in the social sciences. This mass mailing was done in the spirit of assembling volunteers for an ad hoc "postal committee." Such a committee was necessary since the evaluation research community had developed no consensus on these issues, and a solitary background paper might precipitate inadequately debated regulations. Some 75 persons responded, almost all with detailed comments. Of these, 45 also expressed their preferences on the ballot that allowed specific proposals to be endorsed, rejected as "too protective," rejected as "not protective enough," or rejected for other reasons. These conscientious and thoughtful reactions were compiled and returned to the commentators in a report consisting of

73 single-spaced pages of written comments and a 23 page written summary.[2] Ernest House, whose comments follow, provided one of the most extended expressions of the "not protective enough" point of view. Norman Bradburn, whose comments follow, was one of the strongest defenders of the "too protective" position.

In April 1977, a revised version of the paper was prepared. It eliminated six of the earlier proposed regulations that failed to achieve an endorsement by the majority (most dissents being in the "too protective" direction), though discussion of these issues was retained. Several new proposed regulations were added, especially in the area of informed consent. This second version of the paper appears as chapter 12 in Appendix II of the report of the Commission (NCPHSBBR, 1978). This version was also circulated with ballots to previous commentators, plus a few others. Responses from some 30 persons were received. These results again were assembled, duplicated, and redistributed. These results are reported in the text that follows. All of the proposed regulations were endorsed by a majority of this group, all but one by more than 70%. Similar support was found in the first survey for those proposed regulations that were retained. The proposed regulations that follow remain essentially the same as those of April 1977, with minor modifications in wording.

Events have moved swiftly since these recommendations were developed and critiqued. The Commission has released its report containing recommendations for institutional review of research (NCPHSBBR, 1978; Veach, 1980), which were transformed with some degree of fidelity into proposed federal regulations (DHEW, 1979), then into final regulations (DHHS, 1981), to replace the regulations that proved unsuitable for contemporary social research (DHEW, 1974). While the Commission's report and the recent federal regulations address some of the issues raised in this chapter, by and large these areas of research will remain unregulated.

To some it may seem that our suggestions for regulations are out of step with the times. The final federal regulations exempt from their restrictions many of the areas of research we would include, thereby avoiding some of the issues we confront. But these proposals address persistent problems of applied social research. If the pendulum again swings to favor regulation of these areas, it will be necessary to devise a regulatory scheme that offers adequate protection while permitting the goals of the research to be realized. Presentation of these proposals may offer guidance in such an event, as well as acknowledge the contributions of all of those who were helpful in shaping the recommendations.

Our proposals for regulation are offered in this specific form to provoke detailed discussion. Some of this discussion is already under way, as evidenced by the extended comments of House and Bradburn following this chapter. The controversy over the recent revisions to the current federal regulations for institutional review of research involving human subjects suggests a continuing division of opinion over the need and appropriate means of offering protection in these areas (Breger, in press; de Sola Pool, 1979; Gray, in press; Levine, 1979; Robertson, 1981; Wax, 1981). To demonstrate the contrast with our recommendations, summaries of the

---

[2] These documents are available from the present authors, and are an archive for any future work on this topic.

Commission's recommendations and the proposed federal regulations will be offered when relevant to our own. Since the final regulations exempt many of these low-risk areas of applied social research, our commentary on the final regulations is limited. However, excellent reviews are available elsewhere (Breger, in press; Gray, in press).

Proposed Regulations

1. Scope of Review and Review Boards

Let us start with a concrete recommendation.

1a. Evaluation research, social indicator research, social survey research, secondary analysis of research data, and statistical analysis of data from administrative records are to conform to federal policies and regulations developed for these areas. The federal government or reviewing institution will review such research to the full extent of its authority, regardless of its sponsorship.

There is general agreement that these areas of research should be subject to some form of review, though the research involves little risk to participants and there are essentially no publicized cases of violations in these areas. However, there is less agreement on the limits of federal authority to conduct such a review (Boulay et al., 1980; de Sola Pool, 1979; Pattullo, 1980; Roberton, 1981; Swazey, 1980). We see no necessity to limit the review function only to those programs that have been funded directly by the federal government. To the greatest extent possible, we would extend this review authority to all research without regard to its sponsorship, including all university-related research, research by profit and nonprofit research corporations, and even unfunded private research. The restrictions on this review function will be determined by the constitutional and legislative limitations on federal authority to conduct such a review, and not by the nature of the research. Without attempting to determine the limits of such authority (Robertson, 1977), our effort is intended to construct a scheme for the conduct of applied social research when the regulatory power is extended to its limit. Of course, if research institutions choose to adopt a similar voluntary system of review, then the special nature of applied social research may require consideration of these suggestions.

Our proposal to require institutional review of low-risk research would permit broader review than either the past or recent regulations. The past federal regulations did not clearly specify the scope of review, and institutional review boards varied in interpreting their mandates. In the past at least some institutional review boards felt obligated to review some of the research in these low-risk areas, even though the research was not federally funded. The Commission sought to clarify the scope of review and recommended institutional review of all "research" with "human subjects," broadly defined to include the areas of concern in this chapter with the exception of analysis of anonymous records. The proposed federal regulations followed, for the most part, the definitions proposed by the Commission, and suggest review of all research conducted by an institution receiving federal funds, to the extent that existing statutes and regulations permit. However, the final regulations extend to individual research projects (rather than institutions) that are federally supported. Furthermore, a number of exclusions are included that would deregulate survey research (unless the information may be harmful to the individual survey participant), most educational research, and most research with anonymous records. Consequently, our suggestion that research in these areas be reviewed by the research institutions would require greater regulatory authority than that suggested by the Commission or by the current federal regulations.

The problem raised by the broad scope of review we propose is the monstrous bureaucratic burden of requiring this vast area of low-risk research to go through formal institutional review processes. In response to this problem, we suggest a process of *conditional clearance by affidavit*. As an expeditious means of reviewing certain low-risk research in these areas, the suggested procedure should be superior to the kind of mass-produced perfunctory clearance that institutional review boards would tend to employ in these areas.

1b. *Procedures for conditional clearance by affidavit and full review by institutional review boards.* Before soliciting funding or initiating a research activity in the low-risk areas of evaluation research, secondary analysis of research data, or statistical analysis of data from administrative records, the principal investigator(s) shall file with the institutional review board a full research proposal and a "clearance affidavit," constituting a detailed affirmation that the rights of the participants are not jeopardized in any of the ways specified by federal policies and regulations developed for these areas. At the discretion of the review board and the request of the principal investigator, this affidavit may constitute a conditional clearance of the review process, permitting funding requests and research to proceed forthwith, unless or until the principal investigator, the institutional review board, or the funding source, requests delay for a full review by the institutional review board. The institutional review board may conduct such a full review at any time during a research proceeding under conditional affidavit clearance, and may order the cessation of research found to be in violation of the regulations.

Conditional clearance by affidavit for these low-risk areas of research might be implemented through a detailed questionnaire, signed by the principal investigator(s). These affidavits and research proposals would be kept on file by the board for the length of the research project and the subsequent period of project liability for participant injury. For these designated low-risk areas, the funding and research process could proceed if the principal investigator(s) does not choose to have a full review, and files the research proposal and clearance affidavit. The board would have the right to examine these materials in any way it chooses. Certainly a board would want to have a staff or board member examine each affidavit for combinations of features that might indicate possible risks. Since sampling is an efficient technique for quality control, perhaps a board should give full review to a random one-tenth of conditional affidavit clearances. Such sample verification should discourage abuses. The board would have the right to request at any point the cessation of research activity (funding applications, data collection, data analysis, etc.) until a full review had been conducted. Such a delayed decision to hold full review or a veto of the research would be rare for these low-risk areas of research and a principal investigator would be likely to choose a conditional clearance rather than a full review by a board.

From the investigator's point of view, conditional clearance speeds up and simplifies the review process, but prolongs the project's vulnerability to a negative review board decision. Conditional clearance may increase the likelihood that law suits will be brought against the researcher, and increase the likelihood that the board will check whether ongoing research corresponds to the proposed procedure, especially if the board receives complaints about a project.

Both the recommendations of the Commission and the recent federal regulations permit an institutional review board to offer a procedure for "expedited review" of proposals in certain low-risk areas of research. The proposed procedure for "expedited review" differs from our proposal for "conditional clearance by affidavit" in that the procedure for "expedited review" permits a single member of the review board to review and give final approval to the research. The single member of the review board must verify that the research is within a category not requiring consideration by the full review board, and that it involves no violation of ethical principles governing research with human beings. This procedure is unlike our proposal in that it would not be conditioned on subsequent verification, and the principal investigator would not be required to go through the affidavit procedure indicating why the research qualifies for the expedited procedure.

Consideration must be given to the effects of reviewing program evaluation on the functioning of review boards. One recommendation is obvious:

1c. Institutional review boards shall be available to review research conducted by independent investigators, profit and nonprofit research organizations, governmental agencies, etc., as well as research conducted through universities.

The proper location of these review boards becomes a problem. It would be desirable for them to be locally available to the research participants so that complaints can easily be placed and heard. This role for review boards becomes particularly important in monitoring the conditional affidavit clearance procedure.

Presently, institutional review boards are set up in the institutions doing the research. Neither the recommendations of the Commission nor the proposed federal regulations anticipate any change in the location of the review boards. Since most research has been conducted in universities and hospitals, the research participants have had easy access to a review board. However, program evaluations may be conducted by a more distant institution. Even if the research institution has a review board, local institutions (such as public schools) whose members are frequent participants in evaluation research may wish to set up their own institutional review boards to ensure adequate access to their membership.

Local review boards seem impractical for broad public opinion surveys. City, county, and state boards are conceivable, and should be given jurisdiction if they request it (local jurisdictions that require licensing of opinion survey interviewers could insist on approval by review boards). However, it would be unreasonable to require local review boards for national surveys interviewing only a few people in any one local jurisdiction. For these, a national review board is appropriate.

Enforcement of the review requirement will be most effective when tied to funding. This suggests that each major source of funding, governmental and private, set up review boards. While some commercial and private political opinion research may avoid review, this may be the practical limit of the enforcement power. Opinion survey interviewing merges into investigative journalism, detective work, credit investigation, neighborly curiosity, and information collection activities more generally. It is in these areas that the interests of participants are in greatest jeopardy, yet we are unlikely to see such "research" activities subject to formal institutional review.

1d. Where there are several appropriate institutional review boards, one review is sufficient if the review board most directly responsible for the well-being of the respondents does the review or concurs in it.

Currently, the institution receiving research funding must conduct the review. This proposal would shift the obligation to the institution most directly responsible for the research participants. Research by a university team on hospital patients would provide one example. In such a case, the hospital has the primary responsibility for the well-being of the participants and should conduct the review. If a community drug abuse treatment agency required data from high school students to be collected through the schools, the school district review board would be the one with the primary responsibility for protecting respondent rights. Proposed regulations recognize the problems posed by multiple review, and suggest that joint review may be approved for institutions participating in cooperative research projects.

To adequately protect research participants' rights, it is essential for the participants to know the extent of their rights and to whom to complain if they feel their rights are in jeopardy. Fully informed research participants will be necessary to monitor the conduct of research approved under the conditional clearance procedure.

1e. Research participants should each be given a printed statement informing them that the research is required to conform to federal legislation and regulations and their rights under this legislation, and providing the address and telephone number of the review board to which inquiries and complaints should be directed.

In the case of a national project review board, this might include a toll-free telephone number. This recommendation is one of several that could be implemented with a statement in writing that could be left with the respondent.

Does the inclusion of the program evaluation, survey research, etc., have any special implications for the selection of review board members? A recommendation characteristic of these areas of research would be that review boards contain members of the groups from which participants are being drawn, or in the case of children, parents of such participants. Such suggestions arise out of experience with neighborhood boycotts of survey research. It is probably true that potential participants in program evaluations are more competent to judge when their own interests are threatened than are participants in medical research. A brief training program could supply the technical knowledge necessary to make an informed judgment. While we approve of having such persons on institutional review boards along with a substantial proportion of nonresearchers, we have been unable to develop a recommendation that would ensure such representation and still be feasible. A recommendation in an earlier draft for participation on review boards by representatives of organizations received the lowest approval rating by all the commentators. It is difficult to develop a method that would ensure representation of the interests of the members of the community while limiting the intrusion of narrow political issues into the review process. If such community representatives were given veto power, this would in effect recognize class or category rights, contrary to the recommendation in section 7.

2. The Borderline Between Administrative Reports on Social Service Delivery and Program Evaluation

While we favor review of a broad range of research activities, we do not suggest that the review extend to nonresearch functions. The difficulty is in specifying the boundaries of research. For example, where is the borderline between a social work department delivering its regular services and a similar department testing out new procedures or giving a special evaluation to its standard method of operation? Where is the borderline between the regular instructional activities in a school and the comparative evaluation of alternative practices? Thus, parallels exist to the medical profession's problem of specifying when the doctor's exploration of alternative therapies with his patient becomes research. Neither the Commission nor the recent regulations attempt to specify the boundaries of research, beyond describing it as a "systematic investigation" to develop general knowledge.

While the borderlines for program evaluation should be recognized, these problems seem less serious than those in medical research, and it is probably wise to employ a narrow definition of program evaluation to *minimize* the coverage. Social service programs, employment offices, adult education programs, schools, police departments, and administrative agencies of all kinds have, in the past, had wide latitude in varying their modes of operation. It is unwise to add regulations curtailing this freedom, or adding to the bureaucratic difficulties of initiating change. Thus, it might be necessary to distinguish between variations in the services and variations in the information collection activities.

2a. Changes in mode of operation of a service agency that are within the legal or customary latitude for change enjoyed by the agency will not be interpreted as research within the jurisdiction of the regulations, except with regard to any novel data collection activities initiated for the purpose of evaluating the change as a program alternative capable of being adopted by other similar units.

There is an ambiguous borderline between information collected for use in an annual report of an operating agency and that collected for a program evaluation done by an in-house staff. Clearly it would be unwise to include annual reports or even special-topic operational analyses done to monitor regular operations.

2b. Data collection and analysis done by an institution for monitoring of its own operations (as opposed to evaluating program alternatives as policy items capable of being disseminated to other units) will not be regarded as research within the jurisdiction of the regulations.

These proposed regulations have obvious ambiguities, but rather than suggest specific refinements, it seems better to wait, allowing operating agencies to define their activities as they choose until specific problems emerge. We must remember that there are risks of exploiting others in every social institution and profession, public and private, whether doing research or not. These regulations address such problems only as they arise in a research setting.

The expressed purpose in the authorization of programs may provide guidance.

2c. Where funds are specifically designated for evaluation of program effectiveness, construction of social indicators, statistical analyses of administrative data, etc., the activities undertaken with these funds are "research" activities that should be examined by an institutional review board.

This proposed regulation does not cover the treatment (although the following one does) but merely the data collection introduced for the evaluation. Such an emphasis on the risks arising from data collection is unlike medical research, where the dangers of the treatment are usually the major concern of an institutional review board.

Consider a borderline case like Title I programs of compensatory education in public schools. In this massive national program, all districts and schools meeting specified poverty criteria are eligible to receive funds to spend on a variety of special remedial activities of their own devising or choosing, but limited to children designated as educationally deficient. While a great diversity of innovative and traditional remedial activities are involved, these are still within the range of standard operating procedures, and the program is funded as a nationwide activity, not a pilot program. However, effectiveness of a sample of Title I programs, employing new data collection activities, opinion surveys of parents, students, and school personnel, specifically administered achievement tests, etc., would be considered research under this regulation.

There are, however, instances in which the treatment as well as the informational research procedures should be reviewed.

2d. Where the enabling legislation specifies a trial or experimental pilot program or demonstration project as well as an evaluation budget, and where the research contract or grant funding covers funds for treatment development and treatment delivery as well as for evaluative information collection, institutional review boards should review the treatment as well as the informational research activities of the project.

Usually the terms of the evaluation contract or research grant will provide adequate information for determining whether the treatment should also be reviewed. While the illustrations have involved governmental programs, privately supported programs also come within the scope of the recommendations.

3. Informed Consent—General

Extension of notions of informed consent from laboratory research into areas such as program evaluation and survey research may require considerable change from current practice. These changes may result in considerable opposition from some segments of the research community. The most common modification in research procedure requested by institutional review boards is in the area of informed consent (Gray & Cooke, 1980). However, informed consent is so fundamental to the protection of the interest of research participants that we recommend the endorsement of this extension.

3a. Individually identifiable participants in social experimentation, survey research, and other areas of program evaluation, must be informed:

3a-1. That research is being conducted;

3a-2. Of the procedures they will be experiencing;

3a-3. Of the risks and benefits reasonably to be expected;

3a-4. Of the purpose of the research;

3a-5. Of the anticipated uses of the information;

3a-6. Of the names, addresses, and telephone numbers of the researchers;

3a-7. Of the names, addresses, and telephone numbers of the sponsors of the research;

3a-8. That they are free to ask questions and may refuse to participate; and

3a-9. That they may later withdraw from the research, and the consequences of such withdrawal (cancellation of income subsidies, etc.).

3b. The exact wording of these statements must be approved by the institutional review board. The board may approve modifications of the elements of the informed consent agreement when:

3b-1. The risk to a research participant is minimal; and

3b-2. Rigid adherence to the specified elements of the informed consent agreement undermines important objectives of the research.

The elements of this informed consent agreement contain all of the elements typically required for consent in biomedical research. However, certain elements have been added to accommodate special problems that arise in the context of program evaluation.

Informed consent must be obtained only from "individually identifiable participants" in social research. This results in two important limitations. First, restriction of the informed consent requirements to "participants" in the research will not require the researcher to obtain the consent of nonparticipants who might be affected by the treatment, such as landlords in a housing allowance experiment. Second, restriction of the requirement to "individually identifiable" participants would exempt anonymous observational studies, etc., which involve no jeopardy to the interests of the individual participants. In rare instances these restrictions may preclude consent by persons whose interests are directly affected by the research, such as in family research where one family member gives information about another. In such situations, as in instances of anonymous participants and nonparticipants who may be affected by the research, the broad representation of interests on the institutional review board should ensure that the rights of such persons will be respected.

Even if consent is restricted to individually identifiable research participants, major changes in the conduct of social research will result. Social researchers will be explicitly required to obtain some kind of informed consent of the participants. Opinion surveys will be required to identify the sponsors and purposes of the survey, as well as the research firm conducting it.

In keeping with the recommendations of section 5 below, the statements of the purpose of the research (3a-4) may stop short of telling the participants about the experimental treatments that they are not receiving. Still, even such limited information may influence the degree of cooperation by participants or modify their responses (Gardner, 1978). It is this latter possible effect that will most disturb the social research profession. However, data collected under these conditions can be almost as useful as present surveys. It is comparative differences under common contexts that are most informative. Present surveys do not provide "absolute" opinions, but rather opinions conditioned by a heterogeneous set of respondents' surmises and suspicions on the very issues that this recommendation would make explicit. Of course, the more explicit nature of this information may result in greater attention by respondents to these issues, and researchers should anticipate the resulting biases.

Recommendation 3b permits the institutional review board to modify the elements of the informed consent requirements when the risks to the research participants are minor and information regarding one or more of the elements of informed consent would undermine some important research objective. This recommendation should permit the flexibility to accommodate a wide range of social research settings. In certain extreme instances, such assessment of the impact of Title I funding, consent of the participants in the research (e.g., consent by the parents of the school children) may not be required by the institutional review board. This would be appropriate when an institution rather than an individual is the focus of the study. In such a situation a similar informed consent can be obtained from an institution representing the interests of the participants (such as a school board or local government body).

The elements of the informed consent agreement listed in recommendation 3a anticipated the elements of consent recommended by the Commission, with the exception of our suggestion that participants be informed of anticipated uses of the information. Our commentators on earlier drafts were also suspicious of this particular element of informed consent, suggesting that such uses are difficult to anticipate. In any case, we agree with the Commission that participants should be informed of information that they may reasonably be expected to desire in deciding whether or not to participate. The recommendations of the Commission indicate that consent would not be necessary in studies of identifiable documents where the importance of the research justifies the invasion of privacy and the institutional review board protects the interest of the participants. The recent federal regulations give little guidance in this area since most program evaluation, survey research, and social experimentation are either exempt from regulations or permitted great flexibility in structuring the standard for consent. In studies where consent is required, it may be unnecessary that such consent be documented. In major experiments such as the New Jersey Negative Income Tax Experiments, participants are asked to sign a written consent form. Such formality is usually missing from survey research, even in panel studies where repeated interviews are envisioned. This recommendation anticipates that in most instances the written consent of the participant will be obtained. In situations such as telephone surveys, where it would be difficult or awkward to obtain written consent, some other means of obtaining consent will be permitted. However, researchers must bear the burden of showing that the individual was properly informed and consented to participation in the research, and therefore may wish to require a signed consent form for their own protection.

It has been suggested that separate consents be solicited for the experimental treatment and information collection components of social research (Kershaw, 1975). Such separation can improve the control and estimation of attrition bias (Riecken et al., 1974, pp. 58-59). For the most part, in program evaluation, social indicators research, etc., and for control groups in experiments, only informational consent forms will be required.

These proposals on informed consent were not reviewed in their present form by our cooperating readers, and should be regarded with more caution than the better-tested sections of this chapter. Moreover, insofar as the content of these recommendations was covered in earlier drafts, no favorable consensus was found.

4. Rights and Interests of Respondents in Informational Surveys

A major part of social and behavioral research involves soliciting information from and about respondents by interviews and questionnaires. Respondents certainly have interests and risks with regard to the information they provide about themselves. Their interests must be recognized in determining the proper uses of any information that identifies them as the source. They also have rights to information provided by others in which they may have been identified. (It will be argued below that respondents have no rights that are jeopardized in transfers and uses of such data in which they are not identified as a source or target of the information.) The rights of participants in survey research, polling, and interviewing have received relatively little attention compared to the attention these issues have received in other areas of research. This overview will touch on these problems.

The data solicited by interview and questionnaire for program evaluation and social indicator development (or for descriptive surveys serving social science or journalistic purposes) often involves information about illegal acts. For example, information about income and income sources may indicate violation of tax or welfare laws. Disclosure of such sensitive information could result in personal embarrassment or discomfort to the respondent, and conceivably could be subpoenaed and result in the arrest of the respondent.

The procedures of survey sampling make the identity of the respondent known to the interviewer in door-to-door and telephone surveys. Procedures for checking on the honesty and accuracy of interviews through reinterviewing a portion of the respondents require recording this identity, as do research procedures involving reinterviews of the same respondents (e.g., pretests and posttests) or linking respondents to program treatments and other information sources.

Subpoena and government audit. In the New Jersey Negative Income Tax Experiment (Kershaw & Fair, 1976; Watts & Rees, 1977), the Mercer County prosecutor requested information about the participants as a part of a broad search for cases of welfare cheating. The power of governmental agencies to subpoena such information can jeopardize the interests of research participants. The decennial census and the interim surveys conducted by the Bureau of the Census are made exempt from such subpoena by acts of Congress. Limited statutory protection exists for certain areas of drug abuse research and criminal justice research (Boruch & Cecil, 1979). But most program evaluation research lacks such protection, and the data will be vulnerable to subpoena. In some cases researchers have gone to jail or risked going rather than release confidential information, while in other cases confidential information has been released (Carroll & Knerr, 1976).

In the Mercer County case the evaluation project and the prosecutor reached a compromise; the project gave the prosecutor names of participants and the amounts of money they received from the project, but no information on income or anything else that respondents provided the project. We believe that this was a proper resolution of the dispute, and sets forth the policy that should be followed by statutes providing for the protection of research data. Research agencies must be accountable for their research findings and their expenditures of public funds. However, sensitive research information provided by respondents should be shielded from scrutiny by governmental officials (Nejelski & Peyser, 1975). Such protection should cover the information in all its data processing stages, rather than just in the interviewer-interviewee communication. If law enforcement agencies want this information, they should ask the respondents directly. However, such broad protection seems unlikely, and one must assume that sensitive information will be vulnerable to a subpoena by law enforcement authorities.

Required audits of federally sponsored social experiments may result in similar threats to the confidentiality of identifiable information. The General Accounting Office (GAO), pursuant to a request from a senate committee considering preliminary analyses from the New Jersey Experiment, sought to audit and verify interviews. The project staff gave these auditors full access to the computer data from interviews with individual identifiers deleted, and the GAO produced its own parallel analyses of income guarantee effects. The staff also permitted GAO access to a sample of individually identified files to audit the accuracy of the transfer from individual files to the record systems used in the analysis, which may have been in violation of the project's promise of confidentiality. Such access was sufficient to meet the purpose of the audit without requiring GAO auditors to reinterview the respondents. A similar issue has been raised between the GAO and the Housing Allowance Experiment operated by the Department of Housing and Urban Development through The Urban Institute, Rand Corporation, and Abt and Associates (Baratz & Marvin, 1979).

Because program evaluation data are assembled as a part of a governmental decision-making process, it seems essential that audit, recount, reanalyses, and other verification processes be possible. In ordinary public opinion polls, verification by sample reinterview is a standard procedure for checking interviewer honesty and competence. This would seem to be a desirable feature for government auditing to verify sample surveys by selecting and interviewing independent samples of the same size drawn according to the same rules. But since this rarely will be feasible, it seems undesirable to preclude verification contacts with the original interviewees. It also seems undesirable to violate pledges of confidentiality to the respondents. In most cases slight changes in those pledges so as to mention the rare possibility of verification interviews to check interview honesty would suffice without reducing respondent cooperation on sensitive material. If, despite these precautions, the information is so sensitive that the threat of recontact would substantially impair participation in the research, other less intrusive means of establishing response validity should be considered (Boruch & Cecil, 1979; Committee on Evaluation Research, Social Science Research Council, 1978).

The possibilities of subpoena and of release of names to auditors for verification interact crucially with informed consent. The institutional review board should examine the specific wordings of the explanation of research purpose and pledges of confidentiality made to respondents to ascertain that relevant risks and threats to privacy are mentioned and that the investigator has not promised more protection than can be given. Recommended wording might eventually be prepared. The risks involved will depend on the type of information being requested and degree of cooperation promised by local prosecutors and police.

4a. Where the material solicited involves no obvious jeopardy to respondents, a general promise of confidentiality is acceptable. For example, "These interviews will be summarized in group statistics so that no one will learn of your individual answers. All interviews will be kept confidential. There is a remote chance that you will be contacted later to verify the fact that I actually conducted this interview and have recorded your answers accurately."

4b. Where full and honest answers to the question could jeopardize a respondent's interests in the case of a subpoena, the respondent should be so informed. For example, "These interviews are being conducted to provide statistical information in which individual answers will not be identified or identifiable. We will do everything in our power to keep your answer completely confidential. Only if so ordered by court and judge would we turn over individually identified interviews to any other group or government agency. We believe that this

is very unlikely to happen, because of the assurance of cooperation we have
received from _____.''

4c. Where the researcher has made the data invulnerable to subpoena, as by relin-
quishing control over the key linking names to code members, this being stored
beyond reach of subpoena or in some agency immune from subpoena, like the
Census Bureau, or where the researcher has used other procedural or statistical
techniques that ensure the anonymity of the sensitive information, the warning
of possible subpoena may be omitted from the background statement to the
respondent.

The devices are discussed more fully elsewhere (Boruch & Cecil, 1979; Campbell
et al., 1977). While they have not been tested in the courts, they seem sufficiently
sound, and the dangers of a subpoena are sufficiently remote, so that omitting
mention of the possibility of a subpoena creates no real jeopardy. While in general
our commentators approved of these recommended regulations, a strong minority
found regulation 4b not protective enough. There was general approval of statistical
and procedural devices to protect sensitive data.

Subpoena is probably a rarer threat than accidental release of individual information in the form of gossip. Blackmail, though a rare event, is also possible. Thus,
respondents' rights are involved in the degree to which the data processors have
access to the data in an individually identified form. We endorse the following three
recommendations from the Report of the Committee on Federal Agency Evaluation
Research (Rivlin et al., 1975).

4d. Sensitive information should not be collected unless it is clearly necessary to
the evaluation and is to be used.

4e. Where it is feasible and does not undermine the validity of the evaluation, the
anonymity of the respondent should be preserved from the beginning by not
collecting identifying information at all.

4f. Identifying information, such as name and address or social security number,
should be removed from the individual records at the earliest possible stage of
analysis and replaced by a code number. The key linking this code number to
the identifying information should be stored in a safe place and access to it
severely limited. This key should be destroyed as soon as it is no longer needed.

Even with individual identifiers removed, individual data probably should not be
stored on time-sharing computer systems, as this makes possible a repeated access-
ing of the data, using publicly available variables so as to discover the identities of
some individuals.

5. Rights and Interests of Participants in Social Experiments
   with Regard to Treatment Variables

5a. All participants in an experimental program should be informed in advance of
all features of the treatment and measurement process that they will be experiencing that would subject them to any obvious risk or jeopardy and that would

be likely to influence their decision to participate in the program or their conduct as participants in the program. Institutional review boards should be provided with copies of the statements made to potential participants when seeking their consent.

All researchers would probably concur in this recommendation, even though there will be many settings in which living up to it will produce less valid data than if participants were not informed of certain aspects of the treatment variable, or kept in ignorance of the fact that an experiment was going on. For example, in the New Jersey Experiment, it was recognized as essential that the recipients of the income supports understand clearly that it was for three years only. (This has been the source of such serious criticisms about the validity of the experiment for purposes of extrapolating the impact of a permanent national program, that in later experiments small groups are getting guarantees of up to 20 years.) Were the experiment to be redone again today, the recipients should be warned that information about the payments made by the project to them would be released to government officials if requested.

There is a further degree of informed consent, however, that methodologists recommend against; that is, the informing of each group of what the other groups in the experiment are getting. In particular, methodologists caution against informing the control group of the desirable treatments the experimental groups are getting. The Social Experimentation Committee of the Social Science Research Council discussed this issue at length, and ended up approving this position, since the interests of the control group are not jeopardized and since more complete disclosure would have potentially destructive effects on the conduct of the research. For example, in the New Jersey Negative Income Tax Experiment, the control group members were not informed about the maintenance payments of up to $1000 or $2000 per year to the experimental group members. As it was, some 26% of the control group were lost from the experiment in spite of being paid $15 per interview four times a year, while only 7% were lost from the best-paying experimental group. Envy and resentment, coming from awareness of relative deprivation of the control group, would almost certainly have added to this differential dropout rate.

Of course, there are cases in which failing to inform an untreated control group of the availability of the treatment being offered the experimental group represents a harmful deprivation of rights. The Tuskegee syphilis experiment (Brandt, 1978; DHEW, 1973; Jones, 1981) was such a case. When begun in the 1930s, the informed consent of the participants should have been secured, but the available "cures" were so ineffective that the use of a control group restricted to traditional treatments was probably not unethical. However, once penicillin became available, the dramatic (even if only quasi-experimental) evidence of its effectiveness and its plentiful availability made it unethical to withhold it from the experimental group. While a similar situation is extremely unlikely in the realm of program evaluation, the possibility should be kept in mind.

Of course, beneficial treatments are recognized and adopted through a consensus of expert judgment and popular demand. If such a consensus is present, quasi-experimental evaluation designs not involving equally needy control groups may be employed. If the treatment is in short supply, an especially powerful quasi-experimental evaluation design not involving equally needy control groups may be employed. If the treatment is in short supply, an especially powerful quasi-experimental design is made possible by making quantitatively explicit the degree of need and assigning to treatment on this basis (Riecken et al., 1974, chap. 4).

5b. Where there is already expert consensus on the value and feasibility of a treatment and where there are adequate supplies of the treatment available, needy control groups should not be deprived of the treatment.

It should be noted that pilot programs, experimental programs, and demonstration programs are not within this exclusion. These testings of potential policies should be done so as to learn in the most precise way the social costs and benefits of the program, and this will usually require random assignments of participants to experimental and control conditions. If there is expert consensus on the costs, benefits, feasibility, etc., then the program could just as well be adopted as national policy at once; if controls cannot ethically be deprived of the treatment, then usually the pilot program is not worth doing. However, without such a consensus, the drawing of lots, random assignment, is a traditional equitable method of assigning the boon. In such circumstances, the controls are not being deprived in relation to the general population, but only in relation to the temporary experimental recipients. (This condition definitely did not hold in the syphilis study.)

6. Reanalysis of Research Data and Statistical Analysis of Administrative Records

Here is an area in which some current interpretations of research participants' rights are needlessly hampering useful science. Let us begin by proposing an exclusionary rule.

6a. The reanalysis of research data and the statistical analysis of administrative records jeopardize no individual rights as long as no individually identifiable data are involved. For uses of research and administrative records meeting this requirement, the informed consent of the respondents is not required.

There are horror stories about institutional review boards requiring consent by each of the original participants for the statistical reanalysis of 20-year-old intelligence test data, even though names and other identifying information have been deleted from the data. This seems a totally unnecessary requirement. The Russell Sage Foundation's guidelines for the maintenance of school records (Russell Sage Foundation, 1970) suggests parental approval of *each* research use of a child's record. The proposed federal regulations on research involving children (DHEW, 1978) go far in protecting the privacy rights, but do not clarify the rights of children and parents to restrict access to anonymous data. Certainly each of these guidelines should be changed to require parental permission "for each research use involving the release of individually identified records," and not for release of anonymous records for research purposes. The report of the Privacy Protection Study Commission (1977) suggested that greater access to statistical and administrative records for research purposes be permitted. Several bills have been introduced in Congress to increase research and statistical access to federal records (Alexander, in press).

As an example of the practice recommended in 6a, data of the New Jersey Negative Income Tax Experiment are now available to social scientists through the Institute for Research on Poverty, University of Wisconsin. The data have been stripped of identifying information, such as names, addresses (but not cities), Social Security numbers, names of the family doctor, and so forth. Data archives go to great lengths to permit data sharing without compromising the privacy of the research participants (Clubb, Austin, Geda, & Traugott, 1981).

6b. Individually identifiable data from either research or administrative record systems may be released to new users for statistical analysis only with the permission of the identified individual.

While this rule is consistent with the spirit of the Privacy Act of 1974, the report of the Privacy Protection Study Commission suggests that the Privacy Act be amended to permit greater access to identifiable *research* information without the consent of the individual participants, so long as the information is not used to make a determination about any individual (PPSC, 1977). If the Act is so amended, we would support such greater access to research information.

6c. Release of research or administrative data to new users for statistical analysis when done without the express permission of each respondent must be done so as to adequately safeguard individual identities.

Procedures for achieving this have been described elsewhere (Boruch & Cecil, 1979; Campbell et al., 1977). Usually this would include deletion of the participant's name, address, Social Security number, specific birth date (but not year), and specific birthplace (but not geographical region). Where some of the research variables are publicly available and can be associated with identifiable individuals (such as lists and descriptions of members of a school or a professional association), it may also be necessary to delete this information or use crude report categories for the variables that are in these accessible lists. Even where multiple tables of frequencies or percentages are presented, rather than individual-level data, it may be possible to deduce the identities of individuals. Restrictions on minimal cell frequency and randomized rounding may be required in such cases.

6d. The original custodian of research or administrative data may generate and release to others statistical products in which individuals are not identifiable, including statistical products not anticipated by the individuals initially providing the data.

In the future the requirements of respondent confidentiality and of meaningful program evaluation will be resolved by increasing the data-analysis capabilities of administrative record files. Through the "mutually insulated file linkage" (Campbell et al., 1977), the records of two files can be *statistically* linked without exchanging any individually identified data, thus conforming to this rule. But this procedure requires that the custodial file be able to do standard statistical analyses as well as internal data retrieval for individuals. For many ameliorative programs, government records on subsequent earnings and unemployment compensation would provide accurate and inexpensive measures of effects. While these procedures have their own problems, almost certainly they would avoid the differential attrition rate found for the interviews in the New Jersey study. Accordingly, it would be in the government's interest to increase the internal data retrieval and statistical analysis capacities of private health insurance, auto insurance, educational testing agencies, hospitals, schools, etc., so that these data can be used in program evaluation and social indicator generation in ways precluding identifying individual data.

For many psychological studies in college settings, it would be desirable to statistically correlate laboratory performance and general intelligence or grade point average from school records. This could be done either with individual permission, or through mutually insulated file linkage, in which regular registrar staff members are paid to work overtime to retrieve the relevant data on specified lists of persons, transform these to means and standard deviations by lists, and then return only these summary statistics by list.

It should be noted that privacy legislation curtailing the use of Social Security numbers as all-purpose individual identifiers hinders the uses just described. Greater protection of individual privacy can be achieved by prohibiting unified data banks. No abuse of privacy has resulted from the limited use of Social Security numbers in research. The prohibition of the use of Social Security numbers for research purposes is a needless and harmful precaution.

7. Future Controversial Issues

The previous sections have sketched some of the current areas of concern, and also represent to a considerable degree a consensus among the social scientists who responded to our survey. (The recommendations concerning informed consent in opinion surveys may have gone beyond this consensus.) This consensus, however, may be seen as but the current form of a growing shift in attitude about the rights of research participants as a part of an increasingly equalitarian participatory democracy. It may help to consider what the parallel set of standards ten years hence might also contain. The following three topics are included for this purpose.

Respondents' interests in the topics on which data are collected. A recent trend in criticism of research on social problems, including evaluation research, goes under the name "blaming the victim" (Caplan & Nelson, 1973; Ryan, 1971). There is a recurrent option in program evaluation and social indicator research as to whether evidence of a social problem is indexed as an attribute of the individual or as an attribute of the social setting and the social institutions present. When the data are indexed as individual attributes (ability, morale, personality, employment status) this predisposes the analysis to end up "blaming the victims" of social system malfunction for their lot in life. Many times there are options in the wordings of questions that can make big differences in social causation implied even while collecting very nearly the same data. Standards could be developed requiring that articulate representatives of the program recipient population be asked to check on the research instruments in this regard. Or more specific recommendations could be developed, such as recommending the social setting attributional format wherever the option existed. Shifts of this kind might be of practical value as well. In many urban ghetto settings, opinion surveys meet with mass boycott, greatly hampering the evaluation of new alternatives in social welfare services delivery. In most such instances, the program evaluation purposes would be served just as well by substituting "Is this service effective?" questions for the "Are you sick?" questions. The conceptual shift is to turn the welfare recipient into an expert on the quality of welfare services delivered rather than a source of evidence about his or her own inadequacies. This shift, and the shift recommended below concerning participants' rights to the results, will almost certainly increase the cooperation received, and turn the informational survey into a useful vehicle for communicating neighborhood complaints. We have not developed a recommendation in this area, and the reactions of our panel of commentators to the earlier draft shows that no consensus exists to support such a recommendation. In fact, proposed regulations in earlier drafts that would have permitted participation by representatives of various groups in the development of research instruments were among the least popular of all the draft proposed regulations. Most critics felt that these recommendations exceeded the appropriate degree of community participation in the research process. Note that the "blaming the victim" theme is only one illustration of such respondents' interests. The more general issue is discussed in the next section.

Class or category, privacy, interests, and rights. This chapter assumes that the rights of research participants are individual rights. Most discussions of rights of research participants join us in this. Jeopardy to the rights of a class or category to which the research participant belongs has not been considered. If "class" is interpreted broadly, recognition of class rights could preclude most social science research. We recommend that such broad class rights not be recognized in making determinations about research ethics, but we make this decision self-consciously, with some recognition of the issues we are neglecting. Following are some examples.

The American Council on Education prepared a profile from anonymous surveys of college students of the activist campus radicals who had been involved in destruction of property, disruption of speeches, etc. No respondent was placed in jeopardy by confessing to past acts, since the data were collected anonymously through a mailed ballot. However, the interests of current and future radicals were jeopardized. For example, college admissions offices seeking to exclude such students, could do so on an actuarial basis by asking applicants the profile questions about backgrounds, interests, activities, and values, and excluding those applicants who fit the profile. In such a case, the proper protection may be to increase the accountability of college admissions procedures by prohibiting the use of anything but academic competence criteria. However, regulation of research to protect the interests of such classes or categories seem to us to be unacceptable.

A statistical analysis by the Bureau of Internal Revenue might show that medical doctors in certain specialties have twice the income of other professionals. This jeopardizes the interests of these medical doctors by increasing the frequency with which they are approached by fund raisers, confidence men, and burglars, and by the focused zeal of Internal Revenue agents. Yet such descriptive statistics for occupational and social classes seem essential for the governance of a democracy in which governmental decisions are a major determinant of income inequities.

Black leaders are justifiably disturbed about social statistics reporting on invidious black-white comparisons in achievement test scores and crime rates. Perhaps even data on income and rental costs could be regarded as prejudicial. Yet these data seem essential background evidence on which to base governmental policies seeking to remove the traditional environmental disadvantages under which blacks live. The civil rights movement has had to reverse itself on this within the last 25 years. For example, in 1950 those working on reducing segregation in the Chicago schools had as their goal color-blind assignment of children to school districts and setting of school district boundaries. At that time open or covert records indicated the race of every child and teacher. Within 10 years, the Chicago school system was frustrating those pushing for more integration by asserting that it had no way of telling which of the teachers and pupils were black. To achieve integration, racial identification had to be known and counted by categories. Affirmative action and school integration would be impossible without it.

At the present time, the no doubt environmentally produced black-white difference in school achievement tests has been so redundantly documented and is so regularly misinterpreted as evidence of an innate racial inferiority, that one of us has called for a cessation on all such research unless accompanied by thorough measurement of the black-white differential in opportunities to learn the specific items that tests employ (Campbell & Frey, 1970). Considering the problem of class or category rights as a whole, however, we are reluctant to see any such appeal made a compulsory rule.

Respondent rights to data produced. It will be increasingly argued that the participants in research, the interviewees in public opinion surveys, etc., are coproducers of the research product, and should be co-owners of that product with a right to know the results and to use that information for their own purposes. This could lead to the rule that all respondents to an informational survey should be provided with the statistical results produced. Such a rule could be implemented by having these results published in a local newspaper or placed in the public library nearest to each respondent.

Another way of arriving at such a proposal is to recognize that where such surveys are a part of governmental decision making, the voting booth rather than the animal laboratory becomes the relevant model. Just as voters get to know and use the results of elections they have voted in, so too they should know and be able to use the results of surveys and interviews they have participated in. This equalitarian emphasis is supported by an analysis that sees researchers as a potentially self-serving elite who may exploit the cooperative efforts of the respondents by producing products that may be used to harm the interests of the respondents. Unlike much medical and physical research, the results of social research will be meaningful and useful to the respondents. Participants' access to research results as advocated in an earlier draft of this chapter was rejected by a majority of the commentators. However, we believe the trends in political conscience are such that in 10 or 20 years we will have to live with these limitations.

Acknowledgments. Donald T. Campbell is the Albert Schweitzer Professor at The Maxwell School, Syracuse University. Joe Shelby Cecil is a Research Associate at the Federal Judicial Center. The basic work on this manuscript was done while both authors were at Northwestern University. This paper represents a cooperative effort of over one hundred persons who have taken the time to review and comment on earlier drafts of this manuscript. While we regret that an individual listing of their contributions is impractical, some of them are probably relieved. Special thanks are due to Bradford Gray, Miriam Kelty, and Hunter Moorman, who offered guidance and suggestions concerning the work of the National Commission for the Protection of Human Subjects of Biomedical and Behavioral Research and the proposed federal regulations, as well as comments on earlier drafts of this chapter. This effort has been supported by the National Commission for the Protection of Human Subjects of Biomedical and Behavioral Research, National Science Foundation Grants G SOC 7103704, BNS 76-23920, and DAR7820374. The opinions expressed in this chapter are the authors' own, and should not be attributed to any of these persons or agencies.

References

Alexander, L. Proposed legislation to improve research access to federal records. In R. F. Boruch, J. Ross, & J. S. Cecil (Eds.), *Solutions to ethical and legal problems in applied social research.* New York: Academic Press, in press.

Baratz, S. S., & Marvin, K. E. Privacy and confidentiality as problems in the audit and reanalysis of social research for policy. In R. F. Boruch, J. Ross, & J. S. Cecil (Eds.), *Proceedings and background papers: Conference on ethical and legal problems in applied social research.* Evanston, Ill.: Department of Psychology, Northwestern University, 1979.

Boruch, R. F., & Cecil, J. S. *Assuring the confidentiality of social research data.* Philadelphia: University of Pennsylvania Press, 1979.

Boruch, R. F., & Cecil, J. S. (Eds.). *Solutions to ethical and legal problems in applied social research.* New York: Academic Press, in press.

Boulay, H., et al., Comment on Pool's analysis—Protecting human subjects of research: Proposed amendments to HEW policy. *P.S.: Political Science,* 1980, *13,* 202.

Brandt, A. M. Racism and research: The case of the Tuskegee Syphilis Study, *Hastings Center Report,* December 1978, 21-29.

Breger, M. Randomized social experiments and the law. In R. F. Boruch, J. Ross, & J. S. Cecil (Eds.), *Solutions to ethical and legal problems in applied social research.* New York: Academic Press, in press.

Campbell, D. T. Prospective: Artifact and control. In R. Rosenthal & R. Rosnow (Eds.), *Artifact in behavioral research.* New York: Academic Press, 1969.

Campbell, D. T. Comments on the comments by Shaver and Staines. *Urban Affairs Quarterly,* 1971, 7, 187-192. (a)

Campbell, D. T. Methods for the experimenting society. Duplicated lecture, American Psychological Association Convention, September 1971. (When revised to appear in *American Psychologist*) (b)

Campbell, D. T., Boruch, R. F., Schwartz, R. D., & Steinberg, J. Confidentiality-preserving modes of access to files and to interfile exchange for useful statistical analysis. *Evaluation Quarterly*, 1977, *1*(2), 269-300.

Campbell, D. T., & Frey, P. W. The implications of learning theory for the fade-out of gains from compensatory education. In J. Hellmuth (Ed.), *Compensatory education: A national debate* (Vol. 3), *Disadvantaged child*. New York: Brunner/Mazel, 1970.

Caplan, N., & Nelson, S. D. On being useful: The nature and consequences of psychological research on social problems. *American Psychologist*, 1973, *28*, 199-211.

Carroll, J. D., & Knerr, C. R. Law and the regulation of social science research: Confidentiality as a case study. Presented at the Symposium on Ethical Issues in Social Science Research, Department of Sociology, University of Minnesota, April 9, 1976.

Cecil, J. S. 1978. Regulation of research record systems by the Privacy Act of 1974. Research Report of the Department of Psychology, Northwestern University, Evanston, Illinois.

Cecil, J. S., & Griffin, E. Legal issues in obtaining access to data. In R. F. Boruch et al. (Eds.), *Access to research data*. A report submitted to the Panel on Data Sharing, Committee on National Statistics, National Research Council, 1981.

Clubb, J. M., Austin, E. W., Geda, C. L., & Traugott, M. W. Sharing research data. A report submitted to the Panel on Data Sharing, Committee on National Statistics, National Research Council, 1981.

Committee on Evaluation Research, Social Science Research Council, Audits and experiments: A report prepared for the U.S. General Accounting Office, U.S.G.A.O., October, 1978.

de Sola Pool, I. Protecting human subjects of research: An analysis of proposed amendments to HEW policy. *Political Science*, 1979, *12*, 452-455.

DHEW, *Final report of the Tuskegee Syphilis Study Ad Hoc Advisory Panel*. Washington, D.C.: U.S. Government Printing Office, 1973.

DHEW, Protection of human subjects. *Federal Register*, 1974, *39*(105), 18914-18920.

DHEW, Proposed regulations on research involving children. *Federal Register*, 1978, *43*(141), 31786-31794.

DHEW, Proposed regulations amending basic HEW policy for the protection of human research subjects. *Federal Register*, 1979, *44*(158), 47688-47698.

DHHS, Final regulations amending basic HHS policy for the protection of human research subjects. *Federal Register*, 1981, *46*(16), 8366-8392.

Gardner, G. T. Effect of federal human subjects regulations on data obtained in environmental stress research. *Journal of Personality and Social Psychology*, 1978, *36*(6), 628-634.

Gray, B. H. The regulatory context of social and behavioral research. In T. Beauchamp, R. A. Faden, J. Wallace, & L. Walters (Eds.), *Ethical issues in social science research*. Baltimore, Md.: Johns Hopkins Press, in press.

Gray, B., & Cooke, R. A. The impact of institutional review boards on research. *Hastings Center Report*, February 1980, 36-41.

Jones, J. *Bad blood*. New York: Free Press, 1981.

Kershaw, D. Comments. In A. M. Rivlin & D. M. Timpane (Eds.), *Ethical and legal issues of social experimentation*. Washington, D.C.: Brookings Institution, 1975.

Kershaw, D., & Fair, J. *The New Jersey income maintenance experiment* (Vol. 1), *Operations, surveys and administration*. New York: Academic Press, 1976.

Levine, C. Social scientists form committee to protect regulations. *IRB: A review of human subjects research*, 1979, *1*, 8.

National Commission for the Protection of Human Subjects of Biomedical and Behavioral Research (NCPHSBBR), *Report and recommendations: Institutional review boards* (DHEW Publication No. (OS) 78-0008, 1978). Reprinted in *Federal Register*, 1978, *43*(231), 56174-56198.

Nejelski, P., & Peyser, H. A researcher's shield statute: Guarding against the compulsory disclosure of research data. Appendix B, in Rivlin et al. (1975).

Pattullo, E. L. Who risks what in social research? *Hastings Center Report*, April 1980, 15-18.

Privacy Protection Study Commission (PPSC), *Personal privacy in an information society*. Washington, D.C.: U.S. Government Printing Office, 1977.

Riecken, H. W., Boruch, R. F., Campbell, D. T., Caplan, N., Glennan, T. K., Pratt, J., Rees, A., & Williams, W. *Social experimentation: A method for planning and evaluating social intervention*. New York: Academic Press, 1974.

Rivlin, A., et al. *Protecting individual privacy in evaluation research*. Final Report of the National Research Council Committee on Federal Agency Evaluation Research, Washington, D.C.: National Research Council, National Academy of Sciences, 1975.

Robertson, J. A. The scientists' right to research, *University of Southern California Law Review*, 1977, *51*, 1203-1279.

Robertson, J. A. The judicial conference experiment: Social experiments and prior ethical review, *I.R.B.: A review of human subjects research*, 1981, *3*, 1-3.

Russell Sage Foundation. *Guidelines for the collection, maintenance and dissemination of pupil records*. New York: Russell Sage Foundation, 1970.

Ryan, W. *Blaming the victim*. New York: Pantheon, 1971.

Schwartz, R. D., & Orleans, S. On legal sanctions. *University of Chicago Law Review*, 1967, *34*, 274-300.

Swazey, J. P. Professional protectionism rides again. *Hastings Center Report*, April 1980, 18-19.

Veach, R. M. The National Commission on IRBs: An evolutionary approach. *Hastings Center Report*, February 1980, 22-29.

Watts, H. W., & Rees, A. (Eds.). *The New Jersey income maintenance experiment* (Vol. 2), *Labor-supply response*. (Vol. 3), *Expenditures, health and social behavior; and the quality of the evidence*. New York: Academic Press, 1977.

Wax, M. L. Memorandum to Judith Jarvis Thomson, Chair., AAUP Committee on Institutional Review Boards; *Response to the "Final Regulations Amending Basic Policy for the Protection of Human Subject Research"* at 1 (February 23, 1981).

Critique of Campbell and Cecil's Proposal:
Subjects Need More Protection

Ernest R. House

There can be little doubt that current bureaucratic procedures for clearing instruments used in Federal program evaluations are cumbersome, inefficient, and counter-productive. For example, Carter (1977) reports a typical case in which the instrument package was submitted in May to the Office of Planning, Budget and Evaluation (OPBE) in the Office of Education (OE). By the end of June, it was resubmitted to OPBE, incorporating the recommended changes. In mid-August, The Education Data Acquisition Council (EDAC), a group comprised of representatives from agencies under the Assistant Secretary for Education, met to consider the package. At the end of August, the package was forwarded to the Office of Management and Budget (OMB). In October, OMB officials met with the OE personnel and requested changes. Throughout October, various meetings occurred with OE to approve the changes. In early November, OMB gave approval to collect data.

Reportedly, none of the reviewers of the instruments had ever visited the kind of institutions under study. None of them had seen the pretest results. Yet, they made recommendations on individual items in the instruments. The clearance process took six months and cost an estimated $155,500.

However odious these bureaucratic procedures for clearance of evaluation instruments may be, they should not be confused with protecting the rights of subjects involved in social research and evaluation studies. Campbell and Cecil have constructed what are on the whole excellent guidelines for protecting human subjects in social research. Their "conditional clearance by affidavit" provides a mechanism for protection of the subjects without undue bureaucratic interference, assuming that the institutional review boards are vigorous in auditing the projects. It is also essential that the studies not be subjected to double jeopardy by having to pass two or more review boards; one is enough.

Although Campbell and Cecil do not advance a concrete recommendation as to how members of representative groups should be selected for the review boards, I endorse the idea that groups impacted by the study should have a say in reviewing the study itself. For example, much of the research in large city school systems involves poor children. It would not be asking too much to have representatives of the poor occasionally review these studies for potential abuses.

I would also strongly support Campbell and Cecil's informed consent provision. This requires that surveys and other studies identify both the sponsors and the general purposes of the research. It seems common decency that the researcher identify who is paying him to ask the questions. At a minimum, such information is needed for the respondent to protect his or her own interests. Campbell and Cecil limit informed consent to cases where the informant is individually identifiable.

Incredibly, a majority of researchers responding to this guideline failed to endorse it. It was the only one rejected by the panel of researchers (47% of the researchers said the recommendation was all right, 43% said it was too protective,

11% rejected it for other reasons, and no one said that it was not protective enough). It is common practice in surveys to sell question spaces to people who want questions answered—often commercial interests—without identifying the sponsor of the question. This is a practice closer to the ethics of a private detective than of a scientist. It would seem to be more a matter of economics than of science.

Campbell and Cecil allow for special studies in which knowing the nature of the sponsor might invalidate the results. I would go further than the guidelines given and suggest that respondents be told the nature of the sponsor even when the respondents are not individually identifiable. Surely, only someone unaware of his or her own interests or intimidated by circumstances would supply data to a group of which he or she is totally ignorant.

Overall, though, the guidelines are quite good and well thought out. I especially like the suggestions that respondents should know when confidentiality is not completely assured; that representative participant groups should have formal representation; that irrelevant sensitive information should not be collected at all; and that the party paying for particular questions in a survey should be made clear to the respondents.

Review of research instruments by an institutional board is far from a sufficient guarantee of freedom from abuse, however. Who constitutes these boards and what criteria they employ are critical. Neither can the best of boards detect strong abuses and injustices simply from an inspection of the instruments. Much damage is done in the interpretation of the data rather than in its collection. Not even the most educated respondents can always guess the use to which certain questions might be put.

There is also the issue of research which does not depend on prespecified questions and answers. It is precisely in evocative, open-ended, highly cathected interviews that one might expect personal and damaging information to emerge. It would be tragic to eliminate such research and impossible to discern its threat to human rights from the questions themselves.

For these reasons and others, it seems inevitable that something must be done with the *results* of research and not simply with endorsing data-collection instruments. A board might review write-ups of the research for threats to personal liberties. Another approach would be to arrange for negotiations over the data between the researchers and the people being researched. This avoids the implied paternalism of overseeing panels. I realize that all this raises a spector of censorship of data, but review of instruments prior to data collection is simply an inadequate safeguard.

Other guidelines I object to are the suggestions for the free exchange and reuse of both administrative and research data. The guidelines imply that evaluation should be based eventually on administrative records. I object strongly to the reuse of data for other purposes and for basing evaluations primarily on administrative records.

The free reuse of data will lead to erroneous and abusive results, particularly in evaluation. Our ability to generalize in social research is severely limited. Findings do not generalize readily from one setting to another; even those that do decay with time. Data collected for one time, place, and purpose are likely to mislead when applied to others. Some of the worst errors in policy making have resulted from basing policy on sets of data collected for another purpose.

Increasing the data capacity of private companies with an eye to relating these data for unknown purposes is particularly mischievous and perhaps the most dangerous of all the suggestions. Can anyone seriously believe that the companies and government agencies will not abuse such information? All evidence we have of use of data and the ethics of agencies and private companies argues against this practice. The likely abuses of such information in an increasingly centralized society are extremely high prices to pay for convenience of data collection.

For example, the use to which school records could be put in relation to insurance files is stunning. What serious insurance executive, ready to do his company a good turn, could resist such temptations? I would reendorse the Russell Sage suggestion that parents know and endorse such use to which school data will be put. The possibilities for abuse in allowing data reuse, even under structures proposed, are far too great.

Consider an example: Suppose a private auto insurance company had access to school files and was able to relate these to accident rates, through a third party, nonmerged negotiation that does not identify individuals. They find the father's occupation and number of siblings as good predictors of auto accidents. From now on, through access to either school files, their own surveys, or government data, they are able to categorize people as high risks, even though the identities of the original subjects are never revealed. As I understand the guidelines, this use of data is permissible.

This potential seems to me to infringe on individual rights in two ways. One is that people should have a right to determine whether they want their personal data to be used to help insurance companies or whatever. They have a right to permit people to use their data—identified or not—just as they have a right to let someone use their car—particularly data collected from them involuntarily or under threat. They have a right to know the purpose for which data are being used. If the data are to be open to general perusal, respondents should certainly be informed of this at the time of data collection.

The other objection I have is about the weakness of social science predictions. It is quite possible that the generalizations found in this case will not apply well to other situations. Certainly the findings will decay with time. So there is a high inherent error factor that is unfair to individuals.

Consider an analogous situation. A graduate student of mine is doing a dissertation on the tort liability of school districts with a view towards making suggestions for legislation that would relieve the heavy strain that school districts bear for accident liability. In order to do that study, he must have some idea of how much money is paid out in claims by insurance companies, as well as how much school districts pay in premiums.

For more than a year he has tried to obtain information on which public policy is presumably based. No individual insurance company need be identified. Yet he cannot obtain this information. Instead, he is confronted with varous stall tactics and diversions by the associated insurance groups. Why would we want to make available to these companies all the data collected by public monies so that they can use them to their own advantage? When access in such a relationship is so one-sided, it is a good indication something is seriously wrong with our ethics.

The fundamental issue, I think, is that having data on people, whether individual or categorical, is a power relationship. It gives the one who knows power over the lives of those known. The issue is not simply privacy. I think that people should agree on the uses to which this information is put. They have a right both to know the purpose of the data analysis and to veto it, should they choose to; or at least I would so argue.

I think we must eventually renounce the neutrality of data collection. Holding data on someone is a power relationship, and it should be so treated. Campbell and Cecil have put it nicely, I think. The analogue for our social research on human subjects should be that of a person going to a voting booth rather than that of a rat running through a maze.

Reference

Carter, L. F. Federal clearance of educational evaluation instruments: Procedural problems and proposed remedies. *Educational Researcher*, 1977, *6*, 7-13.

Critique of Campbell and Cecil's Proposal: Don't Throw Out the Baby with the Bathwater

Norman M. Bradburn

Campbell and Cecil's thoughtful proposal of procedures to ensure the protection of the rights and interests of participants in social research is, on the whole, an excellent document. All of us involved in social science research are indebted to them for their efforts to formulate a set of recommendations that try to balance the interests of all parties involved in social research. While there is much to praise in their effort, the purpose of this critique is to point out several problems that their recommendations may cause for certain types of research of low risk to participants. Although necessarily critical in tone, this should be read with the understanding that most of their recommendations are sensible and worthy of adoption. There are, however, several recommendations that seem to me to pose considerable threats to the ability of social scientists to conduct research of the highest quality, and in some instances, to do research at all. I shall comment on these problem areas under three rubrics: (1) review boards; (2) informed consent; and (3) permission to use existing records.

Review Boards

Some sort of responsible review board is essential if there is to be meaningful protection for participants in social research. I have no quarrel with this notion. At the same time, the review process must not be allowed to become so cumbersome that it defeats the purpose for which it is established or so politicized that it puts requirements on research designs that undermine their integrity by, for example, invalidating a sampling plan or causing biased questions to be introduced into research instruments.

There are several cautions that should be noted in the Campbell and Cecil discussion of review boards. First, they suggest in their discussion of Recommendation 1c that enforcement of review requirements will be most effective when tied to funding and then suggest that each funding source set up its own review board. This part of the recommendation is unnecessary and potentially dangerous. It is unnecessary because all funding agencies can (and most already do) require that there be a local institutional review board that is responsible for all of the procedural clearance of research projects undertaken by a particular research organization or researcher. It is not necessary for the review board to be lodged in the funding agency in order for it to be tied to funding. All that is necessary is that approval of the review board be obtained before the funds (or at least the portion of them involving actual data collection) can be spent.

Campbell and Cecil seem comfortable with the notion of institutional review boards lodged in universities, but worry about research conducted by either non-university-based organizations and/or (it is not clear) by research that takes place in a number of geographical locations remote from the researcher. I do not see this as a problem insofar as one is willing to accept the idea that review boards are to be guided by ethical principles and professional responsibilities exercised in the light of the requirements of good research design rather than by political or personal interests of the research participants.

Although it is not spelled out, there is an apparent assumption in the Campbell and Cecil discussion that the review boards should be responsible to the research participants (e.g., students, the general public, program participants, and hospital patients) rather than to some general body charged with considering both the interests of the participants and of the research goals which are, in some sense, "society's" interest. If the quality of research is not to be impaired, review boards must be professionally oriented, that is, guided by general principles and norms that protect the interests of all parties involved, participants and researchers, as well as the general good. One is most likely to get such a board when it is lodged in a context that insulates it as much as possible from political pressures, but at the same time does not make it subservient to the researchers' interest, more narrowly defined. In practice, institutional review boards lodged in universities, hospitals, large research organizations, and, sometimes, schools, have been able to maintain the necessary independence, while at the same time exercising their function responsibly.

The danger of multiple review boards lodged in the various funding agencies is that of excessive delay in clearance, remoteness from interaction with researchers who may have to modify procedures or answer questions, and the development of differing and inconsistent procedures among the agencies. Anyone who has had much dealing with governmental agencies (or any set of bureaucracies) knows that it is impossible to get them to coordinate their rule making and procedures so that they are working on the same set of forms and procedures. Anyone who has had to get Office of Management and Budget (OMB) approval for a questionnaire knows that difficulties and delays in getting clearance through the levels of bureaucracy in the funding agency, even before the final clearance by the OMB. This problem is not the result of individual incompetence or malevolence, but the natural consequence of large bureaucracies that attempt to deal fairly and impersonally with vast amounts of work generated by rules and regulations, such as those that are here recommended to protect the rights of research participants. One should not add to the burden already being carried by funding agencies if there is some better way to attain the same goal.

One of the important advantages of single institutional review boards that deal with the same types of researchers over a period of time is that they can develop an operational set of standards for the protection of research participants and apply them consistently to relevant research projects. As review boards gain experience with the requirements of different types of research projects, they develop a "case law" in which actual procedures for protecting research participants are worked out. Because the risks and requirements of biomedical research are so different from those of social science research, many institutions have established two boards, each dealing with only one type of research. Such an approach allows for more differentiation of protection procedures in line with the differing risks involved. If separate review boards were established within funding agencies rather than at the research institutions, this development of a differentiated, yet consistent, set of procedures would be much less likely to develop.

There is a further problem with the Campbell and Cecil Recommendation 1e, which suggests that research participants be given a written statement which, among other things, inform participants that any complaints should be directed to the review board at the given address and telephone number. While I can sympathize with the authors' desire to provide a complaint procedure, I think that the review board is not the proper place for action on complaints, although I agree that there should be some way for them routinely to know about complaints. Most review boards that I am familiar with are composed of volunteer members who serve out of a sense of duty and obligation to the integrity of the research enterprise. To also make them the policemen and enforcers of procedures would be to place an intolerable burden on them and discourage all but those who have a vested interest from serving. On the other hand, it is important that the boards get some feedback about problems that approved procedures may be causing so that they can revise them in future cases (or even modify them for ongoing research). I would suggest as an alternative that in the first instance, complaints be directed to the researchers themselves, who have the greatest direct interest in dealing with the complaints, since they may jeopardize the quality of their research. Review boards should be informed by researchers about complaints and how they were handled. In some cases, the board might want to follow up the researchers' actions with an inquiry to the complainant about how satisfactorily the complaint was handled.

Informed Consent

In general, I am in agreement with Campbell and Cecil's recommendations about informed consent, although I would stress more than they do the importance of the review board's exercising discretion about the amount of information researchers are required to give all participants in low-risk situations. In low-risk cases, such as general population surveys involving nonsensitive questions, requiring that all respondents be read or given a long statement detailing all of the possibly interesting information about the study would be viewed as loading the potential respondent down with more information than most people are interested in having about a survey. I would, however, insist that any respondent who asks about a particular point, e.g., the address of the sponsor(s), be given it. It is important that any information the respondent wants be supplied without, at the same time, going overboard in supplying information that many respondents will not want.

The one point I do object to, however, is the view that "in most instances, the written consent of the participant will be obtained." For most sample surveys such a requirement is simply overkill. In surveys that contain questions that might be sensitive or very personal, the respondent should be told explicitly that such questions will be in the interview schedule, but that they do not have to answer them if they do not wish to do so. Written consent is not typically obtained, nor do I believe it should be, because it is clear that participation in a household survey is voluntary. Indeed the problem in an ordinary household survey is more one of "informed refusals," since most refusals to participate occur before the interviewer has an opportunity to tell the potential respondent anything about the survey. A recent methodological experiment (Singer, 1978) indicates that requests for written consent reduced the response rate in a nationwide probability survey. Singer concludes:

> Since the request for a signature appears to function largely as another sensitive question, the requirement that researchers obtain a signature to document consent seems unnecessarily burdensome. The same protection is afforded respondents by the right to refuse the interview, or to refuse to answer particular questions within the interview (p. 159).

> The important point here is that the requirement for written consent should not be involved automatically. Indeed, the entire procedure for obtaining informed consent should be proportional to the degree of risk involved in the research. The greater the risks to the participants, the more fully informed they should be about what they are getting into and the more fully documented should be the consent.

Permission to Use Existing Records

One of the more vexing problems in social research is the degree of "informed consent" necessary about the use of data in existing data files for secondary analysis, that is, analysis other than for the purpose for which the data were originally collected. Campbell and Cecil's Recommendation 6b, which calls for the researcher to obtain permission to use the data from the individual described by and originally generating the data, appears much too restrictive to me. On the surface this recommendation would make impractical much potentially valuable research even when it does not involve linking data records from several record systems, a more special case in which there is a better argument, although not always a totally convincing one, about getting individual permission.

Consider, for example, a study of the relation of tardiness and school absence to school achievement over a ten-year period in a sample of schools. Assuming that the schools' records could provide the necessary data on the relevant variables, would one be barred from doing the study until one had contacted all of the former pupils in the school and obtained their permission to use the records in this manner? If so, it would probably not be possible to do the study, given the costs involved in trying to locate and obtain the permissions and the possible biases that might be in the data due to differential difficulties in location and in gaining permission. What if the more successful students were more likely to move away? Or if those that were frequently tardy failed to respond to the investigator's pleas for cooperation? The difficulties are formidable and probably more costly than the study would justify.

I find it difficult in this case to agree that getting the permission of the individuals, is, in fact, necessary in order to protect their privacy. The goal of the research is to establish functional relationships between variables, not to say anything about individual pupils who might have been tardy or absent frequently. The names are needed only to make sure that data on the different variables refer to the same individual. Perhaps the school officials could devise methods for linking the records without the investigator ever knowing the names. However, using reasonable precautions to ensure the trustworthiness of the investigator, school officials would most likely prefer to have the investigator undertake the tedious task of assembling the data. Ultimately, these questions about who has access to the raw data reduce themselves to questions of trust and responsibility. If someone is really out to breach the confidentiality of a file, it will be very difficult to stop them.

Conclusion

In this critique I have pointed out several places in the Campbell and Cecil recommendations in which I feel they have gone too far in the direction of protecting the research participants' rights at the expense of decreasing the quality of social research. The principal problem is to strike the right balance between protecting the rights of individual participants and the requirements of good research design; what can be given up in the service of one principle without too severely jeopardizing the other? Such balancing requires complex judgments, which I feel are best done by review boards comprising professionally and ethically trained individuals assisted by informed and serious nonprofessionals. Developing guiding principles and actual operations to translate these principles into research procedures is not an easy task and should be approached with considerable humility and flexibility, rather than with a fixed set of rigid rules on procedure. I am suspicious of placing such review boards in governmental funding agencies because of the bureaucratic pressures that occur in those settings and their remoteness from the actual research operations and settings. It is of overriding importance to have review and control mechanisms that can take into account the differing amounts of real risk in different types of research and adjust the requirements accordingly. The research world, as well as the real world, is too complex and multifarious to be reduced to simple, universal procedures to be implemented in all cases. I would like to see flexibility built into every stage of the review process. Don't throw out the baby with the bathwater.

Reference

Singer, E. Informed consent. *American Sociological Review*, 1978, *43*(2), 144-161.

Chapter 6

Regulation and Education: The Role of the Institutional Review Board in Social Science Research

Elizabeth Decker Tanke and Tony J. Tanke

Since its origin in the policy and regulation of the Department of Health, Education and Welfare (subsequently renamed the Department of Health and Human Services), the Institutional Review Board (IRB) has made consideration of the interests of human subjects an important and formal stage of social scientific research.[1] Social scientists are directly affected by the IRB in their roles as (1) investigators who must obtain IRB approval of research projects; and (2) potential IRB members who must review the research of professional colleagues.

In this chapter, we discuss three major tasks confronting IRB members as they review research proposals: (1) identifying and evaluating risks to subject interests; (2) ensuring that subjects give their informed consent to research participation; and (3) structuring the review process to focus scarce IRB resources on the review and monitoring of proposals presenting the greatest risk. Then, we discuss the interaction between the IRB and the research community. We suggest several ways in which social scientists, as IRB members and as investigators, can improve the review process through more effective communication. Finally, we stress the importance of a vitalized educational role for the IRB. We focus on broad general problems of IRB functioning rather than on specific current regulatory or ethical issues such as those raised by the IRB recommendations of the National Commission for the Protection of Human Subjects of Biomedical and Behavioral Research[2] (1978) or by the 1981 Health and Human Services (HHS) regulations for IRBs, which deregulated certain kinds of social science research.

---

[1] As used in this chapter, "social science research" refers broadly to studies designed to obtain knowledge of human behavior in experimentally created and naturalistic settings. Such research generally provides only indirect or incidental benefit to the research subject. The term, as we use it, does not include research which is conducted in conjunction with medical or psychological/psychiatric treatment or counseling of subjects.

[2] The National Commission for the Protection of Human Subjects of Biomedical and Behavioral Research was created in 1974 to study certain aspects of the ethical

The IRB and the Review Process: Examining the Research Proposal

The IRB is a creature of DHEW regulations designed to protect the interests of human subjects at risk as a result of DHEW (now HHS) funded activities. A combination of complex factors, including the biomedical design and imprecise construction of the regulatory scheme and the heavy workloads of individual IRBs, has created some confusion and inefficiencies in the review of social science research. The 1981 HHS regulations have increased the efficiency of the review process by deregulating several classes of social science research. Subsequent changes in social science research regulations may further affect the character of the review process. But whatever the content of regulations, the same fundamental concerns remain for social scientists and their IRBs: risk, informed consent, and the structuring of priorities in the review process.

The Identification, Assessment and Management of Risk

Under the HHS regulatory scheme, the task of the IRB is the protection of human subjects *at risk*. The usual risks to participants in social research, e.g., possible embarrassment, anxiety, invasion of privacy, or breach of confidentiality, are not always susceptible to precise measurement and evaluation. Unlike biomedical research risks, the risks of social science research generally cannot be assessed against a background of clinical and professional experience.

Because there is little evidence available to challenge its conclusions, the IRB has broad discretion in identifying and assessing risks. This discretion is subject to abuse; IRBs may ignore the legitimate interests of subjects in order to promote research or arbitrarily restrict the investigator's right to conduct research. In view of their broad discretion, it is essential that IRBs focus clearly and explicitly on their task and avoid roles which conflict with the performance of that task.

The IRB is in practical effect a goverment-created institution originally designed to regulate the conduct of research investigators so as to safeguard the "rights and welfare of subjects at risk" in HHS-supported activities. (45 C.F.R. §46.102(a)). As such, it was designed to concern itself only with significant risks to the interests of individual humans *as a consequence of their research participation* (45 C.F.R. §46.103(b)). It has not been authorized by any regulation to act as: (1) a peer review organization passing on experimental design or research significance; (2) a censor of research which might have adverse social policy implications or result

---

conduct of research and report to the Secretary of NEW. One of these aspects involves "[m]echanisms for evaluating and monitoring the performance of Institutional Review Boards ... " Section 202(a) (1) (B) (v) of the National Research Act, Pub. L. 93-348, 88 Stat. 348-351 (1974). See Historical Note, 42 U.S.C.A. §2891-1, pp. 396-400 and supplements. A summary of Commission and DHEW action on these recommendations is contained in Herbert (1978). For the sake of convenience, the transcript of the Commissioner's hearings on IRB will be referred to as "IRB Hearings" and its recommendations as "IRB Recommendations."

in lawsuits; (3) a presenter of Golden Fleece Awards; or (4) the moral conscience of the research investigator. But unless IRBs take action to exclude these functions from the review process. they may become latent functions which detract from human subject protection (Gray, 1977).

IRBs can assume latent functions and overstep their authority when they consider so-called "social risks" to subject interests. IRBs have jurisdiction over risks of injury to individual subjects which arise from *the conduct of research*, but not over risks to social or political groups or interests which might conceivably occur *as a consequence of the dissemination or application of research findings*. For example, a study of the relationship between ethnic background and performance on IQ tests may produce data showing the inferior performance of some ethnic groups, although the subjects themselves are exposed only to the common and incidental "risks" of taking a written test. The IRB can properly consider only risks to research subjects *as subjects;* it is not the arbiter of what kind of research results are politically or socially acceptable (Gray, 1977; Smith, 1976; IRB Recommendations, p. 24). Any other interpretation would make the content of research investigations subject to the social and political views of IRB members.

The proper function of the IRB is to protect the legitimate interests of human subjects in the research process. In the ordinary conduct of most social science research, subjects have two general kinds of interests which may be affected. First, they have an interest in maintaining a steady emotional state, free from extraordinary emotional distress and discomfort. This kind of interest might be placed at risk by, e.g.: (1) questions on questionnaires or in interviews which remind the subject of unhappy experiences, thus creating self-consciousness and embarrassment; (2) required behaviors (e.g., taking a skills test) which may create feelings of humiliation or failure; (3) extremely long or frequent data collection procedures which subject the participant to inconvience and/or boredom.

Second, subjects have a related interest in personal privacy and in maintaining the confidentiality of personal data. Kelman (1977) has identified three specific concerns related to the invasion of subject privacy: (1) violation of private space; (2) participant's control over self-presentation; and (3) public exposure of private information. If research procedures require disclosure of sensitive personal information, e.g., sexual preferences, criminal records, etc., important subject interests may be affected. These interests are also related to emotional state, e.g., a subject might experience present discomfort in providing sensitive information about homosexual preferences and future embarrassment if such information were disclosed to others. Disclosure of information can also have serious legal consequences. As Knerr suggests in Chapter 9, companion volume, incriminating data provided by subjects may be the basis of their arrest and criminal prosecution when those data are subpoenaed from the files of the investigator.

It is the IRB's task to identify and assess risks of the types described above. The focal point of this process is the interests and reactions *of the subject*, not the personal preferences of the IRB member. If persons of the same age and mental and physical state *as the subject* could resonably be expected to experience distress of invasion of privacy which they would not have experienced in the absence of the research, possible risk is present. In assessing that risk, IRB members will necessarily be confined in most instances to their own armchair assessments of risk. While the experience and commonsense judgment of IRB members in reviewing individual proposals cannot be reduced to a formula, certain general considerations obtain in the risk evaluation process.

First, IRB members should bear in mind that the low risks of most social science research can be managed or assumed by normal adult subjects. If no coercion is involved, such subjects are generally able to protect themselves by refusing to participate in the research, which in any event usually provides no more "risk" than that encountered in daily living (Pattullo, 1978). For example, some laboratory research in the social sciences involves mild deception, e.g., telling a college student subject that he or she will interact with another student who is pictured or described, when in fact the interaction will not involve the pictured or described student. Such deception does not pose a significant risk to the human subjects of the research, especially when full debriefing is accomplished. It should not absorb significant IRB time and resources.

Second, when the IRB reviews research using subjects from special populations, i.e., subjects who are not normal, noninstitutionalized adults, risks of subject abuse increase and more comprehensive IRB review becomes necessary. Such subjects may be more susceptible to particular kinds of injury or may be more vulnerable to pressures to participate than other subjects. It is important that IRBs reviewing such research develop an understanding of the kinds of risks and pressures peculiar to such a population. An IRB that reviews research involving such a population should retain consultants or have a membership that (1) contains some persons who have professional knowledge of the relevant population, e.g., mental health professionals for retarded or mentally ill persons; and (2) contains some persons who can objectively represent the interests of such subjects. Professionals who work with special subject populations may not, because of bias or conflict of interest, be the best representatives of subject interests. For example, as Loo suggests in Chapter 5, companion volume, teachers of autistic children may overestimate the risk to such children presented by a study of crowded conditions, because they may be forced to contend with disruptive behavior resulting from the study. Thus, IRBs may have to look beyond professional groups to attract members who will give objective consideration to subject and research interests.

Third, regardless of subject population or type of social science research, IRB members should recognize that their primary task in the risk assessment process is the *management of risk*, not the acceptance or rejection of proposals based on excessive risk or even the balancing of risk against benefits. In social science research, most risks can either be managed through procedures or changes in design or consented to by informed subjects.

In the University of Michigan Survey Research Center Study of IRBs,[3] outright rejection of social science proposals occurred in only 1% of the cases surveyed.

---

[3] The University of Michigan Survey Research Center conducted extensive IRB research under contract and reported its results to the Commission in November

In the authors' two years of collective experience on the University of Minnesota IRB—Social Sciences Panel, no rejections occurred. IRB members who review social science research are typically in the business of requiring some risk reduction (e.g., through anonymous collection and storage of data to ensure confidentiality), or of allowing risk assumption through consent procedures. Only rarely are risks so serious and unmanageable that a true balance between subject and research interests must be struck.

Risks in social science research can often be managed by procedures and research designs that have no impact on the validity of the research. For example, perhaps the most common and significant risk to subjects in social science research arises from the possibility of disclosure of confidential or private information given by the subject (Bond, 1978). Procedures to safeguard subject identity and the confidentiality of information, from the simple expedient of omitting names from data to more complex procedures (see Boruch & Cecil, Chapter 10, companion volume), can be devised and even standardized by IRBs. In this way, an investigator's certi-

---

of 1977. We will refer to its report as the "Michigan Study." Some cautionary comment about the study and our use of it is necessary. The study examined IRB review at 71 institutions and covered a wide range of topics including informed consent, risks and benefits, types of research reviewed, and IRB performance. Its overall results reflect a predominance of biomedical research review in the sample. For example, biomedical research constituted 63% of all research conducted in the participating institutions, but behavioral research made up only 25% (Table I.1, p. 92; patients were 67% of all subjects in reviewed projects (Table II.3, p. 99); 53% of reviewed research involved drug administration or evaluation of bodily products, but only 23% involved questionnaries, psychological tests, or behavioral observations (Table I.2, p. 93).

Despite the predominance of biomedical research, the Michigan Study does reveal some results of interest to social scientists. Certain results are reported as responses of behavioral/social science investigators and IRB members or as responses to behavioral science research. We will report these results in this form only where they are relevant, with the caveat that samples of only 100-200 investigators were used.

In addition, the Michigan Study classified IRBs into several categories including university IRBs (whose institutions conducted 71% behavioral research) and medical school IRBs (whose institutions conducted 77% biomedical research) (Table I.1, p. 92). These categories are not necessarily indicative of subject matter of research reviewed, e.g., "medical schools" included panels which reviewed social science research. From the manner in which the results are presented, it is often difficult to determine how IRBs behave in reviewing social science research. We will occasionally give results from university IRBs, which apparently reviewed primarily social science research, but we caution the reader that the university IRB sample contained only 17 boards.

Because of its broad coverage, the Michigan Study is not particularly helpful in analyzing specific problems of social science research. More study of those problems is needed. For purposes of this chapter, we have used the Michigan Study primarily to suggest possible trends and to offer tentative support for some of the more casual observations of those involved in the social science review process.

fication that he or she will use an IRB-approved procedure can expedite IRB review. When such procedures are combined with assurances that the subject has freely consented to participate, the IRB's regulatory function is usually complete.

Informed Consent

Consistent with the manageable nature of research risks, the central concern of IRB review in the social sciences is the assurance of informed consent.[4] In fact, one IRB member at the University of Tennessee estimated that 75% of the discussions at meetings of his IRB concerned informed consent (Konnert Testimony, IRB Hearings, p. 583). This estimate is consistent with the authors' experience on the Minnesota IRB.

Nature of consent. Informed consent involves two central concepts: (1) the absence of coercive pressure to participate; and (2) the presentation to the subject of information material to his or her decision to participate. While most IRB members and investigators would agree that coercive pressure should be absent in any research setting, how much and what kind of information is required for informed consent is a more complex question that necessarily involves the risks and circumstances underlying the research.

The absence of coercive pressure is by definition the critical element in any kind of consent. While the usual incentives, i.e., small payments and academic credit offered to normal subjects, pose few problems, special subject populations may give cause for special concern, especially when research participation could be viewed by the subject as a condition to further education or treatment. If an IRB reviews research with such populations, e.g., children or mental patients, it should exercise care to ensure that coercive pressure is minimized and subject interests are identified and protected. Initially, institutional pressure should be minimized. Classroom teachers, treating physicians, or other persons who normally influence the subject should avoid assuming the primary role in seeking subject consent. Special precautions should be taken to divorce research from treatment or education in the subject's mind. If subjects are not fully capable of consent, legal representatives should give consent in place of and, if possible, in addition to the subject. If the IRB routinely reviews research involving particular subject populations, it should also develop guidelines to resolve recurrent questions, e.g., one central question in

---

[4] There is some dispute as to whether the IRB should even consider the problem of informed consent in research which presents no significant risk to subject interests. DHEW's Office for Protection from Research Risks (OPRR), which monitors IRBs, has instructed institutions that informed consent is required even in the absence of risk (IRB Hearings, p. 43). But 45 C.F.R. §102(b) and §109 of the DHEW regulations suggest that informed consent review occur only after a threshold decision that "risk is involved." This latter view is supported by one of the few judicial decisions concerning IRBs, *Crane* v. *Mathews*, 417 F. Supp. 532, 547 (N.D. Ga. 1976), in which the Federal district court stated: "[T]he regulation requires such consent only from individuals determined to be subjects at risk. . . ."

school research is what combination of child, parent, and educator consent should be required when the subjects are school children of particular ages.

The second aspect of subject consent, that is, presentation of information material to a subject's decision to participate, sometimes poses difficult problems in social science research. In some cases, full information about the purpose of the research is inconsistent with the research design and would invalidate results. Nondisclosure of certain aspects of purpose or procedure, or even actual deception, may be necessary to obtain certain kinds of social scientific knowledge. In addition, the subject may not need to know or even want to know all available information about the research. Indeed, providing such information may serve to prolong the research experience and to confuse or bore the subject.

In analyzing problems of information disclosure, IRBs should consider the impact of disclosure on risks to significant subject interests under all of the circumstances of the research. For example, if nondisclosure of a particular item of information, e.g., the purpose of a questionnaire study, *does not conceal or increase the risk* of psychological harm or invasion of subject privacy, full disclosure prior to research participation might not be required. It is sufficient in such a case that the subject be provided in advance with adequate procedural information about the study, e.g., that it will involve a 10-minute conversation with another person and a 15-minute questionnaire on general attitudes. In short, the degree of disclosure should vary with the potential impact of disclosure on subject risk.

Deception research poses special problems of informed consent. A subject may give his or her informed consent to specific experimental procedures, such as filling out attitude scales and interacting with others, but may be intentionally deceived by the experimenter about the experiment's true prupose or some of its possible discomforts. In such a case, deception might conceivably have an impact on subject interests. First, some commentators have suggested that deception per se may affect a possible abstract interest in receiving truthful information, thus violating "individual autonomy." Damage to this interest may also have an adverse impact on the reputation and value of the social sciences as well as the "normative order" of society (Smith, 1976). Second, in addition to impairing an interest in truth in the abstract, deception may violate specific interests of the individual subject. For example, a subject may be led to believe erroneously that another subject or confederate has rated him unfavorably on personality traits; this may cause embarrassment or loss of self-esteem. Or, a subject may be led to expect a personal benefit, e.g., when the study is misrepresented as a job interview or therapy session. This expectation interest is frustrated when no benefit is received.

The reference point for considering these interests is the reasonable expectation of and risks of injury to the subject under the circumstances. For example, subjects in a research laboratory may resonably expect some deception or trickery as a part of that artificially created situation. While abstract considerations of the "normative order of society" may be appropriate when social scientists consider professional ethics and responsibilities, they are not relevant to IRB-imposed regulations of research for the protection of subjects. If deception does not violate specific interests of the individual subjects, it should not be censored by the IRB to further the social or ethical views of its members.

In analyzing deception research, IRB members should consider the following questions

1. Whether deception is necessary for the goals of the research.
2. Whether the deception conceals risks of participation or materially increases those risks.
3. Whether the research subject may be expected to find the deception reasonable.
4. Whether the subject is free to withdraw the data when the deception is revealed.
5. Whether the investigator has provided the means for detecting and removing any negative effects of the deception, e.g., through debriefing.

(derived in part from the American Psychological Association, Ad Hoc Committee, 1973):

Question 2 above is the critical consideration in an IRB decision to permit deception research. As Kelman (1977) has commented:

> [D]eception is not permissible if it is designed to circumvent informed consent by withholding information, e.g., about potentially adverse effects that might be material to a subject's decision to participate. (p. 181)

If deception does not affect risk, it may be permissible without violating basic concepts of consent. The IRB should then consider whether an investigator has removed or minimized possible adverse effects through debriefing and disclosures after the research has been completed.

Manner of consent. With some exceptions HHS regulations provide that informed consent must be obtained *and documented.* The standard means of obtaining and documenting subject consent under the regulations is a formal written consent document signed by the subject (45 C.F.R. §46.117). But such formal written consent following extensive disclosure of information is generally unnecessary to insure that the subject has freely chosen to participate in social science research. It may, in fact, be potentially harmful to both investigator and subject interests under certain circumstances.

In some cases, requirement of written consent may produce biased samples because some subjects, although entirely willing to participate, may be reluctant to sign the form (IRB Hearings, pp. 55-58, 72-73, 239, 342-343, 659). In addition, the use of a signed form may suggest to the subject that his or her name is being kept and might be used to identify data, contrary to assurances of confidentiality (Bond, 1978). This concern might conceivably damage the subject's legal interests, e.g., when a retained consent form is subpoenaed and used to identify subjects and their participation. Finally, a signed form may suggest to subjects that they are contractually committed to participation, notwithstanding assurance of a right to withdraw. The commitment generally associated with a signature in our society may leave subjects with a feeling of less freedom of choice or lead them to believe that they are somehow forfeiting their rights. These feelings and beliefs may lead to more psychological discomfort than the research itself (IRB Hearings, pp. 342-343).

Adhering to formality, some IRBs have required consent forms at the expense of informed consent (Gray, 1975; IRB Recommendations, p. 27). Instead of tinkering with consent forms, IRBs should focus their attention and resources on identifying the significant interests of the subject and devising procedures to protect those interests. In this process, informed consent should be regarded as an alternative means of protecting the subject's reasonable expectations of privacy and psychological well-being. Considering risk and circumstances, a research project may demand formal written or oral consent, or consent may be implied from informed participation or from the fact that the subject has no reasonable expectation of privacy in connection with a particular observed activity. Such a flexible approach is embodied in DHEW's 1971 Guide, which appropriately requires that:

> The review committee will determine if the consent required, whether to be secured before the fact, in writing or orally, or after the fact following debriefing, or whether implicit in voluntary participation in an adequately advertised activity, is appropriate in light of the risks to the subject, and the circumstances of the project. (p. 8).

Priorities in the Review Process

Burdened with crushing loads of new research proposals, most IRBs find their time severely limited and their resources stretched thin. With a constant flow of new low risk proposals to review, IRBs have little time to devote to comprehensive review of high risk research and the monitoring of research in progress. Ironically. these often neglected tasks are the most critical to the IRB's function, which is the protection of human subjects at risk. As one witness at the IRB Hearings pointed out, unnecessary review of low risk research has several adverse effects. It serves to (1) slow the review process and take time from necessary work; (2) dull the commitment and sensibility of reviewers; (3) diminish the credibility of the review process in the eyes of investigators; and (4) impede progress toward important ethical objectives (Sprague testimony, IRB Hearings, p. 133).

In order to focus increased attention on the review and monitoring of high risk research, IRBs must devise ways to become more efficient in the review of the routine, low risk research that crowds their calendars. Efficiency can be improved by the development of (1) expedited review procedures that dispose of low risk research quickly and without full IRB involvement; and (2) standardized research procedures that can be used to minimize or eliminate common risks. Development of these procedures will depend on the particular kind of research and human subject issues presented to an individual IRB, but some general observations can be made.

Low risk research can be deregulated or subjected to an expedited review. This procedure can be implemented in a variety of ways. For example, if a particular research proposal fell within a deregulated classification, the investigator could submit a certification and brief description of the research, which could be summarily reviewed by IRB staff and filed for reference. If a proposal called for expedited review, it could be reviewed by two IRB members as opposed to the entire IRB.

Definition of deregulated and expedited review categories will depend in part on the kinds of research reviewed by a particular IRB. However, the following are some general criteria for low risk research:

1. Absence of physical risk—research involving physical risk is not appropriate for summary review.
2. Normal adult subject population—research using children or institutionalized persons deserves special scrutiny and should not be handled with expedited procedures.
3. Unidentifiable data—if data are collected in such a manner that subject identity can be ascertained, more than minimal scrutiny is necessary.
4. Fully informed consent—if the situation suggests that subjects are not given full information about the conduct of research, further review is necessary.

Consistent with the above factors, much routine obserVeratory and questionnaire research would not need full IRB scrutiny.

In addition to handling low risk research more efficiently, IRBs can promulgate and follow more specific guidelines in their review of all research. The absence of clear guidelines and IRB procedures for dealing with social science research is probably the central barrier to IRB-investigator communication. Several witnesses at the National Commission's hearings complained about the vagueness of review guidelines, inconsistent IRB decisions, and the resulting investigator uncertainty about proper procedures. (IRB Hearings, pp. 58, 262, 263, 267, 288, 309). While some of these problems may be alleviated by the advent of new regulations, the original DHEW regulations have been criticized for leaving the most difficult procedural and substantive issues to the IRB (DuVal, 1977, p. 504).

One way in which IRBs can reduce confusion and inconsistency in decision making is by resolving recurrent issues in policy decisions and creating their own "common law." In many cases, IRBs have been inconsistent in their decisions simply because they have failed to keep records of past decisions and apply the same standards to similar proposals. For example, the second author recalls a situation in which a social science panel of the Minnesota IRB became confused as to whether it should require, in studies using elementary school students as subjects, the consent of students, parents, teachers, and school administrators, or that of just some of these persons. The problem had arisen frequently, but members differed in their recollections of past decisions. The policy issue was not resolved; the board simply made a new decision for the proposal at hand.

When an issue continually arises, the entire IRB should resolve the issue and publish its policy decision. This process allows investigators to conform their proposals to the policy decision and minimize future consideration of that issue. IRBs should also keep records of their decisions in significant cases and publish these decisions. By formally making and applying rules like adminstrative agencies, IRBs will improve their own efficiency and consistency and will become more accountable for their decisions in the eyes of the research community (IRB Hearings, pp. 47, 518).

Communication between the Board and the Investigator

The growing literature on the IRB leaves little doubt that many social scientists view the review procedure with suspicion and hostility (e.g., Pattullo, 1978). This attitude may be particularly strong among social scientists in academic institutions who are not used to regulation of their activities. In addition, the low risk nature of most social scientific research often causes social science investigators to question the legitimacy of heavy-handed regulations.

Notwithstanding some hostility we believe that, in most cases, investigators who are made aware of a particular subject interest they have overlooked will be more than willing to remedy that oversight. However, even in cases in which the IRB and the researcher are working toward the common goal of protection of subject interests, conflict between the two may still result. Often, the source of this conflict is a lack of communication of IRB procedures of the content of specific regulation. For example, an investigator may feel resentful about an IRB's enforcement of regulations with which the investigator is not familiar. On the other hand, if a researcher fails to supply adequate information, he or she may unwittingly generate conflict. If a researcher fails to supply adequate information about the risks involved in a study seeking potentially sensitive information, the IRB is faced with a dilemma. It must choose between requesting additional information, thus risking damage to the research and/or a protest from the investigator. Both of these actions inconvenience the investigator and impede the review process.

IRB members and investigators share the responsibility of improving the communication aspects of the review process. In this section, we will suggest several ways in which social scientists, as IRB members and as investigators, can facilitate this interaction through self-education and the education of others in the review process.

The Role of the Board

In order to minimize problems of communication, IRBs must undertake the responsibility of educating their own members and their institutional constituencies in the function and the importance of the ethical review process. This educational function may be the most important, and most neglected, aspect of IRB performance.

Unfortunately, many IRB members begin their positions as reviewers with little preparation for their task. According to the Michigan study, most social science IRB members learned about their roles through experience, briefing by IRB members, and some written instruction; only two percent received any formal training in the form of seminars or workshops (Gray, Cooke & Tannenbaum, 1978 p. 162). Given this lack of preparation, it is not surprising that reviewers have difficulty assessing intangible subject interests and applying informed consent regulations.

Perhaps, as IRBs become a more firmly established aspect of research activity, fewer researchers will be in this position of relative ignorance. In the interim, there are methods the IRB can use to prepare its members for their task. Three such methods are (1) training sessions, (2) communication with other IRBs, and (3) solicitation and application of the results of social scientific research in areas relevant to IRB decision making.

Training sessions. IRB training sessions should (1) acquaint new members with the procedures of the IRB and the substance of the regulations which they are to apply; (2) train members to identify the major ethical issues in a research proposal; and (3) give members the opportunity to develop uniform decision rules to be applied to the proposals they will later review.

These goals can be accomplished in a variety of ways. One possible format might include a general session acquainting reviewers with specific regulations, followed by sessions in which reviewers read, discuss, and review sample research proposals. There is no effective substitute for actual group deliberation on research proposals. Proposals for deliberation should be chosen with the following criteria in mind. First, they should raise a wide range of issues which members are likely to encounter in actual IRB deliberation, e.g., potential invasion of privacy, adequacy of informed consent, and special populations. Second, they should include past proposals on which the IRB has actually reached a decision. These proposals will give new members the opportunity to compare their views with those of current or former IRB members, thus identifying potential areas of disagreement which may be resolved through discussion and/or adoption of uniform decision rules. This latter step has the benefit not only of increasing the efficiency of future IRB activity, but also of establishing uniformity or consensus in decision making which will help to alleviate researcher concerns of IRB arbitrariness or inconsistency.

Communication with other IRBs. Even when members of an IRB are trained and experienced in reviewing research proposals, problems may arise when an IRB is confronted with an unfamiliar issue or procedure. In such cases, one IRB may benefit from the experience of other IRBs which may have confronted similar issues or procedures. Through communication with their counterparts at other institutions, IRBs can also expand the information available to them about risks and benefits found to be associated with common research procedures, methods others have devised for handling of minimizing risks, and new ways of dealing with issues of informed consent. IRB interaction may also help to establish some uniformity across IRBs, thus lessening the problem of unequal treatment of researchers at different institutions.

Individual IRBs might open channels of communication by contacting other IRBs in their vicinity and comparing notes. In addition, DHEW and other organizations might consider workshops and publications designed to exchange information and case studies. One such publication, a newsletter called *IRB—A Review of Human Subjects Research,* is currently published by the Hastings Center, Institute of Society, Ethics, and Life Sciences.

Use of research findings. The raw material used by IRBs in their decision making generally comes from past experience with research procedures and the collective professional judgments of present and past IRB members. But IRBs can also benefit from a growing body of social scientific literature on ethical issues per se, as well as basic research bearing on questions raised in IRB deliberation and the experience of investigators, as the following discussion illustrates.

First, there is a growing body of empirical research on questions of research ethics. This research includes studies sampling general public attitudes about research procedures (e.g., Wilson & Donnerstein, 1976) and studies exploring the effects of informed consent procedures on research results (e.g., Garner, 1978; Resnick & Schwartz, 1973). Other studies have suggested ways of recognizing and dealing with specific subject interests. For example, one study has suggested a procedure for gathering information relevant to a decision to conduct research in which deception may be necessary (Berscheid, Baron, Dermer, & Libman, 1973). This procedure involves giving a description of the proposed research and deception to a sample of the subject population and soliciting their reactions in order to detect potential risks.

Second, basic psychological research has been done on topics relevant to decisions about what actually constitutes, for example, "harm" or "informed consent." Some of this research has identified and discussed specific components of "psychological risk," e.g., self-esteem and anxiety. In addition, research on the topic of "perceived freedom" suggests circumstances under which an individual will feel compelled to engage in an activity in which he or she would not otherwise participate (Steiner, 1970). Such research may be relevant to decisions about the adequacy of informed consent.

Finally, the conduct of research itself has occasionally revealed issues that are not readily apparent either to investigators or to IRB members who review their proposals. For example, in Chapter 4, companion volume, Mirvis and Seashore discuss some of the ways in which information collected in organizational research might shed light on ethical issues which would not otherwise have been detected. In a similar fashion, a dialogue among investigators and IRBs on actual research experiences will add to the sophistication of IRB armchair decisions.

Unfortunately, IRBs may sometimes be reluctant to rely on social scientific knowledge. This reluctance was illustrated in testimony before the Commission for the Protection of Human Subjects. According to one social psychologist, the Chair of the IRB at his institution declined his suggestion to put on the board an investigator specializing in research on the unintended effects of experimental manipulations because, according to him, it would be like "letting the fox in the chicken coop" (Kiesler testimony, IRB Hearings, p. 671). Such attitudes do little to increase either the effectiveness of the review process or the cooperation of investigators.

We are not suggesting that the results of attitude surveys or laboratory experiments should substitute for the reasoned judgment of IRB members. However, they can contribute to the pool of information at the IRB's disposal and provide some objective data to guide in decisions which would otherwise depend solely on the subjective analysis by IRB members who are in many respects different from actual subjects. In this way, the reasoned and experienced judgment of IRB members is enhanced.

The above procedures have been suggested as means by which IRBs can educate their own members about all aspects of the review process. There are also a number of ways in which the IRB can minimize potential conflicts with investigators through education of the research community. These include (1) workshops, (2) liaison persons, and (3) communication of decisions.

Workshops. Workshops that acquaint investigators with the review process may alleviate some of investigator problems with the review process. These workshops might consist of periodic meetings between IRB members and groups of investigators (formed, perhaps, on the basis of similarity of research interests) in which IRB members could discuss the working of the board, explain what problems arise in the IRBs deliberations, and work through examples of project proposals, pointing out common errors or omissions frequently made by investigators.

Liaison personnel. The use of liaison personnel to facilitate IRB-investigator communication may be the most efficient approach to the communication problem. Depending on the size and organization of the particular institution, one member of each department or research unit might be assigned to act as a liaison person between the IRB procedures; ideally such a person would have had previous experienceas an IRB member.

The liaison person could bridge the gap between investigators and the IRB in a number of ways. He or she could advise and assist investigators in the preparation of research proposals by explaining the purpose of questions on IRB proposal submission forms of explaining what specific information about the research design might be necessary in the IRB's consideration of the investigator's proposal. The liaison person would also communicate the concerns of investigators to the IRB. He or she could help the IRB to develop better proposal forms in cases where standard IRB questions were confusing or inappropriate for particular kinds of research. He or she could also assist the IRB in identifying areas of research which are appropriate for expedited review or uniform treatment by the IRB, thus improving IRB efficiency.

Communication of decisions. Finally, an IRB might faciliatate IRB-investigator interaction by providing investigators with information about its policies and decisions. For example, the IRB could publish a newsletter in which it communicated to investigators its basic procedural guidelines, a summary of the number and kinds of proposals received and judgments made, and, most importantly, the kinds of problems most frequently encountered and suggestions of ways in which investigators could minimize these problems through changes in the preparation of their proposals. In addition, IRBs should communicate their policy decisions to researchers. For example, if researchers are aware of IRB policy concerning: (1) who must consent to questionnaire research involving children; (2) when written, as opposed to oral, implied, or no consent is required; (3) what debriefing procedures are adequate in deception research and in observations in natural settings; and (4) what kinds of general safeguards should apply in gathering, analyzing, and disseminating data, they could draft their proposals with these concerns in mind, thus avoiding the costly and time-consuming process of revision and resubmission.

This channel of communication, in addition to providing investigators with specific, useful information, would help to dispel an aura of secretiveness which sometimes surrounds the IRB process and creates suspicion among investigators. It would also eliminate false perceptions investigators might have about the outcome of IRB deliberation. For example, as we have discussed above, it is extremely unusual for an IRB to reject a social science proposal, but many investigators may not realize this.

The Role of the Investigator

Investigators can also play an important role in bridging the gap between their research and the activity of the IRB. Social science investigators have all too often been a prophylactic force in the review process, complaining about bureaucracy and threats to academic freedom without making any substantial commitment to assist their IRBs in the difficult and complex process of ethical review. The case of the Psychology Department at the State University of New York-Albany, which incurred a $100,000 penalty (later suspended) and substantial damage to its reputation because of a failure to impliment IRB review, is a lesson in point. As a perceptive New York editor observed:

> Perhaps these are only isolated instances (i.e., the Albany case and another case involving the use of an uncertified substance in recombitant DNA research), but there are reports that scientists elsewhere have also ignored state and federal safety regulations. Scientists are given to complaining that bureaucratic regulation stifles scientific inquiry. They maintain that the scientific community should be trusted to police itself. The surest way to lose this argument and to bring on stringent government controls would be to ignore these recurring signs of trouble. (*New York Times*, November 11, 1977, cited in Lowman, 1978)

Investigators can aid in the review process by educating themselves in the issues of ethical review as well as by promoting ethical training among their own graduate and undergraduate students.

The means by which investigators can aid in the review process through self-education include, but are not limited to: (1) familiarizing themselves with the principles of review: (2) preparing their own proposals carefully; (3) learning to build ethics into their research designs; and (4) undertaking research in areas related to subject interests.

Investigators can greatly increase the efficiency of the IRB by becoming more effective reviewers of their own proposals. One way in which investigators can accomplish this objective is by developing their skill in applying the principles discussed in this chapter to their specific research. This analysis can be aided by a review of relevant ethical principles or codes within the investigator's own discipline. For example, the American Psychological Association published in 1973 a set of principles under the title *Ethical Principles in the Conduct of Research with Human*

Participants (Ad Hoc Committee, 1973). These principles contain practical guides and commentary which will assist the investigator in recognizing common risks and adopting specific procedures to manage those risks.

Investigators can also improve the efficiency of the IRB, as well as prevent unnecessary delays in the conduct of their research by paying careful attention to the preparation of their proposals. While most investigators seek in good faith to comply with review procedures, good faith does not ensure competent proposal submissions. In our IRB experience, social science investigators often submitted proposals requiring IRB revision or requests for further information because they (1) failed to assess and deal with subject interests in privacy and confidentiality; (2) failed to describe fully and clearly information given to subjects before or after experiments; and/or (3) failed to propose consent procedures covering relevant elements of informed consent.

Investigator-IRB interaction is also improved when investigators build ethical considerations into their research designs. This includes taking into account in the earliest phases of planning research many of the issues discussed in this chapter, including who the subjects will be, what their interests are, and how the research proposal impacts those interests. In addition, investigators should insure that the free and voluntary consent of subjects is obtained by developing consent procedures and supervising persons who carry out the research. By planning an ethical strategy, investigators will effectively become reviewers of their own research and their ethical consciousness will improve the performance and efficiency of the IRB.

Moreover, investigators can improve IRB review by offering to IRBs their own data and casual observations of the effects of research procedures. Experienced investigators regularly conduct subject debriefing interviews and observe subject reactions to procedures. Communication of these kinds of investigator observations improves the collective knowledge of IRB members and keeps them in contact with the realities of human subject research. The IRB review process is necessarily an inexact one, but it can be improved by communication of knowledge about alternative research procedures and actual subject reactions to such procedures. Investigators themselves are in the best position to provide such knowledge.

Finally, and perhaps most importantly, investigators are likely to be teachers of future investigators. As they become aware of ethical regulations and principles, they should prepare to communicate them to their students through undergraduate and graduate courses in methodology, as well as special courses in research ethics. Even in basic courses for nonmajors, ethics should be a part of the course, since ethics is an indispensable part of every discipline. An ethical emphasis in social science education will serve to improve not only research proposals, but the reputation and standing of the social sciences in the community at large.

Conclusion

We have examined in this chapter some practical aspects of the role of the Institutional Review Board in the protection of human subjects of social science research.

In the first section, we discussed some of the major aspects of the IRB process. We suggested that IRBs should focus their attention on identifying and managing significant risks to subject interests in privacy, confidentiality, and psychological well-being and should avoid personal assessments of the social value of research. We also emphasized that IRBs should concentrate on the substance of voluntary consent to the specific risks in research, and not on the formalities of consent forms. Finally, we recommended that IRBs develop procedures to review efficiently low risk research in order to enable them to use their scarce resources to review comprehensively and monitor closely high risk research.

In the second section, we described the interaction between IRBs and the research establishment they purpose to regulate. We observed that social science investigators have often viewed the IRB with suspicion and hostility and we suggested several ways in which IRBs might remedy this situation by education both their own members and investigators about the issues involved in the review process. Because of susceptibility of research risks to effective management by the investigator, this educational function of the IRB may be more effective than its regulatory function in promoting the interests of human subjects of social science research.

We have also placed significant responsibility on individual investigators, who ultimately remain accountable for the protection of their subjects and the ethical standards and reputation of their professions. Investigators should make substantial efforts to identify in advance the risks in their research, and to design informed consent and risk management proposals appropriate to those risks. They should integrate subject interest protection into their design as they do any other research procedure. Finally, they should take a positive and active role in educating future investigators in research regulation and professional research ethics.

Ethics and ethical review are a potentially dynamic and humanizing element in the search for knowledge in the social sciences. They are a primary means of keeping investigators in touch with the interests and needs of the society served by their research. If ethical review is to become a fully integrated part of research, and not just a tolerated sideshow, IRBs and researchers must assume the responsibility of bridging the hiatus between broad ethical principles and open-ended regulations and research practices. In this chapter, we have suggested a few tentative approaches toward this end. The quagmires and interstices remain for those who would take up the challenge.

Acknowledgments. E.D.T. served as a social science representative on a social science panel of the University of Minnesota IRB during the academic year 1975-1976. T.J.T. served as a legal representative on the same panel during the previous year, 1974-1975. The second author was a human subject in the Michigan Study of IRBs.

References

Ad Hoc Committee on Ethical Standards in Psychological Research. *Ethical Principles in the conduct of research with human participants*. Washington, D.C.: American Psychological Association, 1973.

Berscheid, E., Baron, R. S., Dermer, M., & Libman, M. Anticipating informed consent. *American Psychologist*, 1973, *28*, 913-925.

Bond, K. Confidentiality and the protection of human subjects in social science research: A report on recent developments. *American Sociologist*, 1978, *13*, 144-152.

DHEW. *The institutional guide to DHEW policy on protection of human subjects* (DHEW Publication No. (NIH) 72-102). Washington, D.C.:: U.S. Department of Health, Education and Welfare, 1971.

DuVal, B. S., Jr. Educational research and the protection of human subjects. *American Bar Foundation Research Journal*, 1977, 477-519.

Gardner, G. T. Effects of federal human subjects regulations on data obtained in environmental stressor research. *Journal of Personality and Social Psychology*, 1978, *36*, 628-634.

Gray, B. H. An assessment of institutional review committees in human experimentation. *Medical Care*, 1975, *13*, 318-328.

Gray, B. H. The functions of human subjects review committees. *American Journal of Psychiatry*, 1977, *134*, 907-910.

Gray, B. H., Cooke, R. A., & Tannenbaum, A. S. Research involving human subjects. *Science*, September 1978, *201*, 1094-1101.

Herbert, W. Panel gives approval to research on mentally ill. *APA Monitor*, April 1978, 11.

Kelman, H. C. Privacy and research with human beings. *Journal of Social Issues*, 1977, *33*, 169-195.

Lowman, R. P. The case at SUNY-Albany. Unpublished compilation of documents, 1978.

National Commission for the Protection of Human Subjects of Biomedical and Behavioral Research, *Report and recommendations: Institutional review boards* (DHEW Publication No. (OS) 78-0008). Washington, D.C.: U.S Department of Health, Education and Welfare, 1978.

Pattullo, E. L. Comment. *American Sociologist*, 1978, *13*, 168-169.

Resnick, J. H., & Schwartz, T. Ethical standards as an independent variable in psychological research. *American Psychologist*, 1973, *28*, 134-139.

Smith, M. B. Some perspectives on ethical/political issues in social research. *Personality and Social Psychology Bulletin*, 1976, *2*, 445-453.

Steiner, I. D. Perceived freedom. In L. Berkowitz (Ed.), *Advances in experimental social psychology* (Vol. 5). New York: Academic Press, 1970.

Survey Research Center, Institution for Social Research, University of Michigan. *A survey of institutional review boards and research involving human subjects: A report to the National Commission for the Protection of Human Subjects of Biomedical and Behavioral Research*. Ann Arbor, Mich.: University of Michigan, 1977.

Transcript of the public hearings of the National Commission for the Protection of Human Subjects of Biomedical and Behavioral Research, April 5, 1977, April 15, 1977, and May 3, 1977, on institutional review boards (NTIS No. PB0270 258). U.S. Department of Commerce, National Technical Information Service, 1977.

Wilson, D. W., & Donnerstein, E. Legal and ethical aspects of non-reactive social psychological research: An excursion into the public mind. *American Psychologist,* 1976, *31*, 765-773.

Chapter 7

Social Science in the Mass Media: Images and Evidence

S. Holly Stocking and Sharon L. Dunwoody

A psychology professor at a West Coast university tells a story of an encounter he once had with a reporter from *The New York Times*. The reporter wanted to know if the psychologist knew anything about women's use of obscenity. It seems a *Times* editor had been cursed out by a woman at a party and had assigned the writer to find out if this were part of a developing social trend.

When the reporter called, the social scientist indicated that he didn't have any evidence on the matter, and he knew of no one who was engaged in relevant research. The reporter had a deadline, though, and pressed for a response. Didn't the psychologist have any views at all on the matter?

"I was almost shamed into it (responding)," the psychologist recalls (Zimbardo, Note 1). He says he told the reporter that "a number of years ago (10 to be exact), in two mental hospitals in Connecticut, in informal observations in the back wards (where chronic schizophrenics were kept), the women's wards seemed to be noisier and to have a greater amount of exhibitionism and obscenity than the men's wards" (Zimbardo, 1977, p. 42).

Not long after, *The New York Times* ran the article: "The use of obscene language among women, from the coeds of the New Left to the proper matrons of swank Manhattan cocktail parties, has risen sharply in the last few years, according to some leading psychologists.

"_____ _____, a _____ University psychologist, said that in observing agitated patients at two East Coast mental hospitals over a long period of time, he noted that the language of the women was more obscene than that of the men" (Zimbardo, 1977, p. 42).

The article contained no references to sources other than the psychologist and no indication that the man's "observations" were general impressions without independent vertifications by other observers, explicit definitions of obscenity, or comparable observations of men. The scientist's reference to "a number of years ago" had become "observed over a long period of time," and "chronic schizophrenics" had become "agitated patients."

It is the kind of "horror" story about media coverage with which many social scientists are familiar. Tales of "scandalous" interactions with journalists are often traded at professional conventions and in professional publications (e.g., Cohen, 1978; Van Dyne, 1978). Indeed, if one were to generalize from some of these informal accounts, one would come away with the impression that social scientists typically have about as much love for journalists as they do for William Proxmire.[1]

Serious public discussions about the popular dissemination of social science information have been rare (Grunig, 1974; National Science Board, 1969; UNESCO, 1974; Yu, 1968). But those that have taken place have done little to contradict such negative impressions. Indeed, the dissemination process has most often been portrayed as a simple, two-sided, and decidedly antagonistic affair a la C. P. Snow (1964).[2]

According to most of these discussions, scientists see the mass media as dominated by reporters and editors whose only goal is to find out something sensational enough to sell newspapers. Journalists, scientists believe, have little respect for the scientific process, and either think nothing of building inaccuracies into their accounts to improve readability, or are not bright enough or educated enough even to realize that they are being inaccurate. This school of thought interprets the popularization process as a never-ending battle between rationalism and sensationalism, as a kind of cold war between the scientist, who wants his or her work to be viewed in its proper, precise context, and the journalist, who needs, and often finds, a "news" angle that distorts the scientist's work and misrepresents the findings.

Unfortunately, such views, while they tend to serve to sensitize social scientists to the existence of problems surrounding the dissemination of scientific findings via the mass media, do little to clarify the nature of the problems or to indicate how scientists might deal with them. The stories scientists swap about the press tend to focus on the embarrassment that may befall those who give science news to the media. They tend to emphasize the helplessness of scientists in the face of media interests and demands, often leaving the impression that the scientist's only recourse is to avoid the media altogether. In our view, such "solutions," while no doubt effective, are needlessly extreme—analogous to that of a scientist whose data on drug addiction have been subpoenaed, who is sued by subjects to whom confidentiality was promised, and who wails, "I'll never study drug abuse again!" Just as there are more sophisticated solutions to the dilemmas of confidentiality (as argued

---

[1] The Wisconsin Senator, at this writing, continues to issue his "Golden Fleece" awards for "outrageous wastes" of the taxpayer's money. A number of social science research projects sponsored by the National Science Foundation have been singled out for this award since the awards were first issued in 1975. These activities do not seem to have won Proxmire many friends among social scientists.
[2] Snow has argued that scientists and humanists are in many ways two different cultures separated by different values, different reward systems, and even different languages. When applying his classic thesis to the mass communications situation—substituting journalists for humanists—one finds scientists and journalists poised on opposite sides of a gaping cultural canyon. An excellent expression of this model as applied to scientists and journalists can be seen in Kreighbaum (1967). See especially Chapter 3, "The Clash of the Cultures," pp. 35-49.

in Chapter 9 and 10, other volume), there are more sophisticated solutions to the dilemmas surrounding the reporting of scientific data in the popular press. The objective of this chapter is to lay the foundation for such solutions and to promote a more accurate understanding of mass media dissemination of scientific results so that ethical researchers who do decide to communicate via the media will be in the best possible position to minimize potential harm to science and to the public and to maximize the benefits.

There are related ethical issues that should be acknowledged before we begin. Do social scientists have an *obligation* to disseminate to the public? Arguments often are made that scientists who do human research and are funded by tax dollars have a moral duty to report what they discover to those who fund their research and might be affected by it (e.g., Walum, 1975; Stocking, Note 2). However, this argument must be tempered with concern for the quality of information that is disseminated. It is often argued that only findings that peers have first certified as "valid" should be communicated to the larger society (e.g., Culliton, 1972; Perlman, 1977). But even this standard may not be adequate. Recognizing this, the Hastings Center Institute of Society, Ethics, and the Life Sciences has undertaken a major project to explore ethical issues surrounding the use of social scientific knowledge in public policy making. One of the major objectives of this project is to determine whether the standards of social science disciplines are themselves adequate to ensure the validity of data that is disseminated to nonscientist publics.

In this chapter, we assume that the scientist already is mindful of these ethical issues, which have been argued at length in other forums. We also assume that social scientists need to know about more than ethics and social science methodology in order to maximize the likelihood of ethical mass media reporting of their research. We focus, therefore, on the *facts* surrounding mass media dissemination, on what scientists need to *understand* about the mass media process as they strive to be ethical.

First, we review a small but growing body of research on science communication, much of which suggests that the views personified in scientists' horror stories about the media are greatly oversimplified—that the dissemination of research via the mass media is a very complex process, controlled by a large number of variables, some of which can be affected by social scientists themselves. Second, we point to issues that remain to be addressed by those investigating the dissemination of research via the media. Finally, we present some practical suggestions, gleaned from this research and elsewhere, for ensuring that findings are disseminated in a responsible and reliable manner.

The importance for social scientists of accurately understanding the process by which mass media disseminate research should not be underestimated. Mass media coverage of the social sciences has grown enormously in the last 10-15 years (Cole, 1974; Olean, 1977).[3] Increasingly, social science researchers are being called on to

---

[3] Research documenting the increase is meager, but Cole's study shows a rise in science news generally, and an increase in social science coverage in newspapers relative to other kinds of science news. Specifically, from 1961 to 1971, news of the social and behavioral sciences rose from 4.7% to 14.8% of all science stories studied

act as sources for media accounts. At the same time, social scientists themselves seem to be realizing the need to responsibly share their knowledge with larger publics (McCall and Stocking, in press).[4] How they fare may depend a great deal on what they know about the process, for in this area of activity, as in many others, knowledge about the process can generate the power to affect it.

Research on the Process

Research on science communication in the mass media can be divided into two broad categories: studies focusing on the news-making attitudes and behaviors of journalists, and those examining relationships between scientists and mass media. In this section, we will first examine the evidence concerning journalists and then the evidence that concerns scientists more directly.

Evidence Concerning Journalists

By far the bulk of the research on science communication has focused on journalists: their training, the ways in which they select news, and the accuracy of their accounts.

Training. Research suggests that social scientists may have grounds for concern when it comes to the training of journalists who report about their work. Although we do not really know who is writing most of the mass media accounts of social science research, we do have evidence to suggest that many such accounts are *not* written by science writers, those individuals in the mass media who specialize in the communication of scientific information (Tichenor, Olien, Harrison, & Donohue, 1970). We also know that science writers, whom one would expect to be best qualified to interpret social science information for nonscientists, do not see the social sciences as part of their professional bailiwick, and in fact shy away from them

---

in samples of *The New York Times, The Washington Post, The San Francisco Chronicle,* and *The Minneapolis Tribune.* In the discipline of psychology, Olean notes that the number of reporters officially covering meetings of the American Psychological Association has steadily grown in the 1970s—from 36 in 1974 to 151 in 1976. Anecdotal evidence is more plentiful. Since the mid-1960s, the United States has witnessed the rise of popular social science publications (e.g., *Psychology Today, Transaction/Society,* and *Human Behavior*), a debut of special social science columns and sections in established magazines, and the development of social science specialty writers on some newspapers. Presumably, such developments are due, at least in part, to a general heightened awareness of social concerns. Policy makers and funding agencies have sought to involve social scientists in solving critical national problems; since problems are "news," social science has come to be defined as news.
[4] As George A. Miller (1969) noted in his presidential address to the American Psychological Association, "the enrichment of public psychology by scientific psychology constitutes the most direct and important application of our science to the promotion of human welfare" (pp. 106-107).

(Dunwoody, 1980; Tichenor et al., 1970). The level of training of nonscience writers who communicate about the social sciences[5] is unknown. We do know, though, that among science writers the level of training specific to the social sciences is marginal at best, with most of the writers having taken only general survey courses in psychology and sociology (Ryan & Dunwoody, 1975).

The practical implications of various levels of training, however, are not clear. As far as we know, no research to date has directly tested the proposition that the level of science training affects the quality of news stories that journalists write, although the 1970 Tichenor et al. study does suggest that the reporter's level of experience, as distinct from training, is not associated with the accuracy of reports. However, it does appear that among science writers the kind of training a writer has may affect what he or she writes about. Dunwoody, in studying media coverage of an AAAS convention, found that a science writer's background (biology, physics, etc.) was a good predictor of his or her major writing interests; that is, a biology major was interested in covering biology and medicine, while the physics major had a corresponding interest in physics and astronomy news. Thus, if science writers have little training in the social sciences, they may be expected to write very little about them (Dunwoody, 1980).

Whatever the consequences of training, it should be noted that the level of academic preparation for journalists has been increasing in recent years. Younger science writers have been shown to have more scientific training than do their older counterparts (Ryan & Dunwoody, 1975). Also, journalism schools are designing courses that should expose large numbers of journalism students to information that will facilitate media coverage of the social sciences (McCombs, Shaw, & Grey, 1976; Stocking, 1981). The number of science-writing courses seems to have grown enormously in recent years (Friedman, Goodell, & Verbit, Note 3), and the faculties of some schools of journalism are teaching survey methodology to prepare students to do a more rigorous job of news gathering (McCombs et al., 1976).

News values. Contrary to what one might think given the "two cultures" views of scientists and journalists, several studies indicate that there may be considerable agreement in the way many scientists and journalists view the news and the news process.

One study did find disagreement between scientists and editors on criteria for evaluating science news stories, the editors emphasizing "color and excitement" while the scientists emphasized "significance and accuracy" (Johnson, 1963). However, the same study found little difference between scientists' and reporters' (as distinct from editors') criteria. Another study found that experts in mental health and news media personnel communicating about mental health (writers, producers, directors, and performers in television productions) held similar views on the subject (Tannenbaum, 1963).

---

[5] The "social sciences" have been variously defined, but most often they have been taken to mean empirical investigations in the traditional academic disciplines of sociology, psychology, anthropology, economics, political science, and history.

Moreover, at least three other studies have indicated that scientists and journalists seem to perceive larger discrepancies between their respective attitudes about science news than actually exist. Two studies (Carter, 1958; Tichenor et al., 1970) have found that reporters' rankings of news values were more similar to scientists' rankings than they were to scientists' *estimates* of reporters' values. And a more recent investigation (Ryan, 1979) found that attitudes of scientists and science journalists toward various statements relating to science news coverage and its problems were "remarkably" similar, although, again, each group perceived a larger gap than actually existed.

It would be misleading, however, to make too much of such agreements, for investigations that go beyond pencil-and-paper measures have begun to suggest that journalists' news values vary. Scientists and journalists may evaluate news similarly in the abstract, but as journalists operate amid real-world pressures and constraints, their definitions of news may change. What is news in one place, on one day may not be news in another place, on another day. News, in short, is highly situational.

Studies by Breed (1955a, 1955b), Galtung and Ruge (1970), Halloran, Elliott, and Murdock (1970), Tunstall (1971), and others have indicated that situational factors determining "newsworthiness" include:

Time. Information obtained before a daily deadline may be newsworthy, while information obtained after the deadline may not.

Competition. Information appearing in one news medium may become "news" in other media, regardless of the inherent value of such information.

Editor's Expectations. Information valued by a journalist's editor may be viewed as more newsworthy than information that provokes an indifferent response from the editor.

Perceptions of Audience. If a journalist thinks his audience will be interested in a subject, he may define it as newsworthy regardless of his own perceptions of the subject.

Journalist's Background. Information is likely to become news if the reporter is already familiar with the area and has written stories about it.

Prestige of Source. Information from a scientist who is well known both within the scientific community and without is more likely to become news than information from a scientist with more obscure credentials.

Presence of Conflict. Something is more likely to become news if the information conflicts with everyday expectations or if it contains elements of disagreement or opposition among parties.

Dunwoody, in her study of the news-selection behavior of science writers at an AAAS meeting, identified several situational factors at work, including editors' expectations (Dunwoody, Note 4). Many of the newspaper science writers she studied looked to the wire service science writers (those who work for the Associated Press and United Press International) to set the news agenda, sometimes covering a story just to make sure that they and the wire services had done the same thing. They did so, according to one science writer, because the editors back in the newsroom would evaluate their coverage in terms of what came over the wires.

In sum, given no real-world constraints, science writers and scientists may agree to a surprising extent on news values. It is possible, however, that in some situations where news criteria become much more complex, agreement may diverge.

Accuracy. A number of researchers have examined the accuracy of science stories in the print media, in most cases by showing stories, once they have been published, to scientists who have acted as sources for the stories. Interestingly, most of the errors that scientists have spotted are not objective ones (errors of fact), but subjective ones (errors of emphasis). In one study, scientists, who included social scientists, cited journalists' overemphasis on the unique as the largest problem, followed by omission of relevant information, and misleading headlines (Tichenor et al., 1970). Omission of relevant information was judged to be a major accuracy problem by scientist sources in two other more recent studies as well (Borman, 1978; Pulford, 1976). Although subjective errors are legitimate cause for worry on the part of the conscientious social science researcher, it should be noted that they are not peculiar to journalistic accounts; although we know of no empirical evidence on the matter, it might be reasonably argued that subjective errors are the type that generate most disagreement among social scientists themselves.

If social scientists often express contempt for journalistic "truth," it may be, at least in small part, because they are expected to. Indeed, the findings of one study question the seriousness of scientists' general criticisms of media accuracy (Tichenor et al., 1970). In this study, scientists were more critical of the accuracy of news "in general" than of news specific to themselves. Specifically, 58% thought that science news in general was generally accurate, whereas 94.5% thought news of themselves was generally accurate, and this was not because they cooperated with the "good" reporters, for only nine of the 73 scientists interviewed (or 12.3%) knew anything about the reporter before the article was written.

There is also some evidence to suggest that scientists themselves can affect the accuracy of journalistic accounts by imposing certain practices during their interactions with journalists. For example, Tichenor et al. (1970) found that in general the more reporters adhere to certain practices such as face-to-face interviewing, reading back notes to the scientists, rechecking individual statements, or showing the entire article to the source, the higher the communication accuracy.[6] Tankard and Ryan (1974) also found that stories that were read to scientists prior to publication were perceived as more accurate by scientists than stories that were not read back to the scientists. Thus, the scientist who encourages such practices on the part of a journalist, or who makes such practices a condition for the interview, is likely to encounter fewer inaccuracies than one who does not.

---

[6] Communication accuracy is defined in this study as the extent to which audience statements about the content of media articles appeared acceptable to scientists quoted as sources in said articles.

In addition, Tichenor et al. (1970) found that articles initiated by press releases resulted in higher communication accuracy than articles initiated in public meetings. Thus, it would appear that the scientist can enhance the accuracy of media accounts of his or her work by initially translating the information into a form that is familiar to the journalist.

Evidence Concerning Scientists

Research focusing on scientists in the mass media dissemination process is just beginning. We know of only a few completed studies, but they are noteworthy because they, like many of the foregoing studies of journalists, suggest a complexity of attitudes and behaviors that stereotypical views of the process would deny.

In her highly provocative study of "visible scientists," Rae Goodell (1975) found that those scientists who were among the most visible to college undergraduates had established reputations in their academic disciplines prior to "going public." These scientists, who included social scientists as well as those in the natural sciences, not only did not shun the press, but appeared in many instances to court it.

Goodell's findings, while not systematic in nature, are consistent with those from a French study (Boltanski & Maldidier, 1970). In this study, doctors and biologists in Paris were queried as to their attitudes and behaviors related to popularization. Those who occupied higher ranks in the university hierarchies had more favorable attitudes toward popularization and had participated more in the popularization process than had scientists who occupied lower ranks. Lower-ranked individuals more often refused opportunities to popularize their work, or if they did popularize, they went to considerable pains not to discuss what they had done with colleagues. A more recent study of scientists at two American universities (Dunwoody & Scott, in press) also found a positive relationship between academic rank and both amount of contact with journalists and attitudes toward popularization. It would seem that for scientists who have gained the esteem of their peers, there may be fewer penalties attached to dissemination beyond their colleagues; for novice scientists, however, it may be another matter.

Research Needs

Obviously, research on mass media dissemination of social science information is meager. Although consistencies have emerged from the findings and we now have evidence that extends beyond anecdotal accounts and stereotyped portrayals of the process, there remain obvious limitations to much of the data: Many of the studies deal exclusively with the physical and biological sciences and thus may not provide a sound basis for generalizing to the social sciences; many deal with but one medium (newspapers, for example) and thus say little about mass media coverage via other channels of communication; financial or other design constraints sometimes result in samples that may not be representative of larger, randomly selected populations (e.g., news editors from papers in one state or scientists at one university).

Much more needs to be known about the mass media dissemination process, particularly as it relates to social science information. We turn now to some of the more pressing needs for knowledge about mass media dissemination of research: knowledge about the major actors in the process, and knowledge about the effects of mass media dissemination on audiences, individual scientists, and the institution of science.

The Actors

Journalists. Although we know quite a bit about the journalists generally, we need to know more about the specific individuals who produce mass media accounts of social science. Who are the reporters who are doing the bulk of the writing about social science? What kinds of backgrounds do they have, and what are their attitudes toward social science research? How do these factors affect the dissemination process?

Do the backgrounds and attitudes of editors differ from those of their reporters, and how do such differences act to affect dissemination? Dunwoody, in her study of AAAS meeting coverage, found that science writers typically disliked writing social science stories, but analyses of the stories that subsequently were published in newspapers around the country showed a decidedly different preference on the part of editors (Dunwoody, Note 5); for whatever the reasons (and they remain unclear) editors seemed to prefer the few social science stories that came over the wires to the larger number of hard science stories that were available.

In addition, more needs to be known about how media as economic and social institutions affect what becomes news. How, one might ask, does the organization of a newspaper—its power hierarchy, its economic priorities or the constraints under which its reporters work (autonomy of staff, size of staff, number of deadlines, etc.)—affect mass media coverage of the social sciences?

Scientists. We need to know more about the attitudes and behaviors of social scientists toward mass media dissemination of their research. What distinguishes scientists who disseminate their research via mass media (either directly through their own writing, or indirectly via journalists) from scientists who do not? What are the determinants of these attitudes and behaviors? Do attitudes and behaviors vary depending on the scientist's allegiance to the normative structure of science? Do they vary according to the allegiance of the scientist's institution to such a structure?

Intermediaries. Just as importantly, we need to know more about the intermediaries between scientists and journalists. Who are they? How do they function? In some cases, the intermediary initiates contact between scientists and journalists by sending a press release or setting up a press conference. In other cases, the intermediary acts as a gatekeeper, taking requests from journalists and directing them to appropriate scientists. University news bureaus and public information arms of scientific societies are the most obvious intermediaries, but what about secretaries, department chairpersons, and colleagues? Some of these questions are currently being addressed by one of the authors (Stocking, Note 6). The importance of such investigations is underscored by findings from Dunwoody's study of media coverage of a AAAS convention. She found that the convention organizers—not scientists or journalists—largely determined who would be "read" or "interviewed" at the meeting; they did so by selecting press conference topics and choosing papers to emphasize.

Effects of Dissemination

Most of the formal discussions about the popularization of social science information have been held under the assumption that mass media dissemination is desirable; they thus have focused on barriers to dissemination. But is such an assumption warranted? Research has very little to say on the matter.

Public, policy makers, practitioners. We know that mass media dissemination of social science information has implications for a variety of *audiences.* Most parents, for example, are likely to read popular magazine articles or books on child rearing, many of which are based on social science research (Clarke-Stewart, 1978). Government bureaucrats say they use the mass media for social science information relevant to their work (Caplan, Morrison, & Stambaugh, 1975).[7] Judges, teachers, and social workers may be alerted by the mass media to research findings (e.g., effects of foster care, validity of IQ tests, work aspirations of welfare mothers) that have a direct bearing on their professions. Research in political communications has shown that the mass media create awareness in audiences. They set agendas for people and they seem to perform this function most effectively for individuals who have a particular need to know. They may also stimulate further information seeking (Shaw & McCombs, 1977). But we need to know much more about the effects of media-relayed information, particularly social science information, on audiences. Do mass media accounts of social science research help individuals to live better lives? Do they help people to participate more fully in societal decisions? Or, more realisitically, under what conditions (and for whom) do mass media accounts have differential effects?

Scientists and science. We also need to know more about the effects of popularization on individual scientists and on the institution of science. Does mass media dissemination of social science research information help or hurt the conduct of scientific inquiry? To hear many scientists tell it, the effects of mass media dissemination on *individual scientists* are usually negative. The scientist whose research is distorted by the mass media complains that he or she has been subjected to ridicule

---

[7] In this study, newspapers along with government reports were the most frequently mentioned sources of social science knowledge by high-level bureaucrats. Specifically, 81% of respondents reported getting social science information from newspapers; 70% reported getting such information from popular magazines; 50% reported getting it from TV and radio. Respondents reported using such information to increase bureaucratic efficiency, to improve personnel selection and promotion, and to help meet the special educational needs of low-income and minority children, among other things.

by peers. The assistant professor who fails to get tenure is told he or she "does not have a scientific attitude toward his work" and assumes it is because he or she has published several articles in the popular press. The fact of the matter is, though, we do not really know how mass media coverage affects individual investigators. One can find anecdotal evidence that suggests positive as well as negative effects. One sociologist, for example, admits that the public notice she received for a piece of research presented at a professional meeting opened up a number of publishing opportunities, and thus may have contributed to her promotion. Another sociologist reports a similar experience. It is more than likely, of course, that mass media coverage affects individual scientists in a number of ways depending on a variety of factors, including the medium in which the journalistic account appears (*Harper's* will be more valued, say, than the *National Enquirer*), the quality of the account, the prestige of the individual scientist and of his or her institution, and the level of his or her productivity. However, we lack empirical data on these matters.

We know equally little about the effects of mass media dissemination on the institution of science. It is often argued that "popularization" threatens the very fabric of science. The rewards that are offered by the popular media—public fame and money—exist outside the system of science. Prestige among one's colleagues, which has been the traditional reward in science, is thus said to be undermined; the scientific norm of "objectivity" is compromised. Critics argue that the popular media create a breeding ground for scientific "operators" out for personal gain. Such operators may think little of bypassing the peer review system; bad science, uncontrolled science, thus may be promoted. Indeed, the editors of some scholarly publications in the natural sciences have cited this as a reason for denying publication to individuals who have disseminated their findings to nonscientists before subjecting them to peer review (Culliton, 1972).

On the other side of the picture, it can be and has been argued that mass media dissemination of scientific information contributes to the public understanding of science (Dubas & Martel, 1975). And public understanding of science, in turn, contributes to the welfare of the institution. As Ezrahi (1971) has noted, there is a "growing consciousness within the scientific community of the political condition of science, of the relationships between the popular images of science, and of the welfare of the scientific enterprise" (p. 132). Conceivably, popular journalistic accounts of science, by promoting public understanding of science, promote funding of the enterprise.

More pertinent to the concerns of this volume, it has been argued that popular dissemination of scientific information may serve to increase the public's appreciation of and concern for the ethical components of research. As Sieber (Note 7) has suggested:

> To the extent that the public is educated about the methods, purposes and limitations of science, it will also be in a position to understand the value dilemmas of scientists. When scientific literacy grows to include literacy about value dilemmas in science, then processes such as obtaining voluntary informed consent may take on a different character; subjects may be better able to comprehend their role and scientists, in turn, will have less

temptation to be careless, paternalistic or disrespectful in their relationship with subjects and society at large.

Again, we have many opinions on the matter, but little evidence. And again, it is reasonable to suppose that effects of mass media dissemination on the institution of science are not uniform, but rather depend on a variety of factors, including the quality of the media accounts and the devotion of individual scientists to such established scientific practices as peer review.

Some Implications and Practical Suggestions

Obviously, it will be a long time before we have anything more than anecdotal answers to many questions about the process and effects of mass media dissemination of scientific information. The questions themselves are only beginning to be asked, and empirical answers are a long way off.

Social scientists, meanwhile, are being pressed to act as though they had the answers. Faced with increasing numbers of journalists knocking at their doors, they must decide whether (or when) to open the doors, what to say if they do, and how to say it. Lacking a strong empirical base to guide their actions, what are they to do?

We suggest that responsible social scientists will do what responsible policy makers have always tried to do, that is, make the best of the little bit of evidence that does exist, and when evidence is lacking, take whatever actions that appear on the face of it to be both effective and responsible. In short, they will do what seems reasonable to maximize benefits to individual scientists, science, and society, while minimizing harms.

In the years since the West Coast psychologist had his run-in with *The New York Times* reporter, he for one has discovered a number of strategies for interacting with media representatives, not the least of which is saying "no" to requests for information in areas in which he has no professional expertise (Zimbardo, Note 1). Thus, he would recommend that if a scientist's area of expertise does not include women and obscenity (or holiday depression or delinquent dwarfs) he should simply say so. He should not try to "fake it" or let himself be shamed into answering. The scientists who does may wind up reading his words in the newspapers, then eating them.

This psychologist's experiences and those of other social scientists[8] suggest additional strategies. When journalists call for interviews, for example, it is always a good practice to find out about the media they represent. Media vary in quality. The probabilities of inaccurate reporting, for example, are likely to be lower in a publication like *The New York Times* that has the finances to hire specialty writers and to give them time to produce quality stories than they are on most small-town dailies. Media vary in the amount of time or space they can devote to a piece of

---

[8] We have not identified these scientists because when they offered their suggestions they were not informed they might be quoted.

reporting. Broadcast media work in seconds and minutes; wire service stories average about 500 words; many newspaper and magazine accounts are longer. Ethically minded scientists should find out how much time or space will be devoted to the subject they will be discussing. They should notice how reporters for the medium treat serious subjects. If they are unfamiliar with how the medium treats science news, it may be worthwhile to investigate first.

As noted earlier, research suggests that journalists often lack training in the social sciences. However, a scientist should not automatically assume that journalists cannot evaluate scientific information. Before an interview begins, the scientist may want to ask the reporter about his or her background and establish how much training he or she is bringing to the interview. Many science writers, for example, can apply the evaluative skills they have acquired in dealing with the "hard" sciences to the social sciences.

At the same time, a scientist should expect to have to do at least some educating during the interview. Most reporters, including science reporters, have to cover a wide variety of subjects, from competency testing to recombinant DNA research. Thus, even the best-trained among them can hardly be expected to be familiar with all of these areas. It is reasonable to expect, and perhaps even demand, that the reporter acquire some background knowledge before coming to the interview. (Some scientists, for example, suggest articles to reporters at the time the interview is arranged.) But it is unrealistic to expect the reporter to acquire instant expertise through such backgrounding. Time often will not permit a thorough reading of the materials the scientist suggests; and even if it does, the reporter may require help in interpreting the specialist's jargon.

It is important for scientists to be aware that reporters may be operating under situational constraints (deadlines, competition with other reporters, requests from editors, etc.) that may cause them to define newsworthiness differently from the scientist's assessment of what is important about the research. A scientist does not have to agree with the reporter's selection criteria, and upon finding out what news criteria are being employed, may very well decide not to give the journalist a story. But it is important to take the time to find out. Some questions that may be useful in identifying criteria include: What interests you about this particular piece of research? Why have you decided to talk to me about it? What do you think the angle of your story will be? If the journalist can only respond in vague terms, it may indicate that he or she has not really given the story or the research much thought. In that event, the scientist may very well choose not to be interviewed. On the other hand, the reporter with a fairly clear idea of the purpose of the interview probably deserves the scientist's time.

It would be wrong to assume that media accounts by nature are inaccurate. Accuracy can vary depending on a number of factors, including the controls the scientist chooses to exert when interacting with the journalist. As research suggests, the scientist can minimize inaccuracies by granting the interview on the condition that the reporter meet face-to-face. The scientist can encourage further interaction by offering to check the factual components of the journalist's story once it has been written. Some scientists make this latter request a condition for granting an interview, while others prefer to let such requests vary with their knowledge of the skill and social science expertise of the particular journalist. Not all journalists will be receptive to an offer to check their facts. Deadlines will not permit such a luxury for some, while others may view such checking as a form of "prepublication censorship." However, many excellent journalists with experience in translating technical matters will agree to such conditions (e.g., Perlman, 1974). The important thing is to avoid implications of censorship. The scientist might say, for example, "I know how difficult it can be to summarize all this technical material clearly and quickly. If I can help you by looking over the article (or script) when you are finished, I would be happy to do so. Of course, that would be with the understanding that I am not interested in censoring what you write, but merely in helping you to put together the most accurate story possible."

The scientist should consider issuing a press release. As indicated earlier, research suggests that releases can reduce misunderstandings. Anecdotal accounts by scientists also suggest the value of press releases. The West Coast psychologist mentioned earlier has found they are so effective in reducing inaccuracies that he now prepares them as a matter of course when he decides to go public (Zimbardo, Note 1). Organizers of professional conventions also find them useful in relating to press personnel. The American Psychological Association, in fact, has produced a booklet that tells psychologists how to prepare such releases (Olean, 1977).[9] If the scientist decides to issue a press release, he should contact the public information office of his or her institution. The quality of public information offices varies, but personnel often are drawn from the ranks of journalism and so typically know how to prepare releases that will be attractive to reporters and editors. The scientist should realize, however, that he may have to educate these people just as he would the journalist.

If at all possible, the scientist should take charge of the interview. When being interviewed for a broadcast, for example, with only a minute or two to discuss the topic, the scientist should make the most of every minute. If the reporter asks a question that is off the mark, he or she need not feel pressed into answering it. Instead, he or she could politely suggest that "A better question would be . . ." and then pose a question that allows a summary of the findings in one or two sentences. If there is time to elaborate, he or she may do so, but succinctly. Only after summarizing the findings should he or she elaborate further. Basically, this is the way most journalists structure their stories. They put the most important things first, briefly elaborate on these points, then elaborate further as time and space permit. Reporters will do this regardless of whether the scientist plays a role in the process, but the scientist can facilitate matters, and make sure that the proper points get emphasized, by structuring the interview with the journalist's needs in mind.

It is important for the scientist to consider the possible social implications of the work as one of the important elements to be covered. The scientist may feel some

---

[9] In addition to explaining how to prepare news releases, the APA booklet provides instructions on conducting press conferences and interviews. The booklet can be obtained by writing Public Information Officer, American Psychological Association, 1200 Seventeenth St., N.W., Washington, D.C. 20036.

moral obligation along these lines, particularly if the research has been financed by public monies. But regardless, the reporter will want to know what the researcher's work means for people. This will be true whether the primary objective of the research is to elucidate a process or to develop knowledge that can be applied to practical problems.

Obviously, there are some dangers associated with discussing potential applications of basic research findings. As writers for *Science* magazine have suggested, journalists often "want stories based on solid facts or conclusions or on new concepts . . . there is little room for ambiguity. . . ." As a result, "it may mean that what the scientist perceives as 'a little blip on a very long and slowly rising curve'. . . will appear as a major 'breakthrough' to the nonscientist" ("Science and the Press," 1976). To minimize such dangers, the researcher should take care during the interview to emphasize the limitations of the research. He should make explicit the qualifications that ought to be in the story. Also, he should mention other studies that have been done in the area, noting conflicting points of view and areas where further research is needed. In so doing, the scientist will be helping to educate the public to the process of science, to "demystify" science, and to check the development of unrealistic public expectations.

Experimental research indicates that both scientists and lay persons prefer to read accounts that use simple, direct language with as little jargon as possible (Funkhouser & Maccoby, 1974). Thus, it is to the scientist's advantage to translate jargon into more commonly understood terms. When scientific terms are crucial to an understanding of a research problem, explaining those terms becomes important (Tichenor, Donahue, & Olien, Note 8).[10] The social sciences, because their terminology so often bears a surface resemblance to lay language, may be particularly susceptible to misunderstandings. If the social psychologist uses the word "aggression," for instance, he or she must carefully explain the meaning; to him or her, aggression may mean intent to commit bodily injury, while to the journalist it may mean little more than assertiveness.

If time permits speculation about evidence as well as descriptions of it, the scientist should be explicit about what is based on data and what is not. People tend to speak more loosely when talking than when writing; reporters, though, are likely to transcribe what is said verbatim. If the researcher is not good at thinking "on his or her feet," it might be beneficial to write out the major points ahead of time.

If the scientist discusses sensitive topics during the interview, topics that should not find their way into print, they should be put "off the record." Note, though, that he must tell the reporter that such information is "off the record" *before* he presents it; journalistic ethics do not bind reporters to "off-the-record" requests if such requests are made after the fact.

---

[10] This group of researchers argues that scientific terms in a news article do not hinder audience understanding as long as the terms are clearly defined. In fact, in their field studies "the news article containing a higher number of scientific terms accompanied by explanations seemed to get more meaning across to readers than articles that contained only a few unexplained concepts or none at all" (p. 11).

It is our belief that actions such as these will help the social scientist take a more active role in a very complex communication process, and may serve to minimize some of the problems that have helped give rise to stereotypical views of the process. However, such steps will not preclude all difficulties. Even when interactions with particular journalists go smoothly and the reporting is flawless, distortions can occur. For example, other media can "pick up on" the first medium's account, shorten and simplify it, and run it without even so much as consulting the original source. That is precisely what happened after an Ohio State University sociologist delivered a paper on the familiar male-opens-door-for-female ritual to a meeting of the American Sociological Association (Walum, 1975). A *New York Times* reporter obtained a copy of the paper, interviewed the social scientist, and wrote a very accurate and appealing story for the *Times*. It was only after the story appeared in the newspaper that problems surfaced. The story traveled, via the *Times's* wire service, to a number of newspapers around the country. Editors on many of these publications shortened the information to suit particular needs and in the process altered the original emphasis of the researcher's analysis. In one extreme case, a newspaper extracted only the headline from another medium's story, tagged it a "quotable quote" and attributed it to the researcher. Thus, even in cases where the original news report is precise, subsequent "piggyback" reports may not be.

It is not certain how the social scientist can avoid distortions of this type. Some solutions may lie outside the purview of social scientists—in schools that train journalists in the tools of their trade. Nevertheless, this sociologist feels that dissemination of social science research via the mass media cannot be ignored by social scientists. Walum writes: "For those of us who consider the sociological perspective to be valuable to the layperson, there is a need to present that perspective to the community-at-large. More radically, the knowledge that 'belongs' to sociology and which is communicated to 'relevant' decision makers, should be available to those persons about whom decisions are being made" (1975, p. 31).

Unfortunately, the training social scientists receive gives them no help in learning to communicate with lay audiences via the mass media. As a result, researchers often take a "passive" approach to the problem, an approach that renders them powerless to affect it. If conditions are to change, this sociologist notes, social scientists must learn to "deal with the system (of popularization) actively" (Walum, Note 9).

At the very least, social scientists ought to begin to give thought to the dissemination process, to engage in serious discussions that move beyond traditional "two cultures" views. In some instances, scientists already have taken steps to participate actively in media dissemination. Sessions promoting sophisticated exchanges about mass media and the social sciences have been launched at meetings of professional societies. The AAAS administers a Mass Media Intern Program designed to support advanced students in the natural and social sciences as intern reporters, researchers, and production assistants in the mass media. In addition, some organizations of social scientists have developed lists of members willing to talk with reporters, packets of information on given topics to submit to the press, and seminars for journalists. For a time, the American Psychological Association even considered publishing its own popular magazine of psychology.

These are welcome signs for, if nothing else, they suggest that scientists, who traditionally have placed the burden of responsibility for public dissemination on the shoulders of journalists, may be starting to share in that responsibility. If stereotypes and oversimplified views of the process still cloud their vision, we can only hope it will not be for long.

Acknowledgments. The authors would like to thank the following individuals for commenting on early outlines of this manuscript: Rae Goodell, Thomas Gregory, James Grunig, Marcel Chotkowski LaFollette, Vivien B. Shelanski, Joan Sieber, Phillip J. Tichenor, William D. Timberlake. Technical support for preparation of this chapter was provided by the Library Services Division and the Word Processing Center of the Boys Town Center for the Study of Youth Development, Boys Town, Nebraska.

Reference Notes

1. Zimbardo, P. G. Personal communication. March 1978.
2. Stocking, S. H. Popular dissemination of research: Perils and promise. Paper presented during Symposium on Psychology and the Media, American Psychological Association, Toronto, 1978.
3. Freidman, S. M., Goodell, R., & Verbit, L. *Directory of science communication courses and programs.* Binghamton, N.Y.: Department of Chemistry, State University of New York at Binghamton, 1978.
4. Dunwoody, S. L. *Science writers at work.* Center for New Communications Research Report No. 7. Bloomington, Ind.: Indiana University School of Journalism, 1978.
5. Dunwoody, S. L. Tracking newspaper science stories from source to publication: A case study examination of the popularization process. Paper presented to the Society for the Social Studies of Science, Toronto, October 1980.
6. Stocking, S. H. Visible scientific institutions: Characteristics of medical schools and news coverage of their research. Bloomington, Ind.: Indiana University, Institute for Communication Research, in progress.
7. Sieber, J. Personal communication. February 1978.
8. Tichenor, P. J., Donohue, G. A., & Olien, C. N. Science, mass media, and the public. Paper presented to U.S. Department of Agriculture Science Writing Seminar, 1971.
9. Walum, L. R. Personal communication. March 1978.

References

Boltanski, L., & Maldidier, P. Carriere scientifique, moral scientifique et vulgarisation. *Social Science Information.* 1970, *9*(3), 99-118.
Borman, S. C. Communication accuracy in magazine science reporting. *Journalism Quarterly*, 1978, *55*, 345-346.
Breed, W. Newspaper opinion leaders and processes of standardization. *Journalism Quarterly*, 1955, *32*, 277-284. (a)

Breed, W. Social control in the newsroom. *Social Forces*, 1955, *33*, 326-335. (b)

Caplan, N., Morrison, A., & Stambaugh, R. J. *The use of social science knowledge in policy decisions at the national level.* Ann Arbor, Mich: The University of Michigan, Institute for Social Research, Center for Research on Utilization of Scientific Knowledge, 1975.

Carter, R. E. Newspaper "gatekeepers" and the sources of news. *Public Opinion Quarterly*, 1958, *22*, 133-144.

Clarke-Stewart, K. A. Popular primers for parents. *The American Psychologist*, 1978, *33*(4), 359-369.

Cohen, S. Science and the tabloid press. *APA Monitor*, 1978, *9*(3), 3.

Cole, B. *Science conflict: A content analysis of four major metro newspapers, 1951, 1961, 1971.* Unpublished master's thesis, University of Minnesota, 1974.

Culliton, B. J. Dual publication: "Ingelfinger rule" debated by scientists and press. *Science*, 1972, *176*, 1403-1405.

Dubas, O., & Martel, L. Science, mass media and the public. In *Media Impact* (Vol. 2). Ottawa: Information Canada, 1975.

Dunwoody, S. The science writing inner club: A communication link between science and the lay public. *Science, Technology and Human Values*, 1980, *5*, 14-22.

Dunwoody, S., & Scott, B. T. Scientists as mass media sources. *Journalism Quarterly*, in press.

Ezrahi, Y. The political resources of American science. *Science Studies*, 1971, *1*(2), 117-133.

Funkhouser, G. R., & Maccoby, N. An experimental study on communicating specialized science information to a lay audience. *Communication Research*, 1974, *1*(1), 110-128.

Galtung, J., & Ruge, M. The structure of foreign news. In J. Tunstall (Ed.), *Media sociology: A reader*. London: Constable, 1970.

Goodell, R. *The visible scientists*. Boston: Little, Brown, 1975.

Grunig, J. Untitled article. In N. Metzer (Ed.), *Science in the newspaper*. Washington, D.C.: American Association for the Advancement of Science, 1974.

Halloran, J. D., Elliott, P., & Murdock, G. *Demonstrations and communication: A case study*. Middlesex, England: Penguin, 1970.

Johnson, K. Dimensions of judgment of science news stories. *Journalism Quarterly*, 1963, *40*, 315-322.

Krieghbaum, H. *Science and the mass media*. New York: New York University Press, 1967.

McCombs, M., Shaw, D. L., & Grey, D. *Handbook of reporting methods*. Boston: Houghton Mifflin, 1976.

Miller, G. A. Psychology as a means of promoting human welfare. *American Psychologist*, 1969, *24*(12), 1063-1075.

McCall, R. B., & Stocking, S. H. Between scientists and public: Communicating psychological research results to the general public through the mass media. *American Psychologist*, in press.

National Science Board. *Knowledge into action: Improving the nation's use of the social sciences*. Washington, D.C.: Report of the Special Commission on the Social Sciences, 1969.

Olean, M. M. *Communicating with the public—via the media—about psychology.* Washington, D.C.: American Psychological Association, 1977.

Perlman, D. Science and the mass media. *Daedalus*, 1974, *103*(3), 207-222.

Perlman, D. Scientific announcements. *Science*, 1977, *198*(4319), 782.

Pulford, D. L. Follow-up study of science news accuracy. *Journalism Quarterly*, 1976, *53*, 119-121.

Ryan, M. Attitudes of scientists and journalists toward media coverage of science news. *Journalism Quarterly*, 1979, *56*, 18-26, 53.

Ryan, M., & Dunwoody, S. L. Academic and professional training patterns of science writers. *Journalism Quarterly*, 1975, *52*, 239-246, 290.

Science and the press: Communicating with the public. *Science*, 1976, *193*(4248), 136.

Shaw, D. L., & McCombs, M. E. *The emergence of American political issues: The agenda-setting function of the press.* St. Paul, Minn.: West, 1977.

Snow, C. P. *The two cultures and a second look.* London: Cambridge University Press, 1964.

Stocking, S. H. Don't overlook the "social" in science writing courses. *Journalism Educator*, 1981, *36*, 55-57.

Tankard, J., & Ryan, M. News source perceptions of accuracy of science coverage. *Journalism Quarterly*, 1974, *51*, 219-334.

Tannenbaum, P. H. Communication of science information. *Science*, 1963, *140*, 579-583.

Tichenor, P., Olien, C., Harrison, A., & Donohue, G. A. Mass communication systems and communication accuracy in science news reporting. *Journalism Quarterly*, 1970, *47*, 673-683.

Tunstall, J. *Journalists at work.* London: Constable, 1971.

UNESCO. Proceedings of UNESCO symposium on social science communication. *International Social Science Journal*, 1974, *26*(3).

Van Dyne, L. Dean, under fire for article, says magazine sensationalized it. *Chronicle of Higher Education*, 1978, *16*(2), 6.

Walum, L. R. Sociology and the mass media: Some major problems and modest proposals. *The American Sociologist*, 1975, *10*, 28-32.

Yu, F. T. C. *Behavioral sciences and the mass media.* Hartford, Conn.: Russell Sage Foundation, 1968.

Zimbardo, P. G., in consultation with Ruch, F. L. *Psychology and life* (9th ed.). Glenview, Ill.: Scott Foresman, 1977.

Author Index

(Italics denote entries from this volume, *The Ethics of Social Research: Fieldwork, Regulation, and Publication*)

Abelson, R. P., 59
Abernathy, J. R., 209−210, 221, 223, 228
Abul-Ela, A., 222, 224
Albrecht, M., 49
Alderfer, C. P., 101
Alexander, L., *115*
Alger, C., 47
Altman, I., 45
American Institute of Planners Newsletter, 115
American Psychological Association, 39, 40, 101, 103, 107, 110, 112, 117, *138*
American Statistical Association, 153
Anderson, E. N., 115, 116
Appell, G. N., *25*
Appleton, H., 63
Argyris, C., 31, 22, 42, 93, 101
Aronson, E., 42, 49
Assakul, K., 217, 219
Austin, A. W., 196
Austin, D. F., 172
Austin, E., *115*

Babbie, E., 170, 177, *72*
Back, K. W., 133
Ball, S., 63
Banks, W., 46
Barabba, V. P., 152
Baratz, S. S., *111*
Barber, B., 5
Barker, C. M., 197
Barnes, J. A., *36, 85*

Baron, R. S., 48, *143*
Barth, E. A. T., 174
Barth, F., *26*
Barth, J. T., 224
Bartz, W., 107
Baumrind, D., 47
Beach, M. E., 154
Bean, F. R., 42
Becker, H. S., *82−83*
Bek, Y., 224
Bell, E. H., *81−82*
Bengston, V. L., 128, 131, 133
Benne, K. D., 100
Bensman, J., 174, *72, 80−83*
Berg, D. N., 86, 93, 101
Berge, K. G., 58
Berghe, P. van den, *62*
Berman, A. J., 42
Bermant, G., 24, 91
Berreman, G., *58*
Berscheid, E., 48, *143*
Bickman, L., 59
Biernacki, P., 184−185
Bluebond-Langner, M., *65−67*
Bogatz, G. A., 63
Bok, S., *22, 23*
Boltanski, L., *158*
Bond, K., *138*
Bonham, G. S., 226
Bonoma, T. V., 60
Booth, C., *38*
Borman, S. C., *157*

Boruch, R., 8, 45, 47, 57, 60, 62, 149, 152, 168,
    196, 208–209, 218, 220, *99, 110–112, 115*
Boulay, H., *101*
Bourke, P. D., 209, 222–223
Bradburn, N., 224, 228
Brandt, A., *113*
Breed, W., *156*
Breger, M., *100, 101*
Brody, R., 47
Bromley, D. B., 137
Bronfenbrenner, U., *81–82*
Brown, G. H., 209, 211, 224, 226
Brown, R., 49
Buck-Morss, S., 139
Burcart, J. M., 120, 122
Buss, A. R., 138

Calder, B. J., 42
Calhoun, J., 107
Cammann, C., 83
Campbell, C., 209
Campbell, D. T., 44, 45, 57, 62, 60, 218, 221,
    99, 112, 115, 118
Canner, P. L., 58
Caplan, N., *116, 160*
Capron, A. M., 47
Carlsmith, J. M., 42, 49
Caro, F. G., 63
Carpeter, E., *26*
Carroll, J. D., 195, 204, *110*
Carroll, J. S., 45
Carter, L., *122*
Carter, R. E., *156*
Casagrande, J., *45*
Cassell, J., 5, *10, 23, 25, 33, 7, 8, 14, 16*
Cecil, J. S., 8, 45, 149, 152, 168, 208, *99,*
    110–112, 115
Chagnon, N. A., *24, 34, 35*
Chambers, E., *85–86*
Chambliss, W., *19*
Chernickey, P., 40
Cherniss, C., 122
Chesler, M. A., 100
Chi, I. C., 209, 211, 224–225
Chilungu, S. W., *25*
Chinatown 1970 Census, 114
Chow, L. P., 209, 223–224
Christiansen, G., 47
Chubin, D., 19
Clark, K., 118
Clarke-Stewart, K. A., *160*
Clubb, J. M., *115*
Cole, B., *153*

Committee on Evaluation Research, Social
    Science Research Council, *111*
Conner, R. F., 63, 66, 69, 70, 74, 175
Cook, T. D., 42, 45, 57, 60, 63, 67
Cooke, R. A., *141*
Cormick, G., 91
Coronary Drug Project Research Group, 58
Coutu, W., 49
Cowan, C. D., 159
Cowen, E. L., 122
Craik, K., 107
Crandall, R., *19, 45*
Crane, D., 18
Crawford, T., 47
Culliton, B., *153, 154, 161*

Dalenius, T., 196, 209, 222
Davis, F., *45*
DePres, T., *61*
Deloria, V., *19*
Demallie, R. J., *19*
Denzin, N., *45*
Department of Health, Education & Welfare,
    39
Dermer, M., 48, *143*
Devereux, G., *43*
Diamond, S., *25*
Diener, E., *19, 45*
Dollard, J., *41*
Donnerstein, E., *143*
Donohue, G. A., *154, 165*
Dorr, D., 122
Douglas, D., *16, 54*
Douglas, J., *43*
Drane, W., 220
Dreher, M., *23*
Drevenstedt, J., 132
Drexler, J. A., Jr., 93
DuVal, B. S., *140*
Dubas, O., *161*
Dubois, W. E., *38*
Dumont, J. P., *36*
Dunwoody, S. L., *155, 156, 158*
Dworkin, G., *17*

Eisendorfer, C., 137
Elliott, P., *156*
Ely, R. T., *38*
Emmet, D., *45*
Endruweit, G., 209
Englehardt, H. T., Jr., *14*
Epps, E. G., 118
Erikson, K., *45, 59–62, 64*

Eriksson, S. A., 220, 224
Ezrahi, Y., *161*

Fair, J., *110*
Fanning, J., 173
Fawcett, J., 107
Federal Register, *34*
Federer, W. T., 215
Feige, E. L., 196, 211−212
Feinberg, S., 65
Felton, B. J., 132, 133
Festinger, L., 44, *25*
Feyerabend, P., 18
Fichter, J., *84*
Fillenbaum, S., 42
Finkner, A. L., 154
Folmer, W., 177
Folsom, R. E., 221
Fowlkes, M., *50−53*
Fox, M. H., 197
Fox, R., 62−65
Frankel, L., 153
Frankel, M., 5
Franklin, J. L., 60
Franz, M. M., 173
Frazer, J., *37*
Freedman, A. M., 179
Freedman, J., 42, 49
Freeman, H. E., 57, 68, 69
Frey, P. W., *118*
Frey, R., 42
Friedman, S., *155*
Funkhouser, G. R., *165*

Gallaher, A., *72, 74−77*
Galliher, J. F., *16, 22, 40, 45*
Galtung, J., *156*
Gamson, W. A., 47
Gardner, G. T., *108, 143*
Garfinkel, H., 185−186
Gaylin, W., 68, *53−54*
Geda, C., *115*
Geller, D. M., 40, 50, 51, 172
Gergen, K. J., 133
Gilbert, J. P., 57, 73
Glass, E. S., 47
Glasser, I., 68
Glazer, M., *24, 49*
Glen, N. D., 133
Glidewell, J. C., 100
Goffman, E., 183
Goffman, I., *18*
Gohre, P., *38*

Gold, E., 172
Goldfield, E. D., 159
Goddell, R., *155, 158*
Goodstadt, M. S., 224−225
Goodstein, L., 40
Gorden, R. L., 177
Gordis, L., 172
Gouldner, A. W., 100, *45*
Graen, G., 82
Graeven, D. B., 177, 196
Gray, B., 13, 173, *11, 100, 101, 133, 138, 141*
Greenberg, B. G., 49, 50, 196, 208−210,
    220−225, 228−229
Grey, D., *155*
Griffin, E., *99*
Gronewold, S., *61*
Gruson, V., 224−225
Guetzkow, H., 47
Gunn, S. P., 40, 125
Gusfield, J. R., *49*
Guskin, A. E., 100
Guttentag, M., 60
Guzman, R., 120, 122

Halloran, J. D., *156*
Hamilton, V. L., 42
Handschin, S., 169
Haney, C., 46
Hanson, N., 19
Harding, F. D., 209, 211, 224
Harris, A. R., 174
Harris, Louis & Associates, 140
Harrison, A., *154, 165*
Hartley, S. F., 146, 148, 169−170, 174, 191
Hartsock, S., 220
Haveman, R. H., 62
Hebb, D. O., 173
Henchey, T., 59
Hendrick, C., 52
Hendricks, M., 70
Hessler, R. M., *17, 20*
Hilbert, R. A., *19*
Hill, T. W., *19*
Hillis, J. W., 70
Hoehn, A. J., 220
Hoffman, N. von, *2*
Holahan, C. J., 135
Holmes, D. S., 43
Holton, G., 18
Horowitz, I., 49
Horvitz, D. G., 208, 210, 221−223, 226,
    228−229, 196
Humphreys, L., 1, 2, 44, 183, *17, 18, 54*

Hurlbut, N. L., 136, 137
Hutt, C., 110

Illinois Institute of Technology Research Institute
    and Chicago Crime Commission, 210

Ja, D., 116
Jackson, D., 42
Jacobs, S. E., *20*
Jaffe, D., 46
Janis, I., 7, 11
Johnson, J. M., *22, 27, 54*
Johnson, K., *155*
Jones, E. E., 45
Jones, J., 32, *113*
Jorgenson, J., *45*
Josephson, E., 120, 122

Kahana, E., 132, 133
Kahn, R. L., 81
Kant, I., *23, 14*
Kantner, J. F., 170
Kaplan, D. L., 152
Kardiner, A., *72, 78, 79*
Kasanin, M., 169
Kasschau, P. L., 128, 131
Katz, D., 81
Katz, I., 118
Katz, J., 5, 32, 47
Kaufman, D., 194
Kelman, H. C., 16, 17, 23, 24, 25, 42, 44, 49,
    100, 110, 119, 120, 122, 123, *13, 21, 86,
    133, 138*
Kempthorne, O., 216
Kerlinger, F. N., 59
Kershaw, D. N., 193, *109, 110*
Kilmann, R., 17, 18, 19, 20, 23, 25, 26, 27, 36
King, A. J., 173
Kirkham, 194
Kish, L., 170
Klein, L., 85, 93
Klint, C. R., 58
Klockars, K., 9, 10, *19, 72*
Kluckholn, F. R., *39–40*
Knerr, C.. R., Jr., 149, 163, 168, 173, *110*
Kohn, M. L., 174
Kolb, W., *84–85*
Krovitz, M., 42
Kuebler, R. R., 223
Kuhn, T., 18

Lakatos, I., 18
Lally, J., 5
Lanke, J., 220

Laue, J. H., *62, 91*
Lavrakas, P. J., 225
Lawler, E. E. III, 93
Lenski, G. E., 174
Levi-Straus, C., *45*
Levine, R., *100*
Libman, M., 48, *143*
Liebow, E., *62*
Light, I., 120
Lininger, C. A., 120
Liu, P. T., 223
Locander, W., 224, 229
Leo, C. M., 108, 172
Lorion, R. P., 122
Love, L. T., 153
Lurie, N., *35*
Lyall, K. C., 62

MacIntyre, A., *22, 25, 21*
Maccoby, N., *165*
Makarushka, J., 5
Maldidier, P., *158*
Malinowski, B., *37*
Manheimer, D. I., 196
Mann, L., 44
Mann, L., 7, 11
Marcus, S., 68
Margulies, N., 75
Marquis, K. H., 153
Martel, L., *161*
Martin, M. E., 154
Marvin, K., *110*
Masling, J., 42, 43
Mather, H. G., 63
Mauss, M., *45*
May, J. T., *17*
May, W. F., *21*
McCall, R. B., *154*
McCarthy, P. J., 175
McCombs, M. E., *160, 155*
McKay, W., 23
McNeil, J., 70
McPeek, B., 57, 73
Mead, M., *33, 44*
Messick, S., 42
Metraux, R., 196
Michael, D. N., 87
Migdal, J., *55–58*
Milgram, S., 32, 33, 40, 47, 48, 50, 51, 68, 101,
    12, 211
Miller, A. G., 49
Miller, B., *54*
Miller, J., 174, 215
Miller, J. C., 59

Miller, K., 174
Mills, J. A., 43
Mirvis, P. H., 83, 87, 89, 91, 92, 100
Mitroff, I., 17, 18, 19, 20, 23, 25, 26, 27, 36, 60
Mixon, D., 42, 49
Morrison, A., 160
Mosley, W. H., 223
Mosteller, F., 57, 73
Murdock, G., 156
Murtha, J. M., 183
Myrdal, G., 41

Nadler, D. A., 83
National Academy of Sciences, 151, 153–155, 158
National Commission, 13, 100
Nejelski, P., 110
Nelson, S., 116
Nesselroade, J. R., 141
New, P, K-M., 17, 20
Noblit, G. W., 120, 122
Noel, R., 47

O'Connor, F., 4, 49, 13, 72
O'Leary, C., 49
Olean, M. M., 153, 164
Olien, C., 154, 165
Olson, T., 47
Orlans, H., 72, 99
Orne, M. T., 41, 12

Parsons, T., 191
Partridge, W., 84–85
Patton, M. Q., 60
Pattullo, L., 101, 141
Pauker, J. D., 170
Payne, J. W., 45
Pechman, J. A., 62
Perlman, D., 153
Peyser, H., 110
Pfautz, H., 38
Piliavin, I. M., 44
Piliavin, J. A., 44
Pittman, D., 85
Pollock, K. H., 224
Poole, W. K., 223
Powdermaker, H., 38–49, 41, 43, 44
Price, R. H., 122
Privacy Protection Study Commission, 172, 182, 115
Proctor, C. H., 217, 219
Pulford, D. L., 157

Ragan, P. K., 128, 131
Raghavarao, D., 215
Rainwater, L., 85
Reaser, J. M., 220, 224–225
Redfield, R., 41
Rees, A., 110
Reicken, H. W., 62
Reiss, A. J., Jr., 13, 64
Resnick, J. H., 143
Response Analysis Corporation, 151, 154, 160–162
Rhodes, I. N., 226–228
Rider, R. V., 209, 224
Riecken, H. W., 43, 44, 57, 60, 25, 99, 109, 114
Riegel, K. F., 133, 135, 138
Ries, R. E., 82–83
Riesman, S. R., 42
Risley, R., 81–82
Rivlin, A., 15, 99, 112
Robertson, J., 100, 101
Robinson, J. M., 118
Rohlf, D., 70
Rose, H., 138
Rose, S., 138
Rosenthal, S., 70
Rossi, P. H., 57, 60, 62
Roth, J., 45
Rothman, D., 68
Rothschild, B., 49
Ruge, M., 156
Russell Sage Foundation, 114
Ryan, M., 155, 157
Ryan, W., 120, 174, 116

Sagarin, E., 196
Sanders, N., 100
Sandler, H. M., 224
Schachter, S., 25
Schachter, S., 44
Schaef, R. D., 177
Schaie, K. W., 141
Scheibe, K., 12
Schensul, S. L., 20, 17
Schleiser, K. H., 19
Schmitt, R. C., 115, 116
Schooler, C., 174
Schumpeter, J. A., 191
Schwartz, R. D., 218, 99
Schwartz, R. D., 44, 143
Scott, B. T., 158
Scott, J. C., 159
Seashore, S., 85, 88, 89, 90, 100
Sechrest, L., 44
Seeman, J., 42

Seiler, L. H., 183
Shaffer, A., 63
Shaw, D. L., *155, 160*
Shimizu, I. M., 226
Shulman, A. D., 42
Sieber, J., 40, 75, 100, *161*
Sigal, H., 45
Silver, M., 40
Silverman, I., 44
Simmell, G., *45*
Simmons, W. R., 208, 220–221, 223
Singer, E., 154, 172, *128*
Siskind, J., *34, 35*
Small, J. C., 193
Smith, M. B., *133, 137*
Snyder, R., 47
de Sola Pool, I., *100*
Sommer, R., 115
Spector, A. J., 173
Spradley, J. P., *7*
Stack, C., *62*
Stambaugh, R. J., *160*
Stanley, J. C., 45, 60, 62
Steinberg, J., 218, *99*
Steiner, I. D., *143*
Stephan, F. J., 175
Sternberg, W., 40
Stocking, H., *153, 155*
Stone, E., 101
Stricker, L., 42
Stufflebeam, D. L., 60
Suchman, E., 60, 62
Sudman, S., 224, 228
Sullivan, D., 5
Swazey, J., *101*
Swensson, B., 221

Tamkin, G., 63
Tankard, J., *157*
Tanke, E. D., 110, 111, 120, 181
Tanke, T., 110, 111, 120, 181
Tannenbaum, A. S., *141, 155, 156*
Taylor, S., 45
Thompson, J. J., *96*
Thompson, W. R., 173
Trasher, J. H., 60
Tichenor, P., *154–158, 165*
Timpane, P., 15, 62
Tomich, E., 49
Tong, B., 117
Traugott, M., *115*
Tukey, J. W., 57
Tunstall, J., *156*
Turner, A. G., 147, 159, 167, 168, 191, 196

Tyler, L. E., 122
Tyler, R. M., 194

U. S. Bureau of the Census, 228
U. S. Department of Health, Education and
    Welfare, *113, 114*
U. S. Department of Commerce, Bureau of the
    Census, 151–155, 158–163
U. S. Privacy Protection Study Commission, 200
United States Department of Health and Human
    Services, *98, 100*

Vaizey, J., 110
Veatch, R., *100*
Verbit, L., *155*
Vidich, A., 174, *72, 80–83*
Vinacke, W., 44, 49

Wahl, J. M., 49, 50
Waldorf, D., 184–185
Wallace, R. A., 185–186
Walsh, J., 194
Walton, R. E., 100
Walum, L. R., *153, 166*
Waly, P., 118
Warner, S. L., 8, 208, 220–222, 226
Warwick, D., 24, 91, 100, 120
Washburn, W. E., *19*
Watson, J., 24
Watson, W. B., 174
Watts, H. W., 62, 196, 211–212
Watts, R., *110*
Wax, M. L., 5, *34, 25, 7, 100, 13*
Wax, R. H., *13, 45, 64, 67*
Webb, B., *37, 41*
Webb, E. J., 44
Weber, S W., 63
Weiss, C. H., 62
West, J., *72–83*
West, S G., 40, 48, 125
Westfall, R., 18
Whyte, W. F., 191, *39, 44, 80–83, 89*
Wigmore, J. H., 196–197
Wilkie, F. L., 137
Williams, J. A., Jr., 118
Willis, F., 49
Willis, R., 49
Willis, Y., 49
Wilson, D. W., *143*
Wiseman, J., 184
Wohlwill, J., 107
Wolf, A., 185–186
Wong, C., 120
Wood, M. M., *64*

Woolsey, T. D., 183
Wortman, C. B., 70, 74
Wright, S. R., 57, 60

Yablonsky, L., 194
Young, L., 169–170

Young, N., 116

Zdep, S. M., 226–228
Zelnik, M., 170
Zimbardo, P., 46, 47
Zimbardo, P., *151, 161*

Subject Index

(Italics denote entries from this volume, *The Ethics of Social Research: Fieldwork, Regulation, and Publication*)

Abortions, 209
Acceptance, dying informants' need for, *64*
Accessibility, respondent, 117
Accuracy of science articles in the popular press, *157*
Action researchers, 22, 79
Administrative data, use of existing, 172
Administrative records, used as data, *98*
Administrative reporting and program evaluation, borderline between, *105*
Adversarial stance of fieldworkers toward informants, *54*
Advocate
　for political benefit of the research participant, *53–67*
　for safety of the research participant, 109
Advocacy model of research in fieldwork, *3, 16, 19*
Aggregation of response and BIB designs, 214
Aging and the aged, 127–142
　classroom behavior of, 136–137
　equitable views of, 139–140
　ethnicity of, 127–143
　methodological problems in study of, 127–143
　population characteristics, 127
　professional literature on, 127–143
　race of, 127–143
　ranking and rating behavior of, 132–133
　research on, 127–143
　sex of, 127–143
　social context and why context has been ignored, 138

socio-economic class of, 127–143
　stratum variables in, 128
　use and meaning of "you" by, 133–136
Alternative interpretations of data from cultural minorities, 115
Alternatives to deception, 36
　need for, 42
Ambiguous role expectations of organizational researchers, 36
Analytic scientist, 25–28, 31–38
Anonymity, 82
Anthropology, *33*
Apolitical, science as, 21
Archival research, 191
Archive, centralized data, 211
Areal cluster sampling, 148, 177
　advantage of rigorous, 178
Assessment of attitudes, 46
Assessment of social programs, 57
Assignment of subjects to experimental conditions, 26, 36
Asymmetry between informants and researchers, *8, 14, 17*
Attitudes about surveys, national survey of, 155
Audit, government, of survey data, *110*
Autistic children, effects of crowding on, 106–109
Autonomy of research participants, 14, 24, 31–38, 105, *137*
Autonomy, respect for, *36*

Balanced incomplete block (BIB) designs, 149,
    207, 216
Behavioral methods, 26
Behavioristic models, 25
Beneficial service, assumption of, 68
Benefits, 14, 25, 34
    of research to communities, 120
    of research to organizations, 80
Biases, knowing one's own, 22
BIB designs, 213–216
    aggregation of response, 214
    benefits of, 216
    disadvantages of, 213
Biomedical experiments compared to social
    research, *11*
Biomedicine, origins of concern for human
    research in, 5
Blackmail of research subjects, 26
Blaming the victim, 84, 120, *116*
Bogus pipeline, 45
Boundaries of research, *105*
Bureau of the Census, 151

Case studies, as educational tools, 106–107
Census data, 191
Chain referral sampling, 184
Child abuse, 8
Chinatown, San Francisco, 114
City directories, 176
Codes of ethics of professional associations, 4
Coercion, 26
Cognitive complexity, 21
Cognitive social psychology, 45
Cohort, historical changes in aging, methods for
    studying, 141–142
College students, sampling of, 186
Commitment, avoidance of, 25
Committee on Federal Agency Evaluation
    Research, recommendations on
    confidentiality, *112*
"Common law" created by IRB's, *140*
Communication
    between experimenter and subjects, 31–38
    of decisions, *144*
    with investigator, *141*
    with other IRBs, *142*
Community
    anonymity, impossibility of assuring, *85*
    attitudes towards topics to be investigated, 105,
        117–119
    conducting research in the, 105
    defined, *41*
    needs of, 117
Community studies, *71*

Companionship, as a benefit to survey
    participants, 121
Compassionate analysis of fieldwork data, *67–68*
Compensation for injury, 15–16
Compensatory education, *106*
Competence of investigators, 14, 22
Compulsion of testimony and written records, 196
Concealment, of research purpose, 32–35
Conceptual control of the research setting, *8–10*
Conceptual humanist, 11–18, 21–24, *1–5*
Conceptual theorist, 21, 24, *2–5*
Concern about ethics of social research, origins
    of, 4
Conditional clearance of affidavit, *102*
Confederate discomfort, 41
Confederates, 40–41
Confidentiality, 8, 23, 26, 31–38, 80, 151–165,
    167–189, 191–206, 207–232, *5, 50–58,
    110–112, 114–116, 123–124, 132–134*
    assurance of, 53
    defined, 145, 153
    investigator's guarantee, 147
    promise of, 111, 191
    promise, importance of, 159
    public beliefs about, 152
Conflict between science and society, nature of, 4
Conflicting role expectations in organizational
    research, 84
Confounding, 20
Consent, 31–38, 65, 80, 168, 172, 178–181, *3,
    36–44, 112–113, 122–124, 136–139*
    community, *41*
    deception, and, 39
    involving risk of violating confidentiality, *85*
    manner of, 138
    to risk violation of confidentiality, *85–86*
    to secondary use of data, 174, 178–183, *3, 14,
        34, 36, 44*
    waiver of obtaining, 34
    written, *128*
Constitutional protection of research data, 202
Contamination methods, 149, 207–209
Control group research design, 61
Control groups, 36
Control of the research setting, 31–38, *8–10*
Cornell Studies in Social Growth, *80*
Cornerville, *39*
Cost of aggregation, 212
Costs of research, limiting, 171
Covert fieldwork, *3, 16–18, 22, 37–41*
    disadvantages of, *43*
Criminal aspects of subjects' lives, 191
Criminal justice, 9
Criminal prosecution, 28

Cross-sectional research, 207
Crowding, 37, 105—126
   in a natural community setting, 113
   effects on autistic children, 609
Cultural anthropologists, 27

Death, *62*
Debriefing, 41, 43, 105, *134*
Debriefing, assessing effectiveness of, 105
Decay of data's validity with time, *123*
Deception, 22, 26, 32—38, 39—53, *34*
   alternatives to, 34—37, 39—55
   analysis by IRB members, *138*
   by researchers, 26
   by subjects, 26, 37
   criteria for acceptability of, *23*
   implicit, 40
   reasons for unquestioned acceptance of, 41
   taxonomy of, 40
Decision making—*see* problem solving.
Definition of research problems affected by values
   of researcher, 24
Dehoaxing, 43
Dehumanization, 25
Delay in clearance of research protocols, *126*
Demand characteristics of experiments, 41, 45
Denial of valuable service to eligible clients, 66
Deregulation, *139*
Desensitizing, 43
Destruction of research site, *89*
Detachment of researcher from research
   participant, *67*
Detachment vs intimacy in fieldwork, 27
Determinism, 16
   as the only real science, 17
Deterministic models, 25
Deviant behavior, fieldwork in, 9
Dialectical research, 22
Differences between research methods in social
   sciences, *2—3, 7—31*
Dilemmas, defining, recognizing, solving, 6—8
Direct inquiry, protecting privacy, 7, 207—232
Dirty hands problems, 9—12, 14
Disclosure of data about identifiable individuals,
   71
Disclosure of risk of subpoena, 196
Disclosure, risk of deductive, 211
Disinterested, investigator, as, 21
Disjunctive role systems, ambiguity of, 85
Dispassionate analysis, *67*
Dissemination of scientific information in mass
   media, *152*
Dissemination, responsible, *2*
Distrust, by research participants, 42, 117

Diverse models of social science, 23
Double-blind trials, 57
Draft resisters, *53*
Dying children, research on, *65*
Dying, research on the, *62*

Education
   of IRB members, *141*
   of others by IRB members, *141*
Elderly, stereotyping of in research, 38, 127—143
Elements of informed consent, 34, *136—139*
Embarrassment, 26
Emotional harm, 26
Empathy, *46*
Employee participation, in organizational
   research, 83
Empowerment, 31—38
   of lower level personnel, 83
English, difficulty in conversing in, 117
Environmental deterioration, 107
Equitable allocation of scarce resources, 66
Equitable distribution of social benefits and costs,
   14
Equity, 66
Ethical concern in social science, 1—29
   disproportionate conflict about, 20
   as related to conceptions of social science, 20
   history of, 4—6
   politics of, 4—6
Ethical
   decision making—*see* problem solving
   norms, in flux, 100
   proofreading of manuscripts, *71, 87—89*
Ethnic minority communities, 106
Ethnography, 21, *1—96*
Ethnomethodology, 185
Evaluation research, 57—77
   in the public sector, *93*
Exemption from IRB review, 35
Existing records
   misuse of, 178
   permission to use for research, *125—128*
   relationship with agency providing records, 181
   role of IRB and use of, 181
   sampling from, 178
   solutions to ethical problems of consent to use,
      180
   undermining public confidence through use of,
      179
Expedited review procedures, *103, 139*
   and statistical methods for assuring
      confidentiality, 218
Experimental method, 22, 31—38, 207
Experimental realism, 42

Experimental research, compared with fieldwork, 8
Experimenter bias, 45
Expert witness, 60
External validity, 44
Eye movement recording, as alternative to deception, 45

Fieldwork, 21, 1–96
    analysis of modes of, 3, 7–31
    compared with surveys and experiments, 12
    ethical problems of, summarized, 1–6, 8
    five varieties of, 8
    relationship with informants, 14
    wrongs associated with, 20–24
Facts, as separable from values and theories, 28
Fair allocation of scarce resources, 66
False feedback, 46
Fear of strangers, 171, 49–70
Fears of research participants, 4
Federal authority to review research, 101
Federal regulation, 4–6, 33–34, 198, 97–121
    enforcement of, 21
    optimizing effects of, 21
Federal statutes pertaining to testimonial privilege, 198
Federally funded programs, 98
    audit of, 98
    verification of, 98
    reanalysis of, 99
Fertility control, 209
Field sampling, 148, 183–184
Field simulations, 47
Fieldwork, 1
    defined, 5
    ethics of, 9
    in deviant behavior, 17
File linkage, 98
    mutually insulated, 116
File merging, 98
First-come, first-served selection procedure, 71
Flood victims, 58–62
Freedom of Information Act, 146
Frontwork, 16, 19

Game simulations, 47
Generalizability, 44
Generalization of procedures, inappropriate, 29
Goals of research participants and freedom to choose, 24
Going native, 10, 3, 16, 18, 60
Good ends, dirty means, 9
Government audit of survey data, 110
Grindstone Experiment, 47
Growth, social science as the fostering of, 18

Guilt, 10
    feelings of by researcher, 58, 65–66
    pain of, by researcher, 10

Harm or wrong to persons through publication of research, 84
Harming versus wrong, distinction between, 4
Harm
    and benefit of fieldwork, 2
    determination of, 111
    degree of, 111
    emotional, 26
    fear of, 49
    reversibility of, 111
    to research participants, 111
    to reputation, 15
    to self esteem, 15
    to society, 71
Helping behavior, 44
Historical materials, 191
History of social science, 18
Holistic, 24
Human growth, social science as the fostering of, 18
Humanism, 16, 21, 24, 27, 93
Humanistic relationship with research participants, 21
Humanity, concern for, 14
Hypothesis testing by participants, 41

Illegal behavior, study of, 173
Illegal drug use, 209
Implicit deception, 40
Incentives to participate in research, 136
Individual vs class rights, 117
Individually identifiable data, 115
Inference, valid, 171
Information in return for giving of friendship, 34
Informational surveys, rights and interests of respondents in, 109
Informed consent, 20–26, 31, 58, 63, 105, 145–146, 151, 196, 34–36, 44–45, 107, 125
    adequate, 136–138, 172
    coercive pressure to participate, 136
    concept of, legal and philosophical, 32–35
    deception, and, 137
    defined, 136
    degree of, 128
    derived from biomedical model, 43
    documentation of criminal behavior, 173
    harmful consequences of, 172
    identification of consequences, 14–15
    impossibility in fieldwork, 14
    modification of elements of, 107

nondisclosure of some detail, and, *137*
on-going process, as an, 17, 24, 79—104
presentation of information, *137*
relativity of, in fieldwork, *43*
temporal separation of informing, consenting
    and research, 171
voluntary, 15
Informed participants in social experiments, 65
Institutional pressure, to participate in research,
    136
Institutional Review Boards (IRBs), 6, 34, 59, 91,
    95, *97—121, 125, 131*
  "common law" or policy decisions, *140*
  definition of role, *132, 141*
  educational role of, *131*
  empirical findings used on ethical problems,
    142
  procedures, absence of as cause of problems,
    140
  multiple, *126*
  review process, *132*
  workshops to acquaint researchers with policies
    and procedures, *144*
Institutional Review Board (IRB) members, 27,
    131
  as educators of social researchers, *141*
  education of, *141*
Institutionalized facts, 23
Institutionalized persons, *136*
Interviewing, 44, 161—232
  in politicized environments, *55—57*
  private information, uncovering of, *53*
  resistance, initial, of respondent, *51*
  supporting troubled respondents, *54*
Invalid research conclusions, 115
Investigator, role of in IRB process, *145*

Journal of Gerontology
  a study of the, 127—143
  what research titles fail to tell, 130—131
Journalists' interaction with social scientists,
    151—169
Judgmental vs. descriptive words in research
    reporting, *87*
Judicial authority to compel evidence, 197
Jungian typology of scientific styles, 20
Justice, 66

Knowledge, application of, 16
Kantian ethics, *8, 14, 17—27, 35—36, 46*

Laboratory research on vulerable particpants, 112
Laboratory setting, 106
Legal decisions, 191
Legal shields, 147, 192

Liaison personnel, *144*
Linkage of data, costs and advantages of, 216
Lists, ethical uses of, 176
Lists, sources of for sampling: membership,
    directories, personal, 176
Local rules of disclosure, *23*
Longitudinal research, 207
  confidentiality in, 216
Loss of valuable status or service, 26
Low risk research, unnecessary review of, *139*
Lying, *22*
  defined, *22*
  to the investigator, 7

Manipulation, *24*
  of norms of reciprocity, *34*
Marijuana usage, 209
Mass media, use by social scientists, 43, *95,*
    151—169
Matching race and culture of interviewer and
    respondent, 118
Medical experimentation on human subjects, 32
Micro-aggregation
  costs and benefits, 211
  of data, 207
  methods, 149
Milgram study of obedience, 32
Military occupation, research in area of, *56*
Mitroff-Kilmann typology, 19—20, 25—26
Models of man, 19
Models of social science, 17
Monetary remuneration of participants, 121
Moral community, *84*
Moral maturity, 10
Mothers, unwed, 169, 170
Multilateral research planning, 24, 82—87
Multiple causation, 21—22
Multiple correlation techniques, 44
Multiple data sources, research using, 217
  linkage and confidentiality of, 217
Multisource research, 207
Mundane realism, 42
Mutual self disclosure, 23
Mysticism, 22

National Academy of Sciences' study of
    confidentiality, 151—154, *99*
National Commission for Protection of Human
    Subjects of Biomedical and Behavioral
    Research, 21—22, *93, 99, 131*
National Research Council Committee on Federal
    Agency Evaluation Research, *99*
Native, going, model of fieldwork, *25*
Natural settings for research, 106
Naturalistic observation or experimentation, 44

Nazi concentration camps, 32–38
Neurotic anxieties and ethical concerns,
    distinguishing between, 100
New Jersey Negative Income Tax Study, 62
News values of journalists and scientists, *155*
Newsmaking attitudes and behaviors of
    journalists, *154*
Newsworthiness, criteria of, *156*
Noblesse oblige, model of fieldwork, *3, 15–18*
Noncooperation, legitimacy of subjects', *55*
Nondirective interviewing techniques, *53*
Nonrationality in scientific thinking, 23
Normative assumption, inappropriate, 37
Normative behavioral model, 139
Norms of human research, 14
Nuremberg Military Tribunal, 5, 32
Nuremberg code, 32

Obedience research, 33, 50–52
Objectivity, 18, *58–60, 67*
    of descriptions, *82*
Obligation to disseminate social science to the
    public, *153*
Observing behavioral episodes, 191
Occurrence of service, assumption of by evaluator
    and staff, 67
Oral consent, *138*
Organizational development, 22
Organizational research, 36, *79–104*
    ethical norms in, 90
Overgeneralized populations, 173
Overpopulation, 107
Overstudied populations, 173–174
Overt fieldwork, advantages of, *43*

Pain of words, *50*
Parity of research relationship, *8, 46*
Participant advocate, 109
Participant observation, *40*
Particular humanist, 22, 24, 27, *1–5*
Paternalism, 25, 41
Payment to subjects, 177
Peer review boards—*see* Institutional Review
    Board
Personal approach, 22
Personal growth, social science as the fostering of,
    18
Personally compiled lists for sampling, 177
Philosophy of science, 18
Plainville, *41, 71–91*
Pledge of confidentiality, 152
Policy decisions of IRBs, *140*
Political scientists, 146
Political, science as, 22

Population listings for sampling purposes, 148,
    175
Populations, 127
Postal committee, to critique proposed regulation
    of evaluation, *99*
Power, of investigator as perceived by subjects,
    10
    of the investigator, *8*
    relationship between researcher and researched,
        25, 31–38, *94, 125*
    relationship in fieldwork, *34*
Powerlessness
    of disadvantaged participants, 105, 110
    minimizing feelings of, 123
Privacy, 8, 26–27, 31–38, 80, 145–151, 167,
    207–232, *1–5, 71–91*
    defined, 145, 153
    invasion of, *133*
    of managers, 80
    protection of, *99*
    threat to, 105
Privacy Act of 1974, *115*, 146, 153
Privacy Protection Study Commission, *115*
Problems, ethical, 11–3
    defined, 11–12
    how they arise, 11
Problem solving, ethical
    diligence in, 7
    effective and ineffective, 7–11
    styles of, 11
    when there are no good solutions, 7
Process-tracing techniques, 45
Program effects, evidence of, 66, 71
Program evaluation, *57–77, 97–121*
    definition of, *105*
Promises
    of confidentiality, 151
    of advocacy, *58*
Protection of data from one's professor, *79*
Protection of subjects from harm and wrong,
    31–38
Pseudonyms, *75*
Psychological experiments, compared to surveys
    and fieldwork, *12*
Public confidence and good will, when building
    sampling strategy, 175
    policy, based on inaccurate knowledge or
        stereotypes, 167
    records, 191
    trust in survey research, 148
Publication
    of community fieldwork, 5
    of fieldwork, reciprocity in, *57*
    of secrets, *86*

reporting of demography of samples, 141
titles reflecting nature of sample, 141
Purposeful ambiguity, 21

Quasi-experimental research design, 45, 63, *113*

Racial attitudes, 209
Random assignment, 32–38, 57–77, 58–62, 36
Random assignment, adaptation to social
    experiments, 61
Randomized response method, 149, 207–209
    choice of an innocuous question, 226–227
    continuous quantitative response, 223–224
    dichotomous response, multisample, 221–222
    dichotomous response, single sample, single
        trial, 220–221
    multiproportion and discrete quantitative
        response, 222–223
    pilot studies, side studies, adherence checks,
        227–229
    randomization devices used in the field,
        224–225
    recent research in, 219
Randomized trials, 57
Randomness of sample, jeopardizing, 171
Rationality, 23
Realism, experimental, 42
Reanalysis, and data analysis by outsiders, *98,*
    114
Reciprocity, *1–70*
Refusal, rights of, *50*
Regulation, federal, 32, 25
    proposed, *97–121*
Regulatory agencies, 27
Rejection of social science proposals, *134*
Related question techniques, 208
Relationship, between scientists and journalists,
    154
    and accuracy of journalistic accounts, *157*
    of scientists to society, *93*
Relevance of social research, 5
Reputation and value of the social sciences,
    damage to, *137*
Research on, confidentiality and respondent
    cooperation, 154
    science communication in the mass media, *154*
    the ethics of publishing fieldwork, *89*
Respect for autonomy of individuals and groups,
    14
Respondent cooperation, 117
    rights to data produced, *118*
    interests in the topics on which data are
        collected, *116*
    suspiciousness of, 213

Response Analysis Corporation study of survey
    response rate, 161
Response, behavior to surveys, national survey of,
    158
    rates, survey, 153
    time, 45
Responsibility, for the use of knowledge produced
    by social science, 23
    denial of, 25
    in field relations, *58*
retaliation, fear of, *55*
Reuse of data, *123*
Review boards, location of, *103*
    scope of, *101*
Review
    by representative of the poor, *122*
    of fieldwork manuscripts by informants, *77*
Review process, improvement of, *131*
    priorities, *139*
Rights of subjects, 39
Rigorous experiments, 22–26
Risks, 14, 34, 80
    and benefits of social research, 31–38
    assessment or identification of, *17, 132–133*
    defined, 80, 132–133
    management of, *132–135*
    publication, arising from, *71*
Risks of dissemination or application, empirical
    research on, *133*
Role ambiguity and conflict in research, 81–104
    conflicts of social scientists, 27
    deception, 40
Role-playing, simulation of obedience research,
    51
    as an alternative to deception, 50
    simulations, 47–48
Role systems, organizations as, 81–104
Role theory, 36–37
    use of in organizational research, 81–104
Roles, defining and clarifying, 92
Roles in organizations, 81

Safeguarding individual identities, procedures for,
    115
Sample
    location of, 171
    selection, 171
Sampling, 15, 27
    defined, 175
Sampling procedures, 148
    ethical issues related to four procedures, 175
    from existing records, 175
    in the field, 148, 175, 183–184
    invalid, 169

Sampling procedures [*cont.*]
  from geographic areas, 175
  from listings, 175
  snowball, 184–185
  valid, 146, 170–189
Scarce resources, equal right to, 65
Science, models of, 18–20
Scientific freedom, 20
Scientific utility of control groups, 66
Secondary analysis of research data, 148, 172,
    97–121
Secrecy and mystery as a cultural value, *25*
Selection of subjects, 15
Selection procedures, first-come, first-served, 71
Self determination, 22
  fostering individual, 18
Self report, 45
Self-education, *141*
Self-esteem, 46
Self-selected referral, 70
Seminars with colleagues on ethical problems,
    10–11
Sensitive research data, *98*
Sensitivity of questions, perceived, 152
Sensitivity to community issues, 113
Sensitivity, moral, and dirty hands, 9
Separation between the observer and the observed,
    138
Serving one's own community of interest, 23
Sesame Street, 63
Sharing between IRB members and researchers of
    ethical insights, *143*
Shield, legal, 8
Signed consent forms, 173
Simulation, 44–47
  intense emotional involvement in, 47
Social Science Research Council Committee on
    Social Experimentation, *99*
Social action as an outcome benefit, 121
Social experiments, 57–77, *97*, *97–121*
  interests of subjects in treatment variables, *112*
Social indicators, *97–121*
  injury, 108, 114
  need versus group right, *85*
  programs, effectiveness of, 57
  reform programs, 58
  science and social values, linkage between, 23
Sociologists, 146
Sociology of science, 18
Sociopsychological situation of the population
    being studied, 120
Sponsor, identification of, *122–123*
Springdale, *41, 71–80*
Stanford Prison Study, 46–47

State statutes pertaining to testimonial privilege,
    200
Statistical analysis of administrative data, *97–121*
  data, *98*
  methods to preserve confidentiality, 149,
    207–232
Status quo activities, for control group members,
    64
Stratum variables, 128
Street Corner Society, *39*
Stress, 48
Studying down, *40*
Studying up, *40*
Subjective, 22
Subpoena of data, 8–9, 26, 146–149, 191–206,
    98, 110
  exemption of, 199
  immunity to, 192
  incidents known, 193
Surrogate treatment program, 47
Survey research, 26–27, 145, 167, 191, *97–121*
  compared to experimentation and fieldwork, *12*
Survey Research Center, 155
Survivors, plight of, *58*
Suspicion of deception by subjects, 42, 45
  of the experimenter's motives, 41

Tearoom Trade, 1–8, 14
Technical deception, 40
Technological assistance by fieldworkers for
    hosts, *42*
Testimonial privilege, 197
Textbooks on research methodology, 141
Theory and data as interdependent, 21
Third World peoples, research on, *16*
Time series methods, 45
Timetable of research, 118
Tone of descriptions, *82*
Training
  for journalists, *154*
  of social scientists, inadequacy of, 5–6
  sessions for IRB members, *141–142*
Transparency versus secrecy, 17
Transpersonal psychology, 18
Trobriand natives, *37*
True experimental design, 57–62
Truth as absolute vs relative to context, 16
Tuskegee syphilis study, 32–33

Uncertainty about consequences, 22
Under-generalized populations, 173–174
Under-researched populations, 173–174
Undercover agent model of fieldwork, *3, 16–25*
Underground, going, 113

Underlying premises of social research, 127
Unflattering descriptions, *87*
Unflattering stereotypes, *83*
Unionism, 83
Uniqueness of the individual, 18, 23
United States vs Karl Brandt *et al.* 32
University of Michigan Survey Research Center Study of IRBs, *135*
Unrelated question technique, 208
Unwanted publicity, subjecting individuals to, *71*
Urban poor, 108
Urbanization, 107
Use of research findings, *142*
Uses of science, 17

Validity of methods and interpretations, 14, 31−38, 115
Value free, science as, 4, 18, 21
Value laden, science as, 26

Value of one's own research, weighed against risk, 10, 31−38
Values in social research, 13−17
Verandah model, *3, 14, 17, 20, 25*
Verbal protocol, 45
Victim, blaming the, 84, *116,* 120
Voluntary participation in research, 15, 34
Vulnerability of respondents and researchers, *4, 49*
Vulnerable populations, 37, 108, *134*

Waiver of informed consent, 34
Willingness of respondents to provide personal data, 147
Wills, specification of heirs to data, *78−79*
Wives of doctors, *51*
Women, lack of research on, 174
Workshops, *144*
Written consent, *138*
Wrong, defined, *3, 8, 21*
Wrongs, in fieldwork, *1−5, 20*

The Ethics of Social Research
Surveys and Experiments
(Companion volume to The Ethics of Social Research: Fieldwork, Regulation, and Publication)

Contents

Preface

1. **Ethical Dilemmas in Social Research**
    Joan E. Sieber, Department of Psychology, California State University—Hayward

Part I. Experimental Social Research and Respect for the Individual

2. **Alternatives to Deception: Why, What, and How?**
    Daniel M. Geller, TEAM Associates, Inc., Washington, D.C.

3. **Random Assignment of Clients in Social Experimentation**
    Ross F. Conner, Department of Social Ecology, University of California—Irvine

4. **Creating Ethical Relationships in Organizational Research**
    Philip H. Mirvis, School of Management, Boston University, and *Stanley E. Seashore, Institute for Social Research, University of Michigan—Ann Arbor*

5. **Vulnerable Populations: Case Studies in Crowding Research**
    Chalsa M. Loo, Stevenson College, University of California—Santa Cruz

6. **Old People Are Not All Alike: Social Class, Ethnicity/Race, and Sex Are Bases for Important Differences**
    Eleanor K. Levine, Department of Psychology, California State University—Hayward

Part II. Survey Research and Protection of Privacy and Confidentiality

7. **What Subjects of Survey Research Believe about Confidentiality**
   Anthony G. Turner, U.S. Department of Commerce, Bureau of the Census, Washington, D.C.

8. **Sampling Strategies and the Threat to Privacy**
   Shirley Foster Hartley, Department of Sociology, California State University—Hayward

9. **What To Do Before and After a Subpoena of Data Arrives**
   Charles R. Knerr, Jr., Department of Political Science, University of Texas at Arlington

10. **Statistical Strategies for Preserving Privacy in Direct Inquiry**
    Robert F. Boruch, Department of Psychology, Northwestern University, and
    Joe Shelby Cecil, Federal Judicial Center, Washington, D.C.

Author Index

Subject Index